Across the Open Field

Penn Studies in Landscape Architecture

John Dixon Hunt
Series Editor

Across the Open Field

Essays Drawn from English Landscapes

LAURIE OLIN

University of Pennsylvania Press
Philadelphia

*Publication of this volume was assisted by grants from the Getty Grant Program
and the Graham Foundation for Advanced Studies in the Fine Arts.*

10 9 8 7 6 5 4 3 2 1

Published by
University of Pennsylvania Press
Philadelphia, Pennsylvania 19104-4011

Library of Congress Cataloging-in-Publication Data

Olin, Laurie.
    Across the open field : essays drawn from English landscapes /
Laurie Olin.
        p.   cm. — (Penn studies in landscape architecture)
    Includes bibliographical references and index.
    ISBN 0-8122-3531-2 (alk. paper)
    1. Landscape architecture—England—History.   2. Gardens—England—
History.   3. Gardens, English—History.   4. Olin, Laurie—Journeys—
England.   5. England—Description and travel.   6. Landscape—England.
I. Title. II. Series.
SB470.55.G7044 1999
712' .0942—dc21   99-15965
                                                               CIP

Endpapers: from the first edition of the one-inch Ordnance Survey of England and Wales.
Front, detail of map 70, Oxford and Reading; back, detail of map 71, Devizes. Reproduced by
permission of David & Charles Publishers.

For Jessica and Nathaniel

Contents

CONTENTS

Preface

In 1970, I WENT TO ENGLAND for a three-month visit and rest. What I found changed my life. Trained as an architect, but frustrated with the field as I knew it, I was overwhelmed by the English landscape. This was especially so as I came to see it that summer as a built artifact, a mosaic of designs and purpose. This experience launched me into the study of landscape history and soon led to my pursuit of landscape architecture instead of that of the architecture of buildings. Over the next four years I spent months on end in the field in England, exploring, walking, looking, sketching out-of-doors, alternating with periods in libraries and archives in England, the United States, and Italy, reading and studying the records and accounts of how this landscape came to be. I produced a work of youth but not a book that met my expectations or standards. Worst of all, it didn't in the least resemble the simple thing I had set out to make. This was to have been a modest collection of drawings and straightforward text that conveyed several points. First, it was to be an introduction to the English landscape, not an exhaustive or authoritative work. Second, it was merely to be an appreciation of the field of landscape history and design, not an original contribution to its history, theory, or criticism. Third, and probably most important to me, it was to demonstrate the possibility of human society and nature working together in a densely populated, beautiful landscape in a highly productive and rewarding manner, something that is as desirable now as it was then, but is not the experience of a large percentage of the population of the industrial and developing worlds.

An American, I was then and still am alarmed by the environmental crisis as it was perceived and weary of the all-or-nothing debates between preservationists and advocates of ecology versus the entire apparatus of society, commerce, and government. It seemed to me that there had to be ways that urbanization could take place in conjunction with natural processes and systems. There had to be methods one could develop to preserve and expand agriculture while maintaining the health of streams and wildlife habitats. Large portions of the United States had become such a mess and had been made so in such a short period of time that counteraction was called for. We needed alternative models and habits from those we were using. While I didn't then and still don't think we can or should remake America into a landscape resembling England, I did think there was much to learn from it in terms of strategy and values. I still do. Also while studying in England I began to wonder how many people there really understood their own landscape, and if they weren't about to tear apart what had so carefully been made over such a long period of time.

Although I knew there must be other examples and different applicable models for such issues, I felt I should get on with what I'd found and share it.

After several years in Europe and England I returned to America to teach and began to practice my newly found vocation. Despite my interest in rural conservation and regional planning, however, my own particular skills and circumstances have led to a career in the design of urban landscapes which I have found to be equally engrossing and deeply rewarding. As my responsibilities and workload grew in professional practice and academia, the slowly developing manuscript entitled "Continuity in the Landscape" ground to a halt and became forgotten. In the spring of 1995, for some reason curiosity regarding the subsequent fate of the places that had so influenced me, and an urge to do something — at least with the drawings that have been sitting around all this time — prompted another visit to the countryside of England, to assess the changes, if any, and to test my earlier opinions and conclusions. Having done so, and concluding that my original goals and impressions are still valid, I have winnowed the earlier work down, while adding additional remarks that the privilege of time has allowed me.

While much of this book is about physical and visual aspects of the landscape, more is at stake than aesthetics in our need to understand and be concerned with the health and management of the countryside. First, there is our need to understand the natural world and how agriculture utilizes, directs, and distorts nature and its processes to our benefit without which we would cease to exist, and second, how our particular culture has evolved to produce the habits, knowledge, and pleasures we hold dear. As an American I have been blissfully raised and educated within a broadly progressive and liberal Western tradition and have missed out on the predominantly Marxist-influenced social science and art history prevalent in Europe and Britain for the past fifty years. This has allowed me to read among historians of previous generations (many of whom I find to be well balanced, thorough, and careful in their work) with less disdain than some of my contemporaries. This well may have led me to unfashionable views and an inadequate grasp of some of the issues discussed here, which I accept.

For some time I have been troubled by the gradual disenfranchisement of modern society from the environment. Over the past twenty years in American graduate schools I have faced an increasing number of students from suburban environments. Born and raised in peripheral environments to which their parents have retreated in search of good schools and homes where they can avoid the numerous troubles that have befallen our great cities, many of these students do not really know much about cities, which they fear and dislike, nor much about nature, and nothing at all about agriculture. For them milk comes in cartons from somewhere and meat from counters of frozen or fresh food, where it is wrapped in plastic, precut, measured, and priced, like socks or auto parts — all products of industry — the management of which they probably believe one goes to business school to learn. Estrangement from the rural or natural environment is extreme and common for American college students, and is probably not much less so today for Europeans.

It has caused great difficulties for me in trying to teach design, whether in the context of architecture, landscape architecture, or urban design. Considering that these students and their contemporaries eventually are to manage government, industry, and the design professions with such views and lack of knowledge is thought provoking, to say the least. I have often wondered how they will make informed decisions on protecting our food sources or on urban development.

The gradual but all-pervasive effects of increasing industrialization and burgeoning population, combined with a profound lack of understanding of natural and agricultural systems by urban populations who control the governments of the Western world, has in this century begun to produce environmental and economic crises previously unimagined. The American dust bowl of the 1930s, now nearly forgotten, was held up as a prime example to my generation. In 1995 while revisiting the villages and landscape discussed here, and again in Europe in 1996, I found myself witness to an event that revealed the absolute and fundamental importance of agriculture to civilization, and the fact that its economy and intricacy have been lost on people for some time. This was the "mad cow" disease panic that swept England and the Continent. Throwing government and industry into turmoil, thousands of people were suddenly put out of work in farming-related industries, from auction and slaughterhouses to meat- and food-processing plants and trucking and shipping firms. With a worldwide ban placed on British beef and cattle products of all sorts and a quandary about how to restore the health and safety of British meat and dairy herds as well as public confidence in the farmers and British government, the understanding and ability of those obligated to resolve the problem became an extremely serious issue. This crisis presented a remarkable example of the results of what was either an incompetent or unscrupulous political administration of an almost unimaginably complex and interlocking set of relationships.

As events unfolded it became clear that both the politicians and the electorate had been singularly inept at understanding and dealing with the issues for many years. Beginning with scrapie, a disease of the central nervous system in sheep that has existed for hundreds of years, the problem was allowed to lead to an international debacle. For at least the past forty years, large agricultural feed manufacturers have supplemented their vegetable-based processed pellets with ground animal remains supplied by abattoirs in order to increase the protein level. Old sheep and dairy cattle past the age of breeding or the production of milk or wool were routinely slaughtered and their various parts used in processed foods and for animal feed. Sometime in the 1980s the remains of sheep who had died of scrapie found their way into cattle feed, and under the deregulation policies of Britain's conservative Thatcher government, the temperature at which such material was cooked was lowered to save money on fuel costs by the industry. A few years later cases of a debilitating brain disease began to appear among dairy and beef cattle. Most of these animals were destroyed, but some found their way into the agricultural and human food chain. By 1996, after several years of medical concern and a rising number of cases of a deadly brain disease among humans (British beef already having been banned for years in the United States and Australia), the news broke in Britain and a furor ensued. Within days the industry was paralyzed, thousands were out of work, numerous farmers were reported to be suicidal, and the government was debating how many thousands or millions of cows were to be destroyed throughout the country, as well as how to incinerate or bury them all without further contaminating the country, how many billions of pounds it would cost the country one way or another, and how to restore safety, order, and public confidence.

Concern regarding the need (and cost) to import milk, butter, and cheese to feed its population, let alone the discovery of how many other things from leather goods to bouillon cubes, the basic ingredients for numerous medicines, cosmetics, and soap — it turns out even pork sausages had 20 percent beef offal in them — were derived from elderly dairy cows, came as an aggravating revelation to a population in the process of embracing cyberspace and virtual reality. The need to understand the messy and old-fashioned (real) physical world and an obligation to nurture agriculture and its rural landscapes were suddenly no longer a thing to leave to the horse-and-hound set or to gray functionaries and political hacks. The fact that the landscape and agriculture within it operate along ecological principles and are subject to instability and interrelated biological phenomena, and that they are not merely machinery or a branch of mining and industry, could not have been demonstrated more clearly. This unfortunate incident can be seen as a comment upon the desire of people to cut corners, optimize short-term profits, eliminate regulatory powers of government, and cover up mistakes and cling to power —things that have happened in every country regardless of party or political philosophy — and upon the implications of playing such politics with matters of science, biology, and the environment. While the solutions to this event may turn out to be less severe than first appeared, the lesson could not be more serious.

That a rudimentary appreciation such as this book might help change the situation is not likely. However, in the past ten years I have found that many of those who know more and whose expertise in the areas discussed far surpasses mine are loath to write for the general public or the professional. A few years ago, when I directed the faculty and curriculum of a department responsible for the professional training of landscape architects at a great American university, I discovered that virtually none of the historians qualified to join the faculty was willing to give a survey course in the history of the field or of their subject. All had become specialists and disdained generalists. At the same time I couldn't very well commission amateurs for the task, nor did our students, the future practitioners, wish to take a couple of years' worth of graduate-level studies in the finer aspects and subtleties of each special discipline of the faculty (history, ecology, structures, horticulture, and so on). Survey courses are for undergraduates today and are not tolerated in the graduate programs of research universities, even if the overwhelming population of students is ignorant of the sweep, depth, and content of their chosen field. Historians and social and physical scientists today tend to teach only the area of specialty in which they have worked. Professional design students must browse around and put things together for themselves. The integration of different fields and branches of knowledge is left to those who care and take the time to do it for themselves. This is all right if one slows down and takes the time. But people could be helped a bit more — if not by the faculty, then possibly with a few books. Yet, despite a recent deluge of books on the English garden, on cultural geography and the history of art and architecture of Britain, there have been few attempts to bring these phenomena together and to show their necessary relationships.

I have, therefore, tried to bring together those things that seemed to me important and relevant in the making of one significant landscape — of southern England — without straying into the conservative excesses associated with English heritage and its preservation or into American university curriculum debates, or those of the post-Marxist, post-Freudian, Lacanian, Foucauldian, or Derrida-besotted specialist scholars of our time. I only wish that others might do the same for parts of America, continental Europe, and Asia, for if such books existed, I am certain people would read them with considerable interest. Like an earlier study I made of Skid Road in Seattle, this work grew out of an interest on the one hand and a frustration on the other that there was no such work quite like the one I wished to read. If, as I suspect, all such studies are highly personal ventures of self-discovery as well as histories and travelogues, it follows that such a work about America and its landscapes would probably best be done by a foreign visitor who truly enjoys the place. Many such visitors have already helped to shape our landscape and analyze it — witness the work of Crèvecoeur, De Tocqueville, Reyner Banham, and Rem Koolhaas. As will immediately become obvious to the reader, this is unquestionably a personal book, an American practitioner's subjective view of another's culture and landscape. It is also an affectionate ramble through real places of lasting worth.

CHAPTER ONE

As the Twig Is Bent

*The following of such thematic designs through one's life should be,
I think, the true purpose of autobiography.*

VLADIMIR NABOKOV
Speak, Memory, 1966

ONE DAY NEAR THE END of my first summer in Britain, while visiting Magdalen College, Oxford, the cumulative experience of recent walks, sights, senses, and ideas, the layering of efforts and disciplines that have made the landscape of southern Britain, became overwhelming. Many thousands of people before me have passed through this college and its environs and have been moved by its tranquil cloister, commenting on the charm of the river and bridge, the shady waterside path known as Addison's walk, and the harmony between Sir Christopher Wren's classical building and the earlier Gothic arcades and tower. On this particular occasion I happened to find myself at a corner of its little park beside the Wren building. It was a beautiful warm afternoon, and a small herd of fallow deer was browsing near the railing, their mottled tawny backs moving in and out of shadows cast by centuries-old oaks. It was calm and quiet. Birds chattered and cooed somewhere above. A bell chimed the hour. I studied Wren's graceful facade, the tall window frames and buttery-gray stone of the wall, their cornices, the central arcade, and the vines growing upon it. I turned and found the massive hulk of an ancient tree. Beneath it was a plaque. The text explained that this plant had been one of the first London plane trees to be grown in the seventeenth century in the botanical garden across the road from the college. They had been started from cuttings brought from the very first such plant in London, where specimens of Oriental planes and American sycamores had accidentally (naturally?) cross-pollinated in the nursery of a leading horticulturist who had been actively importing plants from around the world.

The tree and Wren's building were the same age. I thought about the effort and vision of the people who created this ensemble, the optimism and care with which they had attempted to combine the latest science of their day, in this case botany, and the exploration of distant continents with the accident that had produced this hybrid, which has been such a blessing for the great cities of the world ever since, and of architecture and planning — again in this case the use by Wren of the very latest and modern architectural style and technology to produce a bold and handsome building, one that holds its own with the equally strong (and contemporary in their own day) late Gothic buildings it faces, forming a court without rejecting them — and of the deer, themselves a remnant of medieval landholdings and hunting privileges, not to say culinary habits. The trees, the animals, the buildings, the steady and serious scholarship taking place inside, the light-hearted recreation on the river outside, together presented a clear attempt by the men of the seventeenth century who created this ensemble to produce a harmonious world through the combination of art and science, nature and culture. It isn't Utopia, but it is humane in the deepest sense of the word. Also it is beautiful. As I finished reading the plaque the intelligence and combined efforts that produced this ensemble struck me, and I burst into tears.

Not many other physical environments have had such an effect on me. On another occasion several years later, however, I had a similar reaction late in the afternoon at the Villa Lante. I was sitting alone on the edge of the basin of its water parterre, looking at one of the little stone dwarfs with his flower-shaped blunderbuss standing in one of the stone boats that appear to float on the water and are derived from an ancient Roman votive *navicella* recently discovered at the time of the garden's creation, with Cardinal Gambara's delicate pavilions and unsurpassed series of fountains and terraces hanging above in the golden light. I have thought about my reaction to these particular environments and such moments on more than one occasion since. The source of my reaction and the strength of my emotion probably lay in recognition that certain values and aspirations I hold dear were given particularly clear and potent physical form in these cumulative environments. Additionally, aside from their physical endurance (no small feat for a landscape), and therefore the craft and materials employed, there was also an overarching grace and calm present in them that I suppose I have sought to invest subsequently into work of my own.

I was in a particularly receptive frame of mind that summer in England. While I didn't know it at the time, I was entering an intense phase in my education to become a landscape architect. In retrospect it is obvious that I had been headed that way for a long time, but like many people I didn't aspire to the field earlier because I didn't know it existed, and like others, even after I learned of it, I had little idea of its legacy, complexity, and potential. Since then I have learned that a large proportion of students entering landscape architecture programs at America's great universities are changing careers, have come from some other field, have been out of college working for a few years, and as often as not have been drawn to urban centers from small towns or rural environments. Most place a high value upon the natural environment and have a creative, even artistic, urge, often coupled with a sense of social and moral purpose. In several ways I was somewhat of an extreme case. The impact that England, in particular its rural landscape and gardens, had upon me and the sort of landscape architect I was to become are related to the intrinsic properties of these landscapes and gardens, my own personal background, and the timing of the encounter within the trajectory of my life. A brief sketch of that background might help to understand my frame of mind at the time.

I was born in a small town in the middle of Wisconsin during the Depression. My father tried various jobs at an ice cream plant, a plywood plant, an egg ranch with a friend, and tending bar at a roadhouse on the Rock River — none of which lasted long. We moved west soon after the outbreak of World War II and came to live in a small town near where the Snake and Columbia rivers meet in what was then a beautiful valley between the Rattlesnake and Horse Heaven Hills of eastern Washington state. While my father began working for the Defense Department (this was a spot where supplies were sorted out for shipping to the troops in the Pacific and the top-secret Hanford atomic works was under construction), I began kindergarten in a chaotic one-room school with an outhouse in the middle of an asparagus field. My parents had a large "victory" garden where they raised beans, tomatoes, lettuce, radishes, and other common produce, all of which seemed interesting if not tasty to me. Some, like the peas and other vines on their strings and frames, I recall towering overhead in great green walls. There was a lovely small river below our house lined with tall cottonwoods. All around lay desert, where we would drive on the weekends, with sagebrush and jackrabbits. Not far away were the extensive orchards of Wenatchee and Yakima. The two biggest events I remember were a spectacular train wreck and the communal harvesting and dismemberment of an ancient and giant Bing cherry tree that had come down in a windstorm. Surprisingly my father was abruptly drafted into the army — the war effort was quite desperate by 1943 and even thirty-five-year-old men with children were plucked out of defense jobs. My mother (whose father was from Nova Scotia) and I moved to Vancouver, Canada (where she'd been born), to live near her aunt and uncle.

There, while learning to sing "God Save the King" in assembly along with a sketchy history of the Hudson's Bay Company, England, and Canada, while attending all of first and part of second grades at Prince of Wales School, I had my first glimpse of the English landscape. This was in the form of pen-and-ink drawings by E. H. Shepard in a copy of *Winnie-the-Pooh* a young girl had brought from London, where she and her mother had been bombed out in the Blitz. Bundled together with refugees from the Japanese occupation of Asia, we lived in a huge Victorian pile that had become a boarding house to support a woman who had two sons in the Seaforth Highlanders, who at the time were struggling northward against the retreating German army in Italy. Subliminally, I suppose, I must have absorbed a significant amount about England and the British Isles during those years. Certainly I can close my eyes and see E. H. Shepard's drawings for *Pooh*: the old beech trees that housed Piglet and Christopher Robin, the tall scruffy Scots pines, the drowsy midsummer meadows and stream banks. They were superb distillations of particular ordinary aspects of the English countryside.

When the war ended in the summer of 1945, we moved south to Seattle, where my father felt fortunate to obtain a job as a civilian with the Corps of Engineers. With so many men returning from the war, and the armament industry closing down, there was massive unemployment and labor strife across the country. Even so, Vancouver and Seattle were energetic, bustling, and physically attractive to me with their parks and beaches, shops and trolleys, boats and airplanes, bridges and hills. I was dropped into a new school and the stimulation of a racially mixed community of postwar temporary housing. Then in June 1946 my father joined a small group of men who boarded a ship for Alaska to establish a new District for the Corps of Engineers in preparation for the immense construction effort that was about to commence. World War II was hardly over, but the U.S. government believed it was soon going to be drawn into another war, this time with Russia. Fairbanks was a boomtown, awakened from the drowse it had fallen into after the hectic days of the gold rush before World War I. The defense construction was challenging in its scope and central to the intellectual and economic life of the region of Alaska known as the Interior to which we had moved.

I was eight years old at the time, and nothing could have pleased me more. There, in one of the most beautiful and astonishing natural landscapes, I had the privilege to grow up. There I began to draw and paint. There for several years we lived twenty-six miles from town, and I attended two-room schools. My playgrounds were the woods, streams, and hills of the Tanana valley and the large-scale construction projects administered by my father and his colleagues in the Corps of Engineers. Eventually we moved back to civilization, and I had the additional pleasure and curiosity of getting to know the town of Fairbanks and many of its most interesting and eccentric inhabitants, which numbered only about fifteen thousand at the time.

I was a small child when I arrived and twenty-one when I left, having finished university. It was a marvelous place to be a child, to explore, and to witness nature at work over an extended period of time — a privilege few people in the industrialized world today ever have. For a small frontier town, it was an intensely social scene, isolated in some ways physically, yet connected to contemporary life in the United States through radio and magazines, catalogues, books, records, air travel, and the constant influx of workers and military personnel, not to mention fur trappers, Eskimos, Indians, and bush pilots, as well as the usual shopkeepers, priests, doctors, engineers, bankers, housewives, and children. Although Alaska was a territory and not a state (thus we had U.S. marshals for law enforcement, as on the earlier western frontier), Congress had seen fit to provide a land grant college, which by 1946 had turned into the University of Alaska, located a few miles outside town. If you add the moose and bears, the extraordinarily long hours of sun, heat, dust, and mosquitoes in the summers and the darkness, cold, and ice fog in the winters, floods, volcanoes, and earthquakes, it was an unusually stimulating and at times surreal place in which to grow up.

Although I had been happy drawing and building things like most children prior to our move to Alaska, by the time we moved to a construction site twenty-six miles from town where there were only three other children, I was doing so constantly. In fact, from the year when I turned eight onward I began to explore the world about me, walking all around, looking, poking, talking to the people I encountered, and drawing. With the exception of an odd and limited natural history museum at the university and occasional exhibitions of native artifacts, my only encounter with the world of art came through books, reproductions, and articles in magazines such as *Life, Time, National Geographic, Colliers*, and the *Saturday Evening Post*. Books, therefore, became more than a window to other things, but a whole other world in addition to that which I already possessed, and at times a refuge. Part of my good fortune was that my parents liked to read — the only job my mother ever had was that of a librarian — and our various small and inelegant houses were stuffed with books on many subjects. When I was ten we moved back to the outskirts of town, and in my exploration of it, I discovered David Adler's bookstore. Here I found books on watercolor and drawing techniques as well as art and history. My parents found poetry, biographies, and fiction. In the world before television, shops such as his provided basic knowledge, entertainment, and communion with one's heritage and culture.

Nevertheless, the intellectual leaders of a frontier society whose economy is based on mineral extraction and military construction and support services, especially those of transportation and communication, tend to be technocrats, primarily engineers. Despite the few priests, doctors, and schoolteachers, most of the people with a college education were engineers. Even the army officers were engineers. A life in the arts was neither expected nor considered. Already as a child, increasingly as a teenager, and even later as an architect, I was not particularly in step with the attitudes and expectations around me. My educational trajectory took me from study in two-room schools to a small public high school and summer employment first collecting fossils with a world-famous German paleontologist in the gold fields and wandering about isolated villages sketching, next to civil engineering on entering college at Fairbanks and summer employment with the Alaska Road Commission as a surveyor and engineer on the construction of roads and bridges in the Chugach and Alaska ranges and on the Bering Sea, and then south to the United States and Seattle where I graduated with a degree in architecture.

Coincidentally at this moment and as a result of confrontations between President John F. Kennedy and Soviet premier Nikita Khrushchev in Cuba and Berlin, my local draft board in Anchorage let me know that I was to enter the army one way or another. Upon graduation from college, therefore, I journeyed to Fort Ord, California, on Monterey Bay, where my father had been stationed twenty years before. This brought exposure to yet another powerful landscape, a couple of interesting towns, and an important city, San Francisco. The coast from San Francisco south through Monterey Bay and Peninsula, to Point Lobos and the Big Sur is one with a particularly strong and unique ecology and physiographic character as well as a long and elaborate settlement history and a literature that extends from Philip II of Spain and the Law of the Indies to John Steinbeck, migrant workers and labor movements, Beat poets, psychedelic rock, gay liberation, and a revitalization of American cuisine. San Francisco, one of the most vibrant cities in the United States, is where I learned to play boccie, eat abalone, and listen to some of the best jazz in the world at the time while on weekend passes from military duty. So too I was exploring the back alleys, cemeteries, and vernacular buildings of Monterey and Carmel, sketching at the old mission and remnant ranches, reading under the eucalyptus, pines, and cypresses. I was learning an enormous amount about the environment and design, about landscape and communities, but very little seemed connected to the substance of my college training and supposed future occupation.

Leaving the army, I began to work as an apprentice in the offices of gifted designers in Seattle, subsequently moving to New York and exposure to more of what America had to offer in the arts and architecture at the time. In 1967 after three years in Manhattan, culminating in the inclusion of some of my drawings in an exhibition entitled the "New City" at the Museum of Modern Art, I withdrew from the scene and moved to a cabin in Amagansett at the end of Long Island, again to explore, to draw, to examine a particular place, and to try to understand more about the relationships between people, the things they make and do, their setting, and the world of nature and natural process. I took a brief but indelible visit to Paris and Provence. It confirmed things I'd suspected for years — not just that France would have good food and art (which of course it did), but that there was something important about dwelling in a place and developing layers, that cities really were like landscapes and vice versa in terms of their complexity, evolution, and composite systems. They were different, very different, but there were powerful analogies and congruities. I was interested in memory and its use in art in general; years later I would see how that might also apply to landscapes. Then came 1968, and the entire world seemed to come apart at the seams: there was war in the Middle East; America erupted in massive rock concerts and political confrontations. Journeying to Washington with friends, I was equally taken aback by the widespread presence and use of drugs as I was horrified by the tear gas that confronted us at the Pentagon and our disorderly retreat across Memorial Bridge and past the Lincoln Memorial. Traveling through Chicago that summer on the way to a family reunion in Wisconsin — by coincidence at the very moment of the horrific Democratic convention — I was afraid to leave the bus station as I saw jeeps full of armed soldiers rushing to and fro. In one city after another, students and minorities were rioting. Russia rolled tanks into Czechoslovakia to stop the liberalization and progression toward an open, capitalist society. On television one could see Parisian students hurling paving stones at squadrons of riot police followed by the latest bad news from Vietnam. The world seemed to be flying apart.

Leaving New York, I embarked upon a trip across the country that eventually took me partway down the Pacific coast and into the interior of Mexico before ending up back in the Pacific Northwest. Again, I was just looking at and recording what was there: the landscape, the towns, the buildings, and the people. And I drew it a bit more, and a bit more carefully. Returning to Seattle, I also returned to work as an architect, but not as the same one who had left four years before. I moved to Agate Point on Bainbridge Island and rented a small studio in the Skid Road neighborhood, only to become embroiled in the civic politics of preservation, planning, design, and urban renewal. Alternating drawings and paintings of the rocks, plants, stumps, and objects I found about me in the woods and beaches of the island and the denizens of the flophouses, streets, and historic district near the waterfront of Seattle across the sound, I initiated and published an antiplanning tract about the Skid Road community. I advocated a new series of urban parks and worked with others toward their realization. I became vice president of an organization calling itself Friends of the Market, participating in hearings, demonstrations, and a ballot initiative, this last — literally a citizens' revolt — entailed doing the fieldwork over a weekend with one of my teachers to place the Pike Place Market on the National Register of Historic Places, part of our fight and lawsuits against the business community and city government that wished to raze this market and section of the city. It would be a few more years before I came across Francis Bacon's remark from his *Essays* of 1598, which to some may seem a cliché today, having been invoked so often in the landscape press in recent years: "God Almighty planted the first garden. Indeed, it is the purest of human pleasures. It is the greatest refreshment to the spirits of man, without which buildings and palaces are but gross handiworks; and a man shall ever see that when ages grow to civility and elegancy men come to build stately sooner than to garden finely, as if gardening were the greater perfection."

Whether this is generally true or not, it seems that for some people, especially for some designers, it is as true today as when he wrote it more than three hundred years ago. In my case an intense conscious interest in landscape design began in my early thirties. Despite having worked in remarkable offices for distinguished architects on both coasts, despite having designed and built handsome, thoughtful buildings and having drawings and paintings in museums and collections before I was thirty, I had already left the field of architecture twice for extended periods to paint, write, and sort myself out. It was not enough, or at least not for me at that moment. When I returned to the field, largely for an income, I gravitated toward things that seemed more interesting than mere buildings. These included: a series of campus plans; helping a local society of architects propose and explain a series of urban design proposals largely concerned with parks and open space; a master plan for a zoological garden; the conversion of an abandoned courthouse into a county museum of art and history (while figuring out how to recreate a missing Victorian tower that had burned in a fire and for which no drawings existed); dreaming and scheming with a former teacher, the landscape architect Richard Haag, how to save a gasworks and convert it into a park; consultation with a wealthy neighbor on an island in Puget Sound about an unfinished garden and pond in his woods; and a series of skirmishes with the Seattle City Council and its planning department who were hell-bent on wrecking the city they were meant to be leading and assisting.

In a situation of exhaustion, of dissatisfaction, and of searching for alternative models for design and an occupation that suited me, I accepted the offer to come to England and spend time with friends near Oxford. Thus my flight to Buckland and immersion in the countryside, my discovery of the landscape garden and its history, which I fairly quickly realized was not adequately or honestly portrayed in the standard texts of the day, and my subsequent years of study there and in Italy.

Landscape architects and designers work in what might be described as a gap in the differences between the way things are and what might be, a gap that also holds out great potential. The history of society's attempt to create a more beautiful, fruitful, and just place to live, in both town and country, is the history of landscape design. Tools and crops, building materials and legal systems, horticulture and road building, hydraulics and town planning, myths and art, memory, tradition and history, science and industry, all enter into the shaping of our land. Many of those who enter the field of landscape architecture do so because they care deeply about the natural world and the historic legacy of the cultural landscape, the beauty and richness attained over time. The subsequent discovery that their livelihood as design professionals will almost inevitably involve giving shape to new development, to working for people and situations that bring change to the existing world and will replace one older preexisting environment with another newer one has various effects upon different personalities. Some become depressed and leave the field, or drift into preservation, often in government or foundations. Some become exhilarated, and leap at the chance to sweep away the past or whatever stands in their way in an effort to bring forth some personal or received vision of a new, fresh, and improved world or society. Others struggle year in and year out to give shape to the changes that seem inevitable, while trying to preserve and build upon aspects of what has already come to be. For these people the example of a landscape such as that of southern England is both an inspiration and a caution. Things *can* change without necessarily getting worse. Layers of new structure and use *can* be overlaid upon earlier ones to produce a greater complexity and richer environment. At the same time, some changes can wreck the whole fabric and destroy centuries of incremental improvements. Sorting out which are which and how much is critical or provides what might be seen as a tipping point may depend upon scale or location or the degree of finesse or craft with which something is done. These are important things to learn, not least of all because they can be highly dependent upon unique or particular situations. It's not that there can be no rules, but that everything in design and planning is so relative and dependent upon context, how it is done, or even whether it should be done at all. With the exception of creating new gardens within a derelict urban area or on marginal wastes of agriculture or wilderness, nearly every new landscape development, regardless of merit, involves the removal of something else of value. Change is threatening and disorienting to many people, often representing a loss of some sort. On the other hand, it can be invigorating, life enhancing and fruitful if well done. While attempting to deal with the demons raised by my involvement in urban and architectural design in America, all of this and more presented itself to me through one situation and one place after another in the villages and countryside of southern England. While some individuals might have emerged from such an extended reverie as archconservatives or limiting their practice to preservation, it gave me the courage to plunge into landscape design and planning.

Certainly one of the principal reasons for designers to study the past and to visit the creations of other people, other countries, and other times is to find works that inspire, that can serve as models and touchstones for their own imagination and efforts. The ambition and optimism (at times amounting to hubris), the sweeping worldview and wit of

9

those who created the parks and gardens, towns and architecture of the seventeenth and eighteenth centuries moved me then and still does. It is hard to think of a better attitude than that of the poets of the period, who produced (or perhaps erected or flung) their art in the face of corruption and chaos, disease, death, and destruction. Our own period in history, with its tumult and disasters, is sorely in need of such creative and inventive efforts, and I took it as a challenge and obligation to do the same.

It seems to be common for each succeeding generation to think that it is experiencing an upheaval and decline of formerly stable and orderly values, to feel that it in particular is witness to the demise of a coherent and valuable environment created by its predecessors. Some contemporary artists and critics have made careers of portraying their vision of this perceived breakup, focusing on that which seems new and novel and its malaise, while others have countered, taking a longer view and looking instead for continuity in behavior and the physical world that is more universal and timeless, subsequently attempting to produce work that picks up the dropped threads of ideas and art of the past that they find fruitful. It was during my stay in England that I began the transition from an energetic but conventionally aggressive young student of T. S. Eliot and W. H. Auden, Le Corbusier, and Mies van der Rohe, eager to develop a convincing irony and world-weariness combined with a yearning for something that looks and feels absolutely modern and new, convinced that the old must die and be swept away so that the new could take its rightful place, to that of one interested in building upon the past without needing either to erase or imitate it. I became more interested in being good than radical, of making work of lasting substance. How to learn from history and make one's own work without rejecting the past or slavishly being stuck in it seemed to be one of the central problems facing designers of the environment. Picasso showed one route, but so too did the imaginative and playful William Kent. Today I can safely say that most of the modern architecture and design that I admired the most then and still do has about it the characteristics of being a classic, of being good first and also (sometimes) innovative and fresh.

There was also at Magdalen College, as elsewhere in the environment of southern Britain, a continuous dialogue between high art and the vernacular, between the world of the mind and that of the senses, that I found particularly moving and inspirational. While I was somewhat familiar with the history of monuments and great architecture from the large lecture courses with slides and survey texts that most university students — especially those in design — once took, I was not particularly familiar with the evolution and importance of the ordinary and vernacular aspects of the world. Like most people, I had been drifting through life with little appreciation for the basic structure and workings of most of the everyday physical environment around me. The word *infrastructure* would have been a puzzle to me when I graduated from architecture school. I had, however, happened upon a small book that had been written by Sibyl Moholy-Nagy entitled *Native Genius in Anonymous Architecture* and had spent long hours during my college years studying Norman Carver's *Form and Space in Japanese Architecture*. Both books had included long and loving looks at agricultural buildings, presenting them as being just as serious for consideration as cathedrals and villas, largely for their craft and adaptive fit to a particular landscape and available resources.

Repeatedly in recent centuries one generation's way of asserting itself has been to reject the situation, ideas, and values of the previous one, especially those of its immediate parents, while turning to those of grandparents or further into the past, or to that which it has been told to eschew as inferior or inappropriate. In America, for many young architects between 1958 and 1968, this meant the rejection of urban sophistication and European influence and a return to simpler, more primitive, vernacular works, to the frontier or agrarian past. In Europe, also, in many instances it meant an interest in the countryside and the vernacular of agriculture and small villages. Additionally it meant that, for all of one's modernist training and its emphasis on a litany of classical Greek, Gothic, early Renaissance, and industrial buildings, there was a wealth of repressed "other" architecture, that of classical Rome, and of mannerist, baroque, and rococo production, as well as that deemed ordinary, humble, and vulgar, to be discovered for oneself. At the same time that some were dropping out of design schools to go and build geodesic domes in the desert, others began reconsidering the field and its theoretical apparatus. A handful of architectural critics on both sides of the Atlantic, by coincidence, influenced by emerging linguistic and social philosophy, had begun looking for and discussing typologies and perceived "deep structures" in both vernacular construction and some of the most sophisticated architecture built since the Renaissance.

As part of an international revolution in attitudes, university faculty and students on both sides of the Atlantic erupted in riots in Paris and America in 1968. Ostensibly concerned with justice, freedom, and the control of institutions of power, civil rights, and opposition to foreign wars, this revolution led to a shift in many academic disciplines from the study and consideration of a canon of texts, works of art, and individuals — whether that of an intelligentsia or of rulers — to an interest and concern for broader social and economic forces. Fields formerly considered removed from day-to-day politics, such as biology, became wracked with social, psychological, and especially Marxist analysis and interpretation. This was especially so with art and design history. In the United States, and especially at many of the most elite universities, design schools were at the very center of this unrest. Although cultural geographers such as Marc Bloch had begun to look at the development of rural France in new and fresh ways much earlier, it was not until after World War II that the work of a new generation of scholars on both continents began to study the vernacular landscape, the ordinary and common production of artifacts, and the social processes that produced them. Wildly divergent in interest, personality, and results, men such as Fernand Braudel in France, W. G. Hoskins in England, and J. B. Jackson in the United States assessed the world around them, redirected or invented studies of the working landscape, and influenced a generation of students. I arrived in England ready to discover some of what the countryside had to offer. As a result I formed a deep and abiding belief in the importance of healthy, ordinary, well-built things. Lengthy consideration of the successful elements of English farm and village led me to a deep appreciation of the importance of the tradition and widespread extension of "ordinary" things.

This was equally an aesthetic and technical response. A great amount of our lives and experience involve activities that are repetitive, healthy, and productive, done in the service of other things that we consider more important and special. These range from walking and driving about to accomplish various tasks, to sleeping and working, preparing the products of our particular endeavors — farming, cooking, writing and typing, drawing, assembling machines, or whatever. In most cases the sort of environment that we need and want when going about this work is one that stays in the background and neither trips us up nor calls attention to itself. Yet the minute that we look up and stop or go off to find companionship, to rest or to break our routine, we look for stimulus and delight. It is axiomatic, therefore, that much of the built environment should be solid and unobtrusive, while some aspects of it should be remarkable and special. I saw that historically this had been the case. Most rural buildings were handsome but of a modest familiarity, the result of long tradition and an economy of means regarding energy and life-cycle costs. Conversely, communal and civic structures, such as churches and bridges, were more ambitious and aspired to visual stimulus, innovation, and inspiration. Some few places, estates, buildings, and gardens were in every way exceptional, owing to unusual financial, educational, and artistic resources. While many people correctly think that these special places are marvelous, they would in no way be so special if ubiquitous. The great villas and gardens of the past reveal the lengths one must go to in order to produce such masterpieces.

When I returned to the United States and began to practice, it took me a while to understand fully how tied to particular moments in history were the gestures and forms I had come to love so much, how dependent upon an agricultural workforce, a pace of daily activity, and their role in the pastimes of their owners. What was a novelty or provided stimulus and delight to someone in 1750 is not necessarily the same today. In some cases, yes; in many others, no. Proof of how inexorably our tastes change is all around us. Changes in visual taste regarding clothes, furnishings, education, and architecture accompany other changes in our values and imagination. An example of how deep and widespread such cultural shifts are can be gained by listening to some of the most popular radio programs of the 1940s and considering the jokes that today seem broad, simpleminded, and in many cases downright juvenile, insensitive, even offensive or more embarrassing than funny.

The notion of a transcendent functionalism, of the evocative expression of fundamental but elegant forms and natural materials that was summoned through reflections upon the rural villages, farms, and parks of southern England, had a resonance with certain strains of American thought that had worked their way into and through the architecture and landscape design upon which I had been raised. Long before there was a Frankfurt School or before Wittgenstein had altered the direction of philosophy at Oxford,

Ralph Waldo Emerson and Henry David Thoreau had espoused a deep interest in the "ordinary" and had demanded an art of transcendence, one that grew from the particulars of place and encounters with fundamental experiences of natural phenomena and the senses. Few American writers and artists have escaped their influence. Among the more obvious and important leaders in American art that have been pickled in their thought and who express through their work the possibilities implied in the writings of these two Yankees are the architects Richardson, Sullivan, and Wright, the painters Eakins and Homer, the writers Whitman, Twain, and Melville, and the landscape architect Frederick Law Olmsted, his sons, and his protégés. My own teachers advocated ideas, both consciously and unconsciously, that derived from Emerson and Thoreau and through them Wordsworth, Carlyle, and nineteenth-century Germany, especially Kant.

None of this was altogether obvious as I stumped about the country lanes, but as a result of my long walks I concluded several things. One was that if everything were special, then nothing would be special. It seemed to me that many modern architects, urban designers, and landscape architects were obsessed by novelty and engaged in a futile exercise of trying to make everything they touched special, extraordinary, unique, and new. One astonishing structure after another filled the magazines and lined the roadsides of the United States. Fortunately a lot of the environment was not designed by them, but the effect upon others, from developers to city planners, from blue-collar workers shopping for homes to small-town merchants worrying about survival, has led to a visual cacophony and a discordant scene of ill-built structures that are now proliferating and disintegrating at great cost to our society.

I concluded that much of what I was to design henceforth should be ordinary, should understand its context, and if well done would probably seem as though it had already been there. That is not the same thing as saying that it would be revivalist or a copy of anything, only that I would strive to find the traditions and purpose of whatever new things I was asked to make and distinguish which aspects were worthy of being new and unique, of calling attention to themselves, and which were not. While it is great fun to make things that are new and remarkable, and I have not shied away from doing so when it has seemed called for, I also consider it a compliment when something I have labored over and built fits into its environment so as to seem as though it not only belongs but might have been there for some time, or to have someone not certain of just what it was that I have done. This can be a problem when in projects such as the redesign and reconstruction of Bryant Park in New York, many residents and visitors can't quite figure out what all the millions of dollars were spent on. The park feels fine and people can't remember what exactly it was like before we changed it, except that it was awful. Many people have come to expect that if they pay for something, it should show in some sort of conspicuous display of effort. Outside of the performing arts and sports, the effect of labor and intelligence that produces the appearance of effortlessness is not currently a value that has great standing in our society.

Often in landscape design this also becomes entwined with the vexing idea of nature, of what is or isn't natural. As will be emphasized repeatedly in the following essays, there is little that is natural about cultural landscapes, especially those of gardens and parks, yet some of the greatest artifice of this sort evinces a response from otherwise intelligent viewers that they look "natural." In the years since my return to the United States and resuming practice, there have been several occasions when my colleagues and I have been called upon to preserve and protect portions of a landscape that had genuine natural plant communities and water bodies, often mere scraps of former forests or second-growth stands. On occasion I have been asked for or have even suggested the instigation of natural situations, but they have been rare. This is partly because of the predominantly urban context within which I have come to work most frequently, and partly because I don't really think that making copies or fragments of nature is really very interesting or even possible. Despite the infrequency with which I can get away and visit real wilderness anymore, I deeply love it — love to be there, to hike, to fish, to smell it, and be dazzled by its staggering visual richness, its animals and plants, sky and weather. I have no illusions, however, that I can create such sprawling and intricate phenomena. But I do believe that, like many others before me, I can make environments that invoke some of the elements and aspects of the natural world, compositions that are in themselves both stimulating and supportive. This of course is one (and only one) of the many definitions and functions of art. Another aspect, therefore, of landscape design is that of invention, the creation of something new that did not exist before and that engages our imagination as well as our senses. That such a composition may not necessarily look new or startling is not the same thing as being natural or even reactionary.

While in England, I came to see that most things that were new and interesting were almost inevitably made out of older, common, ordinary things that had been around for some time, but that had been put together or had been manipulated in some way as to make them special. This I came to think of as the "perfection of the ordinary." Just as Igor Stravinsky posited in his Charles Eliot Norton lectures the profound theorem (but in need of considerable explication and development) that there are only two choices possible in composition — contrast or harmony — I came to see that there were only two choices in landscape design, repeated over and over: whether something should be ordinary or not. This is as true for a pavement or curb as it is for the position and selection of a tree, the shape of a pond, or the arrangement of a group of buildings. To know what the repertoire of choices, uses, traditions, and issues might be in case after case in order to consider things in such a way, however, requires considerable experience, knowledge of precedents, and judgment about human behavior and response. One of the reasons there are no hard-and-fast rules or quantifiable measures in this activity lies in the infinitude of such decisions and the constant gradient of choices. I could see how brilliant some of those who'd worked in this landscape had been, from farmers and landowners to dilettantes and professionals. I vowed I would strive to follow their lead. I didn't know at the time that the bulk of my work would end up being in urban settings, not in the countryside, and that I'd have to translate and abstract these principles if they were to be of any use.

Saul Bellow once remarked that "a writer is a reader who is moved to emulation." In like manner I could hardly wait to try my hand at some of what I had seen in England. But while I was away delving into the accomplishments of my predecessors, a backlash against Capability Brown and Frederick Law Olmsted was developing in academic circles of landscape design in Britain and the United States respectively, holding them to be bad old boys who had ripped up earlier gardens and promulgated acres of lawn with trees. While it is true that Brown did destroy numerous baroque gardens and parterres, and that Olmsted did help to create many acres of greensward in urban parks, I was incensed that both of these giants of landscape design had been reduced to caricatures by people of far less talent or understanding who didn't know their work well or at firsthand, nor understand their extraordinary accomplishments. If I didn't learn anything else in England, I learned how skillful these earlier designers had been, and from them an immense amount about land form, the shaping of water and the optical possibilities deriving from its position, and the different effects to be obtained in the placement of trees. Although many still can't see it, there even were ideas and subtle instances of narrative and representation in the works of these two. I became eager to try it myself. In the first project I attempted upon venturing to consult on landscape design, I made a hedgerow using some old sassafras and wild cherry trees as an armature, created a lake lined with clay that was fed by local runoff, and built a hill with earth dug from the lake, upon which were established a meadow and a "hat" of eighty beech trees. There was also a courtyard with an updated cloister garden of herbs, flowers, trees, and a basin, as well as a roof (hanging) garden of flowering shrubs. It was a case of exuberant emulation.

A couple of years later, I tried a lake with two islands, and in one way or another have worked with agricultural elements and references ever since. It has been great fun, if unnerving at times due to the enormous costs and constant worry that accompany these performances. More recently, out of several lakes I've constructed, one has been enormously satisfactory because of the way it lies in and on the land, curving away under a handsome bridge that an entry drive I contrived passes over. Another, consisting of two levels with the dam disguised by a well-placed clump of trees, clearly uses devices I absorbed at Buscot and Stourhead. Matters of craft as utilized in such work are not merely an issue of technical details, but central to the realization of design ideas. Likewise knowledge of the many examples of large-scale tree moving and planting and of agriculture (especially soil preparation) and industrial logistics proved to be of great help later when my office became engaged in large urban projects, such as the streets and esplanades of Battery Park City, New York, and the streets, parks, and squares of Canary Wharf, and Exchange Square at Bishopsgate in London, as well as projects for corporate and private estates.

While a generative influence, the English landscape has not been the be-all and end-all of my work. I must also acknowledge the great influence of visits to classical and post-classical sites during the time I spent at the American Academy in Rome in the midst of my English study and subsequently. It was at the academy that I made the earliest design sketches containing many of the postmodern moves that I would develop in the next decade, especially those used in the Wexner Center for the Arts and projects done with Peter Eisenman and others that have since been referred to as deconstructionist or deconstructivist. Setting aside the somewhat disreputable aura that such a label as "de-con" connotes today, this never was an accurate label for my work, which in fact arose from a different motive and process. The projects I attempted in the first fifteen years of my practice in Philadelphia were developed not from taking things apart and the expression of those pieces and their process, but rather from conceptually building them up in layers. In some ways this was directly related to work that was reshaping the field as a result of Ian McHarg at the University of Pennsylvania.

Shortly after my first visit to England and just before I left for the next two years of travel and study, McHarg paid a visit to the University of Washington, where I was teaching part-time. In a series of lectures he outlined much of the material that was to appear in his landmark book *Design with Nature*, which had just been sent off to the printers. In this material he presented a method of landscape analysis utilizing an overlay method to depict interrelating natural and physical properties of a landscape. It was a thunderclap, putting much of what I'd observed and drawn in my retreats and travel regarding human settlement and natural processes, in America and England alike, into order, placing the patterns and geometry of land form, vegetation, even health hazards and disease, into a format that seemed both understandable and useful to designers, planners, and government. There was, however, as in the spirited writings of J. B. Jackson, a pronounced attack upon architecture — and by implication upon art, landscape design, and gardens — that troubled me greatly. At the time I worried that McHarg's urge to turn landscape study and planning into a hard science and his disdain of intuition and art would inevitably lead to determinism, and possibly to a sociology that I would not find acceptable. A few years later as a member of his faculty, I found several of us arguing that very point vehemently in departmental meetings and large student reviews.

While the state of contemporary landscape design in England in the 1970s seemed to me rather dreary and a real comedown from the seventeenth and eighteenth centuries, I discovered several strong individuals practicing there at the time: Sylvia Crowe, Cliff Tandy, Derek Lovejoy, and Geoffrey Jellicoe. I studied their work avidly, for although they were interested in much of the same material as McHarg, each was approaching it differently and producing work of considerable variability and artistic merit. Jellicoe's writing interested me most. He was a modernist deeply interested in history and contemporary art, who was striving to create landscape designs that were as synthetic, abstract, and evocative as other works of art. In his design and the talks and papers he wrote about it, Jellicoe was attempting to reconcile his perception of art and science with landscape design in a manner that I perceived to be consonant with that of the seventeenth and eighteenth centuries that interested me so urgently. Here was a modernist actually interested in iconography, one actually attempting to shift a field that had become vapid and largely instrumental toward one with content and ideas. While the results in his work have proved to be markedly mixed, it was inspirational stuff.

Thus, while I sat drawing on the downs and paced off the widths of allées, I never for a moment thought I would do anything other than strive to make new works, modern landscapes. At the same time I also knew that somehow they would be informed by all of this. I hadn't the faintest idea what the work I intended to make eventually would look like, but conceived of it as being in some way layered and built up with memories, both personal and collective, derived from specific locations, former events and presences, and finally of programmatic uses and everyday materials. Why, I thought, in addition to strategies and content derived from art and science, couldn't earlier landscapes themselves become the subject for reference, form, and representation? Hadn't painting and architecture taken as part of their own subject matter and inspiration earlier paintings and buildings, that is, the history and achievements of these arts themselves? Weren't earlier gardens as often as not abstractions and pared down, refined forms of horticulture and agriculture? While quietly drawing, I ruminated upon the sort of work that might be possible, that might be almost like the world as it was, but just a bit different. It could be one where ordinary things that had been lying around for ages were rearranged, re-presented, with the dials turned up a bit.

In most writing on the environment there is a strong moral undertone. This may in part derive from the character of those attracted to the topic and their background, but it comes also in part from the traditions and history of the subject, the motives for interest in the topic in the first place. In my own case I belong to a generation for whom a strong rhetoric endorsing the federal, state, and populist democracy was absorbed in large doses at home, from the media, and in now extinct civics courses in public schools. Accepting much of these values and ideas, many of us proceeded to act upon them, often to the horror of our elders during the civil rights movement and Vietnam war. I was therefore captivated by the idea that cultural warfare could be carried out in the execution of garden and landscape design, as was exemplified by several of the most famous of the seventeenth-, eighteenth-, and nineteenth-century works that I visited. Dismissing many of these as the personal indulgences and pleasure grounds of a privileged few and therefore of little relevance to contemporary needs, as many practitioners and educators have done for years, struck me as foolish, for here were *ideas* embodied in physical form. The demonstration of such devices was invaluable to me, and I have to admit to a moment of pleasure when I recently discovered that Peter Rowe had singled out the work of my office in his book *Civic Realism*, 1997, and commented upon its underlying moral attitudes regarding society, public space, and behavior as framed in several of our public landscape designs. One of the most important lessons I learned in England was that landscape designs can and do communicate various messages without necessarily producing a narrative as words do. Just what these messages are and the methods or devices of which they consist are of great interest to a new generation of scholars at work today. As a practitioner I consider it part of my life's work to acquire and employ such knowledge successfully, whether I ever manage to explain adequately to others what I have learned and done.

While traveling about the landscape from one historic garden to another, following the trail of the evolution of the English landscape park as portrayed in popular accounts, I began to ponder the assumption of progress and improvement in landscape design and the implied notion of the perfectibility or end state, a culmination or climax of the history of gardens. Landscape history as written two decades ago by British authors had all of garden and landscape history leading to the development of eighteenth-century landscape gardens, with a few remarks about the Edwardian and cottage gardens of recent times. American and European authors tacked on developments in public parks and a few things about twentieth-century developments in California, Holland, and Scandinavia, especially as related to postwar modernism and new town or suburban development. Two dominant styles loosely regarded as formal (predominantly French and Italian) and informal (English) were seen as the principal product of Western history. Although there was considerable detail and development of these, there wasn't much else. Asia was rarely mentioned, except for China and Japan, which also had their many centuries and variable experience boiled down to two caricature styles. An underlying premise that this was all there was to what I was beginning to see as one of the most complex, synthetic, and revealing of human endeavors throughout history didn't seem right to me; nevertheless, many supposedly thoughtful people — professionals, academics, and laymen alike — seemed to share the same shallow view. As recently as 1985, David Coffin, a respected Italian Renaissance garden scholar, stated in an interview in the *Princeton Journal*:

At the present, I don't know where the history of gardens can go. I wonder if it has a future. In a sense it has gone through all the possible relationships between art and nature. All you can do, now, is tend to go back over something. Nineteenth-century gardening does this just as in architecture. There are all the revivals — not just one revival — one man can work in several revivals. With gardens one can do the same thing. It means that there's a change in where you go for further exploration. In architecture the modern movement developed. I don't know where the garden can go.

I find this statement as foolish and irritating now as I did then. There are serious problems with the notions of style as they have been sloppily applied to landscape and garden design. Fortunately, since the time I made the drawings in this book, a generation of new scholarship and thinking has been applied to the topic, extending our knowledge of the breadth and depth of garden design and its history around the world, more of the personalities, and the economic, artistic, and social contexts of its production. I began to have doubts about the standard history, which argued for the unique character and national invention of the "English" landscape garden while looking with wonder and fascination at gardens and estates of seventeenth-century England and those of Italy of the previous era. In 1973 in Rome I shared my doubts with several garden historians — among them Elisabeth MacDougall and Babs Johnson (Georgina Masson) — outlining (what has since been well documented by others) the proposition that so-called "English landscape gardens" could be thought of more accurately as a version of the late humanist garden as executed in a new and different physiographic region (England) by a new generation of artists, and that there were numerous precedents for all of its parts and effects in Italian estates of the previous generation that have subsequently been destroyed or forgotten. Generally agreeing, they showered me with more to read and go see.

I had come to love the gardens of the Restoration and Georgian England, but I didn't think their value lay in their innovation (which I had come to doubt) but rather in their content and how well done they were, how marvelously designers from Isaac de Caus and John Evelyn to Kent and Brown had adapted and reused material of Italian parks and *vigne* to their own purposes. I resolved that the lesson wasn't so much that one need be original as good, that the reuse of preexisting material in fresh ways was the common denominator of one after another of the people I wished to emulate — from Palladio and Inigo Jones to Richard Woods and Harold Peto. Coffin's misperception that nineteenth-century landscape designers were slipping from one style to another in the creation of their work proves to me that he doesn't really understand some of the most fundamental aspects of the nature of design in general and of those particular designers and their work in particular.

Worry about style and what such a thing might be in landscape architecture or garden design was related to another growing doubt that I'd begun to have in the years immediately leading up to my departure for England. This was a discomfort and finally disbelief in the concept of progress in art, a notion deeply ingrained in contemporary society in the West. It was in the winter of 1962 that I realized I no longer believed in what I came to call the "football theory of art." This is the familiar survey history of art with its implicit linear progression and Hegelian undercurrent wherein, in my caricature, cave men kicked off, *it* was caught by Greeks, advanced by Romans, brought out to the fifty-yard line by Renaissance Italians, further progressed with a little loss of ground by the French in the seventeenth, recovery by the English in the eighteenth, and a remarkable rally by Paris in the nineteenth century, with *it* (this fabulous and progressive thing, *Art* and its history) being brought to the goal line by impressionists and postimpressionists, and finally Pollock (or Warhol, De Kooning) going in from the two! Unfair as such a cartoon may seem, there is a remarkable desire to be the chosen people and to live in the culmination of things and to believe that such a thing as progress and improvement have led to our moment and the work of our contemporaries or immediate predecessors. While I don't believe in the contrary notion that the best is inevitably behind us, and all is downhill from some lost golden age, some apogee of sensibility and circumstance, I no longer believe there is such a thing as "progress" in any of the arts.

All of this became clear to me one afternoon during a visit to the Seattle Museum of Art. I had been upstairs looking at some of the Chinese and Japanese hand scrolls. After a time I set off for the lower floor. A small Babylonian plaque with a bas-relief of a dying lioness caught my eye as I went downstairs, and froze me in my tracks. There on what I remember as a small stone plaque, probably less than a foot square, was a shallow carving of a lioness, with several arrows protruding from her back and side, her hindquarters down, dragging on the ground, front shoulders and head still erect, and mouth open roaring in pain and rage. The energy and force of this depiction were astonishing. I kept looking at it, following the graceful outline, the exquisite lines that traced its form, the subtle relief that depicted the musculature, rib cage, expression, paws, claws, and sprung tail. In an instant I realized that no one could ever draw a lion better than this, nor could anyone portray more effectively the sadness and outrage caused by such a violent and premature death, while simultaneously exulting in the energy and fulsomeness of life, the exciting achievement for the archer and his hunting party, the ambivalent triumph and sorrow caused by events such as hunting and war, of the contest between life and death. I began to consider some of the other great drawings of lions that I knew: Rembrandt's ink rendition of a male lion with its head upon its paws, resting; Rubens's quick sketch of a lioness pacing, its great tail switching with visible force; Delacroix's repeated fascination with lions and other big cats attacking horses, or lying about, crouching, and striding in his slashing pen and brush stokes, and finally of the great Sesshue whose works I had just left upstairs, and the peculiar yet charged great cats that occasionally sprang from his memory and imagination. All of these depictions were remarkable, were records of moments of heightened sensibility, of enormous facility and achievement. Yet none of them were any better than this anonymous work of three thousand years ago that I was staring at. No one has ever drawn better, and who could argue that anyone today has a greater understanding or feeling for life and its loss?

On the spot, I abandoned whatever notions I'd ever had regarding "progress" in the arts. Almost simultaneously an alternative belief began to form in my thoughts of a constantly renewable activity, wherein every generation and individual strives to reach similar such moments of elevated awareness and insight, coupled with some sort of expressive facility. "There is the challenge," I said to myself. Over and over, each generation of artists must start from scratch, individually in their own ways to climb toward such achievement. Art is not cyclical. It is not really additive like science. It is barely evolutionary, yet each generation has the enormous advantage of the example — both inspirational and intimidating — of the accumulated works and achievements of the past in craft, technique, and content. It was an exhilarating and scary moment, for I realized how alone in their work all true artists really are. It had little or nothing to do with their personal or professional circumstances, whether they were happy or sad, rich or poor, old or young, male or female, married or not, successful or not, starting out in the world or well established. While it is true that there has been an enormous evolution and change in technology, and it is true that a vast increase in information has accrued to our culture, it must also be acknowledged that in the realm of insight and values, feelings and skills, these can only be developed in each individual in the course of one life, beginning with little else but our endowments as helpless but gregarious primates. Much as I love history, including art history, from that moment on it had a different cast for me. Rather than a continuous upward trajectory resembling a stock market growth curve, or what I have lightheartedly referred to as the "football theory of art," I came to see the long history of art and architecture more as a series of recurrent bumps, lumps, and peaks of varying intensity or height more resembling a cardiogram or a seismograph, with many successes of all sorts. I left my confrontation with the dying lioness with a renewed interest in art history, albeit all sorts of art and all sorts of history. Yet even today, more than thirty years later, I am still surprised how often I encounter or find myself slipping into the old progressive narrative.

From this it is not difficult to understand that all artists are more or less self-taught. Whatever training or study they may have had, whether formal or not, within or without institutions or workshops, they must learn their craft through individual trial and error, putting together for themselves those elements that suit their emerging understanding and imagination. This cannot be done for them by somebody else, whether teacher or institution, because it has to do with personal development and the construction of a unique individual. The strongest and most original, of course, are engaged in creating both themselves and work that hasn't existed before, is fresh or more highly developed in ways that they will discover or invent. The obligation of those who choose art — not as a mere career, profession, or job (in ways that are both similar to and different from a life in science, business, or scholarship) — is to take a different path, to make new situations, rarely predictable and not always easy to accept or adjust to. Theodore Roethke, a wonderful poet with whom I had the good fortune to study while in architecture school, once said while grabbing, shaking, and lifting me by the shoulders off the ground, "What does Art say?!?" — long pause — "Change your life!" Somewhat alarmed, I took this outburst personally for a few days, thinking he disapproved of me and my efforts. Later I concluded he was talking to himself as much as he was to me, although he was also clearly addressing the person I was at the time. Eventually it seemed to me to be the simplest and most useful advice I'd had in college, even though he'd offered no idea of what specifically I should do with myself. That was for me to find out.

It is one of the ironies of our time that at the very moment when large numbers of people at all levels of society have become aware of the magnitude of the environmental issues that beset our landscapes, a serious political and cultural backlash has grown against the controls and attitudes developed since the publication of Rachel Carson's *Silent Spring* in 1962. The Endangered Species Act passed in 1973, and much of the environmental protection apparatus that followed, has come under increasing attack from U.S. politicians and business leaders in the 1990s. For the past dozen years or so, architectural circles in Europe and the United States have been plunged into a series of puerile debates between those, on the one hand, who believe that architecture is and should be a direct functional response to social issues and needs while asserting that modern architecture has failed, largely because it has embraced particular aspects of industrialization and a formal reductiveness largely for reasons of financial economy, and those, on the other, who think that there was in the past an architecture that was the highest expression of form and human imagination in the building arts and that some version of a "classical" style is the only correct way for our society to build — a design version of the flat earth society.

There is another contingent that argues that architecture is primarily an art resembling a language, and that its main purpose is the creation of aesthetically pleasing works that may or may not respond to the social issues of our time; yet another contingent believes in perpetual revolution, that architecture can and should be self-referential and not be held responsible to any of these other standards or causes. As is common in such disputes, future historians will be amazed that anyone today could have held views so narrow and extreme. To those of us who have been teaching and practicing, sometimes on the edge and sometimes in the middle of this (largely journalistic) tempest, it is obvious that both excellent and terrible work has been executed by people holding all of these views, and that excepting the classical revival aspect of the postmodern period, the truth is frequently compounded of several of these views. Buildings and landscapes that accomplish distinct solutions to a specific social program, but are lacking in spirit and a concern for pleasure, are as doomed to failure as those created solely for financial gain or in a frenzy of artistic excitement that ignore the deep and ordering forces of the natural and social worlds.

One consequence of this debate is an overemphasis on the extraordinary, on the masterpiece, on exceptions. This is a characteristic not only of architecture and the "star system" syndrome, but indeed of our entire culture. The overuse of hyperbole and exaggeration frequently results in an inflation of aesthetic judgments. Few people come away from an exhibition without remarking that it was "great," "terrific," "marvelous," or "lousy," "terrible," "disgusting," "depressing," and so on. Rarely are things merely called "good," "adequate," or "weak," which is far more often exactly what they are. In all of this, many architectural critics and some historians behave like addled movie critics with their emphasis on masterpieces, singling out particular buildings, landscapes, or designers for stardom while ignoring the rest or condemning them as beneath consideration. Louis XIV wasn't France, no matter what he thought, and the dome of St. Peter's doesn't shelter very many of us, even in our dreams. They were and remain powerful exceptions to continuous solutions that have wielded enormous influence, and as such need to be carefully considered. Yet a view of history or the environment that does not examine the normal, ordinary surrounding context of these exceptions and masterpieces with as much energy, interest, and understanding as it devotes to them is a totally inadequate view. Just as most of one's days are a norm from which moments of greater happiness, joy, and sorrow can be measured as the exceptions they are, so too we must realize that nearly all of our environment can and should be "normal, healthy, and ordinary." It is against this continuum of an everyday environment that we should plan, design, and build those special events and places that we desire as exceptions. Furthermore, because we are speaking of our own daily lives and the lives of many organisms, it is essential that this "normal" environment be a healthy one. The definition of health has also become a topic of considerable debate in recent years. I agree with those who believe that it is far more than an absence of disease or accident. Health is a state of being, synonymous with a rich, varied, and vigorous life, and this life cannot be separated from the environment that nourishes it. Just what "normal, healthy, and ordinary" might mean in architecture, town planning, and landscape, of course, is the sort of thing one expects professionals and academics, politicians, intellectuals, and reflective laymen to consider and debate in a free and open society.

We should, therefore, demand a view of the environment that begins with an examination of the continuity of settlement patterns and of architectural traditions within particular social and economic organizations. With an understanding of this general continuum, we may then look for the variety and evolution of ideas and forms, within particular traditions and contexts. In this way, one of the most important measures of environmental quality lies in the duration of use and pleasure returned for the investment of energy and labor. Only by shedding our acceptance of an environment that is an amalgam of masterpieces and unspeakable nonentities, and by substituting a view that values an organic and wholesome environment where each piece is often ordinary but good, can we actually see, describe, and understand places like Wiltshire and Oxfordshire.

The great value of such places is rarely to be found in any of the elements taken singly, but rather in the whole as an ensemble: the grotto *in* the garden, the garden and villa *in* the park, the park *in* the farms, the farms *in* the valley, and the valley *in* the region; the church *in* the village; the village *on* the hill; the hill *in* the landscape.

On Buckland and Drawing

First Impressions and Later Observations

Glory be to God for dappled things —

For skies of couple-colour as a brinded cow;

For rose-moles all in stipple upon trout that swim;

Fresh-firecoal chestnut-falls; finches wings;

Landscape plotted and pieced-fold, fallow, and plough;

And all trades, their gear and tackle and trim.

All things counter, original, spare, and strange;

Whatever is fickle, freckled (who knows how?)

With swift, slow; sweet, sour; adazzle, dim;

He fathers-forth whose beauty is past change:

Praise him.

GERARD MANLEY HOPKINS
"Pied Beauty," 1877

THERE IS AN ELUSIVE ASPECT to life in the English countryside. If I were to name any one quality that best describes the feeling of the village of Buckland in midsummer, I would probably choose that of calm, of stillness and quiet. It would be a mistake, however, to presume that Buckland was a ghost town or somehow dull and soporific. Quite the contrary is true. It was busy, humming with activity in fact, but of the quiet, resolved nature of bees moving about the flowers in a kitchen garden. A steady, orderly routine, centuries old, goes on. Farmers rise and leave for the fields early. Children appear on their way to errands or to play somewhere afield with the distant air of commuters. The few village shops open; housewives make their trips to and fro; delivery trucks circulate about noiselessly. A tractor with a wagon purrs past. A dog barks. A cat glides across a road and disappears under a gate. Swallows and larks zip past above. Cicadas drone from the fields and thatch roofs. A car passes. Laundry is hung out, milk is taken in, trash burned. A lawnmower whirs somewhere in the distance. Someone begins to make the small, sharp noises of hoeing weeds in a kitchen garden beyond a wall. All of these noises are those of normal life in a small town or village, and can be heard and considered only because of the larger context of quiet that lies over the valley like a great golden drowse. It is not a numbing quietude like the oppressive silence and weight of the midday sun in the tropics, but rather a calm openness that allows one to move about and to think clearly, to concentrate thoughtfully, uninterrupted for pleasantly long periods of time. Despite the occasional farm machine or airplane purring past overhead, it was in Buckland that I was reintroduced to life before transistors and recaptured a sense known in my childhood but forgotten since of how the world sounded to Lincoln and Beethoven, to Samuel Johnson and William Kent on their rural sojourns. The sounds of life — both human and otherwise — when unamplified provide a marvelous background for thinking clearly about one's work, especially if the subject is the nature of our environment.

In that July 1970 when I arrived in England for the first time, almost by accident my first glimpse of the village of Buckland was from the window of a taxi that I had hired at the train station in Oxford. I knew next to nothing about the English countryside, and aside from a vague concern about what a ride to another town might cost in a cab, I was excited to be seeing an entirely new landscape. I'd little idea what to expect of this small, unknown Berkshire village — now officially in Oxfordshire as a result of political maneuvers that have reduced Berkshire to a narrow strip along the M4 highway from Slough to the west of Reading. As I was to learn later, the drive paralleled the Thames River valley along a low ridge through farming country quintessentially English. To the left, across a

1. Above, the Thames River valley looking north to the Cotswolds from the edge of the village; below, chalk, corn, hedgerows, and clouds above the farms. Buckland, Oxfordshire.

succession of hedgerows and barley fields, lay the Vale of the White Horse, Uffington, and the Downs. To the right lay Oxfordshire, and ahead lay the Cotswolds. After a drive that was brief by American standards, the driver began to slow. To the right, beyond the crest of a field, I saw a series of small gray and honey-colored buildings amid large billowing trees. Passing a bus shelter, we stopped, and then, after a car passed in the opposite direction, the driver swung across the road to the right and turned into the lane leading to Buckland. As only other foreigners brought up to drive in the right lane can understand, this first right-hand turn from the left lane made my hair stand on end, so much so that I nearly missed the sign of The Lamb. Disconcerted as I was by a world so familiar and yet so different, I nevertheless could not fail to notice this handsome artifact. Later I was to become a fancier of pub signs, like thousands of others before me, and would take notice of each new version of the "Trout," the "Swan," the "King's Head," or the more peculiar and wonderful "Green Man." In this, my first encounter, I noted that I should come back and look more closely.

I was filled with a sense of calm as we drove into the village, dozing in the golden afternoon sun. A faint haze compounded of pollen, dust, and smoke hung over the river valley beyond. The streets were deserted, yet serene, domestic, and well kept. We made a brief stop for directions at the village store with its ubiquitous red telephone box that bears the queen's arms and was still at the time, by historical accident, a property of the postal service. A few minutes later we came to the house where I was to spend the next several months with friends. Feeling overworked and exhausted after several years' work on two politically difficult urban design projects in Seattle, Washington, I had come for an extended vacation. Upon arrival, my remedy for whatever it was that I thought ailed me was to go out each day into the village, surrounding fields, or park to draw.

It is difficult to describe an activity that is as personal as drawing. I will try, however, because many people have little or no experience of it. Drawing is not merely a manual skill or craft dependent upon physical dexterity, although it requires a certain amount. Fundamentally, drawing is an attitude and a mode of seeing and being that is essentially *quiet*. There is not much else to say about this aspect, except that if one watches someone drawing, their absorption in the activity appears more strident than the actual activity itself. This is because the movement of the hand and pen is only the end of a process. Far more important than how a person wriggles his wrist is the observation, thought, selection, and connections that the mind makes when quietly observing some portion of the world. For this and other reasons, drawing can be as important to architects, painters, and sculptors as the experience of visiting and experiencing the work of others or of the past. I have done drawings both before and after those that appear in this book that in certain

2. Buckland turn and the sign of The Lamb.

3. A quiet street on the edge of Buckland. As early as 1970 several of these buildings had been converted to residences for people who work in nearby Oxford. This corner of the village was once an active part of Buckland's self-sufficient economy. On the left is the old brewery. The tie rods were added in the nineteenth century to keep it from collapsing. Beyond are the bay windows of what once was a draper's shop, now converted to the village shop, post office, and grocer's. Next is one of two former greengrocer's shops, recently the home of a retired general. To its right is a gate from which a path leads across fields toward the Oxford Road and Pusey. Further to the right and behind a fence is a Methodist chapel and elementary school. In the foreground is the malt house of the brewery.

ways are superior, but rarely have I come face to face with a place that so engaged my interest and curiosity. On my own, without tutor or guide, I had begun to study a landscape and vernacular architecture that predated the American colonies and has left a lasting mark on our society. It was also to have a lasting effect on me.

Through drawing one can begin to learn the physical properties and appearance, the relationships and structures of that which exists. How and why it came to be so, however, is rarely revealed merely through physical presence. It was immediately clear to me that I was almost totally ignorant of the history and evolution of the complex and beautiful

4. A child's sketch of his home, done for me while I sat drawing. The scene is dominated by the decorative end of tie rods, curving wall, and passage back to the garden where he'd spent most of the six years of his life. That his neighbor's house had bay windows seemed to be less important or unknown. Figure 3 is my version.

5. The village shop, post office, and telephone box, Buckland. Since this drawing was made it has been converted to a residence and the phone box moved across the road.

parks and countryside about me. Thus began a series of trips to Oxford and London to purchase books, maps, and guides. The more I read, the more I needed to see. The answer to one question raised others. The more I saw, the more I needed to read. Although the literature and history of architecture are extensive, that of the history of the landscape seemed at first to be quite small. Later I realized that the history of everything else was really the history of the landscape. Everything related. The literature that told the story of the landscape was unending. My early suspicion that the invention of the eighteenth-century landscape garden was neither so simple nor so homespun as the more popular texts of the day asserted was eventually to prove true, as scholars have shown in the nearly thirty years following my initial visit to England as they dug deeper into records and events of the period. So, too, another modest thought, a commonplace to some scholars, I suppose, occurred to me, namely, that new or more evolved modes of life, behavior, or thought normally coexist, often for considerable lengths of time, with the older forms that they are eventually to supplant. This became clear as I rummaged about in sixteenth- and seventeenth-century material. What this means for us today remains to be seen, but it should cause us to think carefully before dismissing some of our changing landscapes and seemingly aberrant or alternative designers and planners too quickly.

The friends I had come to stay with had taken a rambling establishment called Warneford House, rented out to boarders winter and summer by a boys' school that occupied Buckland House at the time. This jumble of gables, stairways, and chimneys was in fact several older houses and cottages linked together. It had all the mass and complexity of a large and moderately important house without a single room of grace or fine proportions. Fortunately, as in countless similar buildings throughout the south of England, it possessed an enormous well-lit kitchen at one end, undoubtedly the entire original cottage, embedded within one of the older houses. Here we spent nearly all of our indoor waking hours. The remainder of the house was a drafty labyrinth of plastered rooms with small windows, low ceilings and doorjambs, occasional and dangerous winding stairs, wood floors that creaked, doves in the eaves, beds with heavy comforters and weak springs, occasional fireplaces, no closets, few toilets, and no heat. With the exception of its generous size, it was a remarkably typical building for the region and much of the country. Good and solid for more than two hundred and fifty years, it will be good for as many more. Designed for life before fuel oil, it will be just fine after. The roof is of stone, supported on oak. The floors are of oak. The windows all open. One can build a roaring fire and make it warm and cozy in the winter. In the summer it is cool and pleasant. In sum, Warneford is not great architecture, but it is a good and sane place to live. In important ways it is better than nearly every structure built today for the ordinary housing market in Britain and the United States.

6. *Looking south into the sun at midsummer, Warneford House on the left and the Common to the right; below, a derelict manger on the Common, demolished since the drawing was made.*

7. Warneford House seen from Buckland Common with a fertilizer spreader in the foreground.

As in the case of this house, the lessons to be learned from the artifacts and lifestyle of a village such as Buckland can easily be separated from nostalgia. Invariably they will be concerned with matters of the human spirit and a sensibility that has sometimes been dubbed practicality or common sense and that in its most modern formulation is termed an ecological view of the world. Unfortunately, just as in the United States, the majority of England's population is now so thoroughly urban that it is very much out of touch with the physical and natural world and how it works. Few people ever consider the agricultural base upon which our entire population and technological achievement are supported, much less the more esoteric relationships between groundwater, forests, songbirds, pesticides, sewerage, and industry. The great fad for things "natural," the rush to be counted among the right thinkers on Earth Day, has waned for the moment. Today a backlash — at least among those in government on both sides of the Atlantic — has begun to set in. Inflation, jobs, housing, floundering economies, crime, drugs, AIDS, looming medical and pension crises, tax revolt, and a nasty "me first" divisiveness, these are the problems. Anything, no matter how temporary or Pyrrhic, is embraced if it appears to offer short-term relief. Few people know or care about the spectacular loss of topsoil and arable land that continues. The dilemmas of the farmer are unwelcome news that does not interest urban society. Worse, recently on both sides of the Atlantic, spokesmen for industry have come out swinging after fifteen years on the defensive, blaming environmentalists for the problems that have beset their aging and badly managed industries.

I was surprised to discover that even today in England, a land famous for nature lovers, many of those who live in the countryside must often take great pains to explain their actions to their urban contemporaries who besiege them on weekends and holiday seasons. The case of the game warden at Buckland is a fairly typical example. Weekend shooting parties and game for the table were still part of the life of Buckland in the early 1970s. Mr. Veal, the warden, patrolled 2,500 acres, of which 1,200 were agricultural. The rest was in woods, park, meadows, or streams. His job was multifaceted. He was in charge of the deer and their park, the pheasantry, the protection of crops from predators, and the general promotion of conservation and protection of birds, animals, and fishes; he was also the sole human deterrent to poachers.

In the summer of 1970, when the historic house was still a private boys' school, there were forty-four fallow deer in the park herd. Since only thirty-five were allowed by the authorities — a sensible ruling based on the acreage of the park — nine would have to be caught and killed. This would have to be done either in the autumn before school started or over the Christmas break when students and faculty were away. Veal told me that the previous year seventeen fawns were born, and the same number of adults slaughtered, and that there had been a particularly nasty protest and confrontation with the city folks at the school who couldn't or wouldn't listen to or accept any explanation of the slaughter. Veal was equally incensed with what he regarded as their bleeding-heart ignorance of how the world really is. In the United States this is commonly referred to as the "Bambi" phenom-

8. *The old garden wall at Warneford and Dower House, whose chimney pots and trees are the source of interminable cooing of doves all summer.*

enon, a particular form of enthusiasm for a fanciful version of nature and a denial of an ecological understanding of population dynamics and the ability of a habitat to support such a population. Recent controversy about fox hunting in England, while frequently pitting the same forces against each other, should not be confused with these issues, even though it is related.

Born to the south in Wiltshire, Veal was the son of a gamekeeper. He had spent seventeen years in Kent before coming to his post at Buckland. Like many in his profession, he knew every acre of his charge by heart, every animal and plant. He knew their needs, and it was his duty to see to the survival of the entire ensemble. Immune to any Disneyesque sentiment favoring one large-eyed species over another, he was particularly frustrated by the deer park protest and baffled by people who would prefer to have animals starve to death while destroying the park, than have a few shot in order to preserve all the species of plants and animals present. To Veal it was a simple matter of husbandry no different from farming or gardening.

The pheasantry was located in the wood southwest of the house. Here he had raised eighteen hundred pheasants the previous year that had been set out for shooting parties in the autumn. Once again, few general readers of the Sunday papers who happen to glance at photographs of shooting parties realize that the large quantity of birds felled over the weekend were raised from chicks on grain from the estate for that express purpose, like the chickens or ducks on their table and in the market. For sanitary reasons, the pheasant pens are moved every three years. In the keeper's words, "the ground gets sour." There is also a constant struggle against foxes, owls, and hawks. The task of raising and setting out pheasants had become such a burden for the lone warden and the pocketbook of Wellesley, the owner of the manor, that finally the following season he withdrew from the shooting association and raised only enough for his own table.

Fox hunting, an activity described by Oscar Wilde as "the unspeakable in full pursuit of the uneatable," was still practiced in this area, which was ideally suited to both foxes and riding. Hunts, today generally scheduled after the grain harvest to minimize damage to the crops, can often raise havoc with other wildlife both during and after the hunt. In order to prevent too easy an escape for the fox, wardens and keepers normally go about through the entire likely area of a hunt on the day before and plug every burrow and hole in the banks and hedgerows. Veal's method was to do this with bundles and faggots. On the day after each hunt he would retrace his steps and remove each one. Considering the many square miles involved, this attention to detail and care would probably astonish most people if they were to know about it. As it was, he was fond of animals such as badgers, which he considered relatively harmless, and he enjoyed the thought of them providing delight for the village children, who sometimes came to watch them puttering about their burrows at dusk.

9. *While quietly sitting on the edge of a field drawing, I was startled by a sturdy figure who suddenly stepped out of this hedgerow beside me. It was Mr. Veal, the Buckland game warden, and his double-barreled shotgun out after rooks.*

10. *Fecund nature and fractals: clouds, trees, wheat, and hares in the late afternoon, Buckland House. Only in the last few years have we begun to have a mathematics capable of describing the most common forms and processes that have surrounded us forever. Nature, still believed by many to be chaotic and disorderly, may indeed be rambunctious, but disorderly it is not.*

To my amazement, nearly everyone in the Buckland village totally ignored the many large rabbits that come out onto all of the lawns and meadows in the late afternoon. Few people eat them anymore, although rabbit stews and pies were once an English country staple. Regarded as a plague somewhat like pigeons or starlings, these ubiquitous creatures were constantly preyed upon by hawks, owls, foxes, dogs, and cats, and except for occasionally successful raids upon kitchen gardens, they were considered harmless. This was fortunate for Veal, who already had his hands full with another of the farmer's archenemies, crows, or "rooks" as they are called in England. Modern agriculture, with its endless acres of grain and a mere handful of people, almost none of whom are armed in any way, is a paradise for crows. It is probably safe to say that one of the warden's main tasks, and certainly the most thankless and hopeless one, was to try to minimize crop losses due to rooks, with whom he waged a constant war, shooting and trapping them endlessly.

11. Time and timelessness, shifting scales: above, mature oak standards, the only remains of a former hedgerow, itself representative of the economic and national defense policies of John Evelyn's day, standing upon the skyline of a cornfield on the chalk down; below, crowds of hoverflies grazing systematically across the tops of the forests of Queen Anne's lace in the headlands of the fields. Buckland, Oxfordshire.

As I went out daily to draw, I was noticed and occasionally followed about by several small boys who reviewed the progress of my drawings. They supplied me with information about England and Buckland village that at times was remarkably erroneous, but just as often was as perceptive and interesting as children's remarks are to adult visitors worldwide. After my first inspection, when I was quizzed about America and whether I liked English football, which I discovered was the ruling passion of their lives, I was queried about why I was drawing their village. This was a difficult question for me at the time, since I wasn't too certain myself, except that it seemed somehow important. I stammered the usual remarks that I did it because I liked to, which seemed satisfactory to the boys.

Eventually, bored by my uneventful behavior and sedentary activity, the boys drifted off and began to chatter away again. One remarked that he had been to visit a relative in a city, which prompted the question, "which city?" When he answered "Witney," another boy laughed, and with the arrogant air of a child who knows something another doesn't, pronounced, "Witney's not a city, it's a town. Cities have got buildings in and cathedrals. Towns are like that, only smaller. And this, this is just a village." Another of the boys went on to explain to the others the finer points of ecclesiastical hierarchy that accompanied this historic truth. I was amazed to hear such succinct and accurate statements that were almost medieval in their derivation. It is true that in ancient England the distinction between a city and a market town, no matter how large or successful, was that cities possessed a bishop and a cathedral. Towns had churches and priests — often several — while villages had only one church or chapel and a vicar. Thus to this day, Salisbury and Winchester are referred to as cities and Oxford and Cambridge are towns despite their size, industry, or importance. Witney, an ancient market town and weaving center across the Thames from Buckland on the edge of the Cotswolds, which deserves to be better known in the United States because of its manufacture of the famous Hudson Bay trading blankets, was truly a town. The boy was right. As it is, Oxford and Cambridge, along with Shakespeare's Stratford and Dover, are probably the only English settlement names well known to Americans that are not cities with cathedrals. The underlying truth in all of this is not that churches are less interesting than cathedrals, but rather that cities are terribly important culturally and are specifically bred to that end.

It would be gratuitous to point out what should be an obvious truth, if it were not for the fact that for nearly forty-five years in both academia and professional planning circles on both sides of the Atlantic, the true qualitative importance of cities and especially of the central, most dense, vital, and problem-ridden portion of cities was denied. The heart of our cities was dismissed as something passé, unimportant, or as merely an old and not particularly good habit. In one paper after another delivered by postwar urbanophobes, we were told that the city center would wither away in a manner similar to that which the Marxists dreamed for the demise of the state. New communications, transportation, and computers would assure the success of this bright new era. One government agency after another allowed money to flow out of the cities in efforts to hasten the day. As people moved out to the sunlight, fresh air, new schools, and the services that made them comfortable, somehow the countryside receded before them. People who used to live in dense, efficient urban communities found themselves cut off from each other and scattered about the landscape. It was impossible to walk to shops, work, schools, or much of anything else. We all know the rest of the tale. Common sense and history have proved that this idea was wrong. Urban centers were and still are vital to society and to their region or country. Today even Los Angeles is experiencing growth and renewal at its historic core. Possibly the most interesting aspect in the planning and creation of new settlements in this recent era is that not only did most of these urban dwellers not understand the nature of the countryside; they did not understand that of cities either. How had such a situation come to pass? As I sat drawing, the conversation of the boys had set in motion a train of thought about explicating and adding to the virtues of cities that I was to pursue for many years.

The English countryside was an excellent place to sit and reflect upon the situation of cities. The age-old pull between the poles of city and country was as strong as ever. As soon as I was ensconced in this peaceful farming scene and had caught up on my sleep, I began to notice and truly miss the remarkable, great, and wonderful — even beautiful — things about cities. Simultaneously, I was delighted to be rid of the irritating, loathsome, and sometimes deadening or frightening aspects of modern urban life. The contrast was made all the more vivid by juxtaposing London, Dr. Johnson's "Great Wen" — my newly discovered "Great City of the World" in all of its bustling, sprawling fascination — with this sleepy little Berkshire village. What city is simultaneously more ugly and beautiful than London, and what rural scene more tranquil and healthful, yet parochial, than that of southern England? Once one knows the choices and has lived in both circumstances, the ambivalence and wisdom embodied in the lyrics of poets from the first century in Rome such as Juvenal and Horace develop an authentic poignancy. They knew about this. The problem is as old as urbanized man. All over the world, in South America, Asia, and Africa, as well as in Europe and the United States, young country folk are still moving to cities in search of employment and a better life, while city dwellers are writing and singing songs about rural life, moving to the suburbs, and swarming to their weekend cottages in the country.

12. This cottage, known as Godwin House, bears witness to the major periods of construction and growth that have transpired here on the edge of the Cotswolds as elsewhere in southern England.

Wherever I turned in this small village, I was constantly presented with particulars that evoked the general. One such example was the improbable-looking device shown in Figure 15, which lived outside my door at Warneford House. Although not the sort of thing discussed by Nikolaus Pevsner in his book *The Englishness of English Art*, to me it was quintessentially English in design. Not possessing the elegance or ideas of Vanbrugh, Adam, or Kent, it called to mind the more humble England of the Austin minivan, of thatched cottages and tea cozies, of Beatrix Potter and Toby pitchers. There is in England and English design a vigorous, frumpy strain of roly-poly, bumbling practicality, equally rooted in finding uses for leftover bits and nineteenth-century romanticism, deep in comfortable middle-class cottages, and in the amateurism made as famous by great and fictional detectives as by lady explorers, which is inescapably noticeable to the visitor. From solid and

13. *The pensioner Albie, mending a wall at the village car park across from the old store. Beyond are the layers of walls, fences, trees, buildings, and gardens that even a village as small as Buckland displays.*

FACING: *14. Plan of Buckland village.*

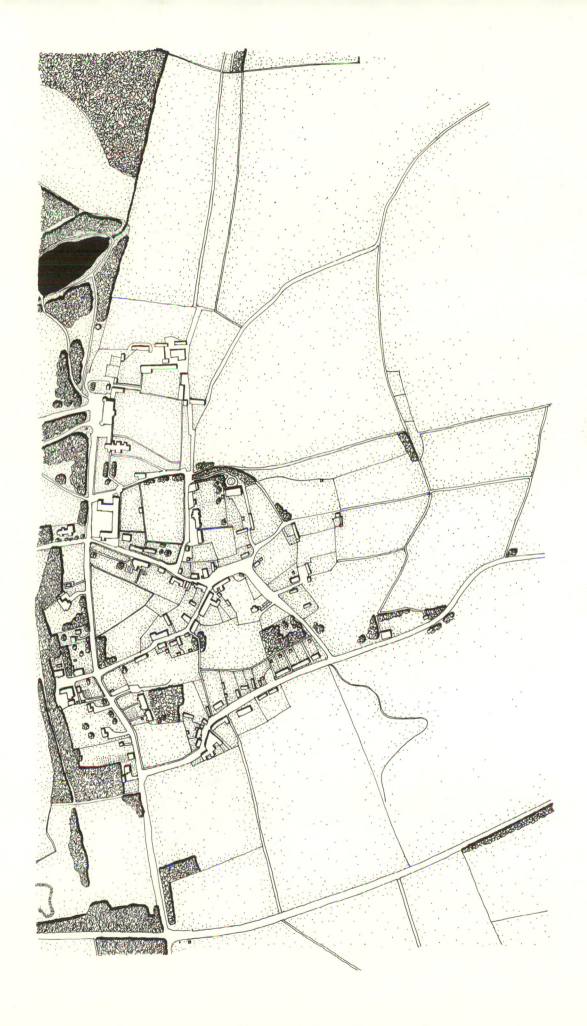

dumpily cut wool clothes and "serious" walking shoes to hideous knit wool hats worn by indomitable elderly women; from Toad of Toad Hall to oddly domestic phone boxes and railway carriages, there is a kind of product that is peculiarly English. One of its most outlandish evocations was presented in the film *Brazil* by Terry Gilliam in the late 1970s, wherein the future is presented as a dystopia haunted by such klutzy gadgets and anarchistic "odd-job" men. The particularly sensible yet somehow amusing contraption outside Warneford House was a trash burner. Its basic element was a corrugated metal trash can — or "dust bin," as it is known in England — that had been modified by the addition of feet, a series of holes to supply air, and a stovepipe fitted into the lid. One American who

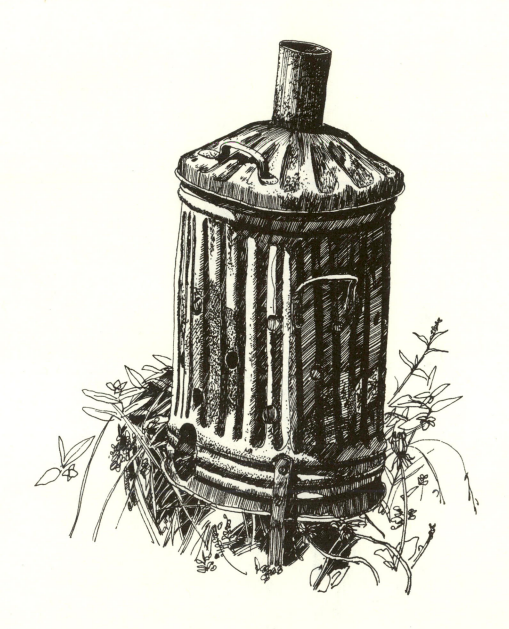

was most English in this particular way, Benjamin Franklin, I am certain would have nod-
ded in approval at this device over his awkward yet effective eyeglasses. Twenty years later,
with the advent of air pollution control and recycling, such things have been replaced
throughout the English countryside by an equally sensible hybrid plastic contraption
known as a "wheely bin," which can now also be seen gracing the curbs of cities in the
United States from California to Vermont and New Hampshire.

I should probably never have concluded that a trash burner could come to represent
or evoke such a long list of design and behavioral phenomena if I had not sat still long
enough to draw it, which prompts me to say more about drawing. I have a firm belief that
drawing is an outward manifestation of thinking in much the same manner as writing or
speech. Just as there are many categories of writing or speech — plain, political, didactic,
satirical, semiliterate, poetry, prose, fiction, nonfiction, biographical, scientific — so, too,
there are many kinds of drawing, and it is not unusual to find the modes mixed. The drawings in this book often began simply as exercises to record information in a relatively fac-
tual way. Like all drawings, they were highly selective from the beginning, exemplifying
considerable editing throughout their execution. Clearly a great amount of visual, physical
material available to me and not presented in the drawings or text is just as real as that presented in this book. Of all the material there was to choose from, this selection represents
a point of view. All drawings, whether topographical or abstract, are always *about* something. Sometimes what they are about is quite simply the subject matter depicted.
Sometimes it is about some relationship within or between the supposed contents of the
drawing, either as observed in the draftsman's world or as depicted on the paper.
Sometimes it is merely some physical property or the result of the very graphics or gestures
on the paper. Sometimes, through inference or suggestion, it is about some thing or event
elsewhere in time and place. It should come as no surprise to anyone, then, to learn that
oftentimes while one sits quietly drawing, the mind races about in all directions, rather like
a dog that has been released from a car after having ridden along patiently for several
hours.

*15. Bricolage in the garden: a trash burner used in the 1970s and now gone the way of hip
flasks and dodoes, replaced by the ubiquitous plastic "wheely bin."*

16. Overlapping and simultaneity: as in one's life, it is difficult to separate things that coexist and may influence each other; so too it is often difficult to draw only one cow. Gregarious, they come in groups and always seem to be arranged in shifting masses like clouds or trees. So, too, the factors influencing patterns on the land — climate, geology, habits of farming, land ownership, mythology, fashions in thought — shift, overlap, and play their part simultaneously. Buckland, Oxfordshire.

Sitting alone motionless and silent before a subject for a long period of time has several effects upon the viewer. First, and most important in terms of knowledge, is that we are slowed down and brought to a complete halt in our normal progress through the environment, thereby allowing us actually to experience something, to be in a place and to feel it, see it, hear it, smell it, and to see the light move and change upon it in more than the superficial manner with which we usually experience our surroundings. Second, in order to draw a thing well we must look at it carefully and long enough to reproduce its likeness from memory when looking at our drawing pad. This means we must observe how a thing is made. We must study its form and order; we must notice how it is positioned in the world among other things and events. As one sits taking in this new information and building the knowledge with which to make a drawing, it is as if one were feeding the visual portion of the brain, which like all creatures develops an appetite based upon its habits and health. A brain used to a regular and rich visual diet chews away with pleasure when given the time before one scene after another. While all of this is going on, it is also as if the more verbally developed portions of our mind become bored and begin to conceptualize, idling along, free-associating about this and that, and poking about at the visual portion. Introspection and phantom conversations ensue. There is a certain amount of seemingly random energy and thought, but with it comes the desire for order and clarity, for the rewarding discovery of relationships and correlations that continually reassert themselves. Two personal examples may help to illustrate this particular semimeditative and associational form of thought that goes on while drawing and leads the draftsman into selecting and editing subject matter in ways that do not appear connected in a more ordinary, cognitive, or causal sense.

Late one afternoon I decided to make a drawing of a Gothicized stable that had been added to the old manor house of the village. It was warm, and shadows were beginning to creep across the drive. I selected a vantage point that included within my view a simple wooden gate, probably with the unconscious thought that there was a certain irony in attempting to restrict access to a building that was supposedly already fortified by means of a gate that any child could open. Obviously, this implied a radically altered social situation, with the further irony that the apparent castle was really only a stable, all tricked out in mock fortifications so as to charm the eye of an eighteenth-century viewer looking

17. Curious as it seems, this building really is what remains of the original manor house that was turned into a stable and Gothicized when John Wood's handsome block of a villa replaced it. Today it has been reconverted into a dwelling for the daughter of the new owner of Buckland House. The tractor below was parked immediately adjacent to the spot from which the upper drawing was made.

down the driveway from the entrance to Buckland House. I was charmed as intended, for I began to sketch the silhouette and fenestration, when a cat, the ultimate symbol of domestic tranquillity, slowly walked across the road ahead. The fierce battlements had become a quaint piece of nostalgia, more suited to the nursery than an agricultural building. Finishing the drawing, I turned to leave and there beside me, parked in a shed attached to the Home Farm quarters were two large, green Massey-Ferguson tractors. With my very first glimpse came a sudden association. Formally and functionally the tractors resembled castles. Like hammers and axes and real castles, the tractors were handsome, tough, functional objects shaped to a complex purpose by clever people. Like hammers, they were tools meant to be used productively in man's labors, and like the crenellations on the castle battlements, the stout metal bars that formed the frame of the driver's cab were actually defenses, in this case to prevent the farmer from being crushed in case the tractor were to roll over in a furrow or on a hill, a fate that has befallen many men since the passing of the draft horse. These roll bars told of danger, death, and the ingenuity of man to protect and harbor life as clearly as any other fortification. Although it was approaching dinner time, I settled down again and began drawing the tractor with an attitude I'd never had before toward one.

Several weeks later I sat drawing on a small canvas stool along the main street of Buckland. The drawing began simply enough as a single vertical image of a wall and houses along the left side of the street. While drawing, however, it became important to me that I represent the opposite, right-hand side of the street, because it occurred to me that one of the most important aspects of the street was that it was not only a divider between two independent rows of buildings, but also the link between them. A dialogue was taking place in time and space between the buildings and inhabitants on one side of the street and

FOLLOWING PAGE: *18. The main street of Buckland clearly reveals how economically successful this manor has been for centuries. Like numerous villages in the Cotswolds immediately to the north, the source of its wealth has been sheep and corn, cattle and corn. Today many of these older homes are owned by comfortable retired individuals and professionals who come from London and Oxford.*

those on the other. The street represented movement and communication. The visual content of the drawing was ostensibly about stone houses and walls, but the psychological content for me while making the drawing became more and more a meditation on the sociability of the street and what it said about this village and possibly about all villages.

What, I wondered, was the small, round structure just inside the garden wall on my left? It resembled the small overnight lockups into which bailiffs used to place prisoners when marching them to be tried at the county assizes. That could hardly be it, I thought, for surely it would have a stone roof if one didn't want the prisoner to escape. After all, a man could untie the thatch and climb out through the roof in such a feeble jail. Then again, I mused, things were different then. Was it possible that the sort of prisoner held there wouldn't believe it his place to escape? Certainly people were as desperate then as today, often more so, I thought, so that argument didn't wash. I kept drawing, finally concluding that it was merely a garden shed, formerly with some other and more pragmatic function unknown to me such as a privy, a granary, or a chicken house. I shifted my attention to the other side of the street.

Mixed among the banal thoughts, the small insights, and new information that accompany nearly every drawing are always questions. The more one sees, the more questions that arise about what one is seeing. We look for order, pattern, meaning, and structure in our world. The more I drew, the more I wanted to read. The more I discovered, the more I wanted to share my findings with others. I was blessed with the greatest luxury of all: time to pursue the subjects of my curiosity.

Although I had walked up and down this street many times and knew where it led and generally what lay along it, while finishing the second half of the drawing, I became more and more concerned with knowing *exactly* what lay beyond the curve in the street at the "end" or "back" of my drawing. I stood up, stretched, and immediately walked to the last visible portion of the street I had drawn. I stopped, sat down on my folding stool, and looked about. Ahead lay the end of the village and a small Catholic church built by the nonconforming owners of Buckland House, who, like many of the upper classes after the English Civil War, had been reluctant to leave their ancestral church. To my left and right were the typical stone walls of the region, seen throughout the hills of the Cotswolds in Oxfordshire and Gloucestershire to the north and west. They were of limestone blocks laid horizontally and topped with stones on edge. The chapel, although only approximately the size of a small cottage, seemed ambitious in its massing. It evoked associations with children's drawings of mountain ranges as well as the contortions of the mind and social order that the struggle between Catholic and Protestant had produced in British history.

I drew the church quickly and matter-of-factly. Oddly enough, at the time I was more interested in some thoughts about mountains than I was in the building. Mountains? I sketched away, filling in the roof. I thought of my childhood in Alaska, of mountains; I thought of drawings I'd made of mountains as a teenager. I shaded the dark trees behind the church. A chill wind blew down from snow on the mountains; I could hear it in the trees. While in this semi-reverie I looked up from my drawing of the church and glanced at the stone wall only a foot from my head. There, towering beside me, was a vast and mountainous landscape. Scale is truly in the mind of the beholder, as recent studies in fractal geometry have proven. The moss and lichens that had crept up the sides of this modest wall suddenly appeared like the relict forests of ancient China that cling to the cliffs and crags of the great Sung dynasty landscapes. I began to draw a small portion of the wall. As I did, I could almost hear the mountains groan and the sound of waters deep within the earth. It was the wilderness of Muziano and St. Jerome, the winter vastness of Wang Wei, it was Leonardo's grotto. After all, wasn't the grotto of Leonardo's vision of the baby Christ and youthful John, later the Baptist, as Chinese as it was Mediterranean or classical?

The imagery of mist-shrouded mountains and boulder-strewn streambeds with pilgrims wending their way across a vast landscape is as deeply rooted in human experience as it is remote from the landscape of the Thames River valley. Yet China and some things Chinese are particularly akin to the English sensibility. So much so, that a lot of excellent scholarship and foolishness have been generated about the Chinese influence upon eighteenth-century landscape gardening. Generally, the rage for things Chinese such as tea came after the fact, and yet the connection is there. The China that one thinks of while in the English countryside is not the China of Kubla Khan, a China of vast and frigid deserts, of invasions and the numbing creation of the Great Wall, nor is it the China of the opium wars or ever more intricate and bizarre decoration; it is not even the China of a moonrise upon a river in spring, of the sound of a flute amid the rustling of leaves, of an old poet sitting in a pavilion by a lake dreaming of journeys in the autumn through the pines and maples of a mountain valley to his family home in the north. Although the differences between the Chinese and the English are almost laughingly obvious, there are profound reasons why these countries have been drawn to each other from time to time.

The most remarkable of these reasons is a characteristic that, although not always in vogue, periodically reappears and separates them from other peoples. This is a shared view of man in nature. There is — or was — in China a vision of Nature as a grand, supreme, all-encompassing flow of force, within which human activity is a small and transitory, if integral, portion, like a cloud passing across the moon. This philosophy and the art it produced struck a chord in the hearts of eighteenth-century English intellectuals. It is related to the mood that produced skepticism in English philosophy and religion, brought kings to the chopping block, and produced political views based upon an idea of natural order that was expressed in large, irregular landscape parks cast in a particular idea of Nature wherein man's works were seen to be small, though celebratory and important.

As different as the Chinese and the English were socially and artistically, there is no doubt that in both cultures man's agriculture and architecture were seen to exist *in* nature, not separate from it. Furthermore, the highest form of art often expressed this view, and, as often as not, the most ambitious works of wealthy landlords were attempts to emulate and create "ideal" or "poetic" landscapes. That they knew exactly what they considered to

be an "ideal" landscape and would attempt to build it was only possible because the topic had been pursued by some of the greatest thinkers and artists in both cultures for centuries. Somehow this confident conceptualization of an ideal hardly seems possible today. This is partly because of a deeply felt distrust of any "ideal" or abstract quest. Many of the worst horrors, wars, atrocities, and dehumanizing processes let loose in our time have been associated with such attitudes. This is no less true for the atavistic and universally faceless and placeless architecture that has grown out of the twentieth-century quest for purity or various attempts to inspire a new social order.

It was growing late, I was cold and stiff. I finished the drawing. The mountain range had been transformed back into a four-foot-high wall. I looked up. The church seemed smaller than before. It looked diagrammatic and poverty stricken. There was little exuberance or detail. Man's work seemed feeble, or at least this one did. I turned to leave but changed my mind. With the perseverance, optimism, and curiosity that characterize our species, I went instead to the church. Why? I guess to look for the saving grace, to find the redeeming feature of this rather humdrum and unwelcome building. Unfortunately, after a quick inspection of the interior, my prejudices were confirmed. This small chapel was lackluster without and within. Both the patron and the faith were to blame, I concluded. As I was leaving, for some reason I looked up toward the sky and gable, and there was what I was seeking! Exuberance, life! Around and above a handsome bit of masonry supporting a fleur-de-lis and bell were a flock of swallows. Feeding on insects lit up by the late afternoon sun as it dipped into the west, they swooped and dove, soared and kited about the belfry. Cheered by the scene and hoping to understand it all somehow, I made another drawing.

19. Changes in scale and point of view: the Catholic chapel built by the Royalist Throckmortons at the top of the village street with the cedars of Buckland House park behind, and vegetation growing from a wall next to my head where I drew the chapel.

And so it goes with drawing. I hope by now it is clear that many of the drawings in this book were not created as illustrations in the conventional sense. Rather than explicating a previously completed text, in most cases they preceded it or generated questions, which subsequently evoked explication. In some cases, for me they carry a major portion of the essay. For years I have wished that I could get people to spend as much time reading a drawing as they do a page of text.

20. Swallows feeding in the early evening above the carved stone finials of Throckmorton's chapel, Buckland village.

When I first came to Buckland, it was still located in the county of Berkshire and hadn't yet been incorporated into Oxfordshire where it now resides. Nikolaus Pevsner in his authoritative guide remarked that Berkshire (then including Buckland) has fewer thrills to offer architectural sightseers than most of the other counties of southern Britain. In the conventional sense of architecture as monuments divorced from life this is true, and even more so now that this county has been reduced to a strip accompanying a motorway. But even if we consider it as it still existed in the late 1960s and early 1970s, there was no cathedral or major city. Only Windsor Castle on its eastern edge could be considered in the monument class. Reading, the largest community, is only an overgrown industrial town, ugly in the manner of such places. There are, of course, various bits and pieces from all periods scattered about throughout the county. Of these, Buckland has several of the most remarkable. There is Buckland House, probably the most important and handsome of the eighteenth-century houses then in the county, with its pavilions, deer park, and lake, to be described later. So, too, is the Gothic revival facade of the stables, which was added to the old manor house in 1790, thereby rendering it somewhat of an eye-catcher. The last of these more special buildings in Buckland is St. Mary's church. Here we are presented with pure English stuff. England is peppered with country churches, thousands and thousands of them. Every one is different in some way. W. G. Hoskins remarked that more than twelve thousand medieval ones alone survived. Certainly St. Mary's in Buckland is as interesting as most, partly because it is so peculiar and awkward. Like most of the wealthy churches that date from just after the Norman Conquest, this building undoubtedly stands on the site of an earlier Anglo-Saxon structure, although virtually no trace remains. From the Conquest on, it was continuously under construction, reconstruction, and repair. The unusually wide nave is twelfth-century Norman, the battlements on the nave are perpendicular gothic, and the dumpy, four-square, crossing tower from the thirteenth century is early English. The bizarre windows in the transepts, which have stone mullions crashing straight and peculiarly into the arches, have baffled several historians. Are they a seventeenth-century repair job? Certainly they aren't original. Odd. But then, too, so are the pretty but incongruous Victorian stained glass windows and the vicar who, throughout the decade of the 1970s, was not on speaking terms with a single parishioner. No single detail makes this church as special as it is, nor any one person the village. Yet the place is special. The entire county is (or was — the logic should still be applied, if only to this portion of Gloucestershire that is now adjacent), despite its paucity of great cities and architectural monuments. Few places on earth are so beautiful, livable, or so manmade.

FOLLOWING PAGE: *21. St. Mary's and its churchyard with the Gothicized stable of Buckland House in the distance.*

22. *One of two gate lodges at Buckland House, both still inhabited. Like every element of the village, even the briefest account of events links them not only to the social history of Buckland but also to that of England in general. It was here that the current estate manager was born and raised. He and his five brothers bathed at the outside pump and trough as children; the coachman would sit here in the sun like a big cat, and various workers on the estate came around and queued up to receive their pay in coins outside what is now the bathroom window.*

FOLLOWING PAGE: 23. *The village of Buckland as it lies along the Golden Ridge, seen from the lane leading up to it from the River Thames in the fields below to the north.*

Village and Farm

Longbridge Deverill, Wiltshire

For my own part, I think there is somewhat peculiarly sweet and amusing in the shapely figured aspect of chalk-hills in preference to those of stone, which are rugged, broken, abrupt, and shapeless.

GILBERT WHITE
The Natural History and Antiquities of Selborne, 1789

He observed that the country was smoother and more plastic. The woods had gone, and under a pale-blue sky long contours of earth were flowing, merging, rising a little to bear some coronal of beeches, parting a little to disclose some green valley, where cottages stood under elms or beside translucent waters. It was Wiltshire at last.

Here is the heart of our island: the Chilterns, the North Downs, the South Downs radiate hence. The fibers of England unite in Wiltshire, and did we condescend to worship her, here we would erect our national shrine.

E. M. FORSTER
The Longest Journey, 1907

AN AGRICULTURAL LANDSCAPE

I WAS NOT IN FACT to return to Buckland, even when I secured funding a few years later and set off for England once again. In returning to the topic of the English landscape with a wife whom I'd met in England during that first summer visit and our six-month-old daughter, I went to a property in Wiltshire that my wife's family had recently purchased. It was on the edge of Salisbury Plain and called Longbridge Deverill. It was not a name that meant anything to me, but at least its position between Salisbury and Bath seemed promising. I was disappointed, certainly, that I'd not be working in Buckland again, but Wiltshire would offer fresh material and expand my direct experience of the English landscape. In retrospect, I cannot imagine a more fruitful location in any of southern England's historical agricultural landscapes than the string of small villages known as the Deverills in which to spend the next several years walking, looking, reading, and drawing and reflecting.

Driving on the A350, the old toll road to Shaftesbury, heading north to the Midlands from the south coast as many heavily loaded goods-lorries and tourists do today, one rushes past the village of Longbridge Deverill. There is the usual clutter of signs, a petrol station and a pub, a few scattered houses, two dangerous intersections, a glimpse of a handsome stone building with a church beyond, and then it is gone. There is a brief pause of meadows and curves before the next hamlet blasts past.

The whole experience lasts less than fifty seconds. An odd name, the terror that a tractor might suddenly lurch out from a hidden lane, once handsome buildings now either abandoned, tarted up, or invisible behind overgrown hedges: a small and slow place seen from a speeding car. This could describe any of thousands of southern English villages. The pattern when seen from outside the automobile, although profoundly affected by it, is nonetheless very different. As soon as one begins to walk around, to explore the world of village and hedge on foot, and to get away from the through traffic routes, the world takes on more complexity, subtlety, and variety. It becomes richer and more beautiful. Longbridge Deverill turns out to have a totally different shape from that first experienced by auto, largely because it was laid out and built by pedestrians. Because of its location, on a clear chalk stream at the edge of Salisbury Plain, it also presents in microcosm the history of man's pragmatic and rewarding relationship with the land of England.

FOLLOWING PAGE: *24. The automotive landscape: even without the worldwide visual horrors of commercialism, the vision of the world from an automobile tends to become more uniform everywhere, in Europe and the United States because of speed, engineering, and mechanical limitation. Entering Longbridge Deverill from the south.*

PRECEDING PAGE: *25. View of the Wylye River valley and Longbridge Deverill from Cow Down. Beyond are the timber plantations of Longleat Estate and Crockerton Common.*

The string of villages known as the Deverills is located — and in this they are like Buckland — near the edge of a great chalk mass radiating out from Salisbury Plain. This upland comprises a group of long, silvery, undulating hills covered with grass or grain (called corn in Britain), and occasional beech woods. The great ridges and arms that reach out and away from this divide are the Dorset Downs, made famous by Thomas Hardy, the south downs of Sussex, the north downs of Surrey and Kent, and the Chilterns ranging north of London to the Wash in East Anglia. All are anchored in Wessex. Nearby are the heavy clay soils that underlie the other half of the south: the great valleys of the Thames, Weald, and Avon. In Wiltshire this difference in soil is referred to locally as the "chalk and the cheese."

Visually and physically Longbridge Deverill hasn't the cohesion of many English villages, nor the postcard qualities of its Cotswold equivalent, Buckland. This is due to the river and marsh that bisect it and the disastrous highway improvements that literally shattered the very heart of it. The community of Longbridge Deverill combines at least two earlier Celtic settlements that faced a marsh, both of which in Saxon times bore the name of the stream, Devrel, like seven other nearby communities, also named Devrel. Eilert Ekwall gives a scholarly guess that this word, which first appears in records as DeFereal in 968, is derived from either the Welsh *dwfr ial*, meaning "the river of the ial" (a fertile upland region), or from the British *dubroialon*, meaning "the ial on the stream." The descriptive qualifier, initially in Latin as *Longo ponte*, is self-explanatory. Somewhat diminished, the marsh is still present, though the long wooden bridge across it, built by the monks of Glastonbury, was replaced long ago by road fill and a shorter stone bridge.

The village stretches out in several directions from this marsh just above flood level on the rich bottomland. It contains small meadows, pastures and allotments, hedgerows, and some very large trees. Because of its situation one can see and step into fields in any direction. The trout-filled river still runs through meadows that have an interesting history of their own and have provided grazing and hay since before the Roman invasion. To the north stands a young plantation of trees, a fragment of the ancient forest of Selwood. Around on all sides the great hump-backed shapes of the Downs, quilted with crops and dotted with livestock, billow and swell against the sky. It is a good place to live, and it was here on the edge of Salisbury Plain in numerous such places that British agriculture began.

From its headwaters above Kingston Deverill to Salisbury, where the River Wylye joins the Nadder, Ebble, and Avon, is thirty miles; it descends five hundred feet and passes thirty village churches. At the beginning of the nineteenth century there were twenty-four parishes alone in the eighteen miles between Warminster and Wilton, each with an ancient strip of valley and its resources that included the river itself, water meadows, side hill, and downs above; as William Cobbett pointed out, they were "pretty near as close to each other as the churches in London and Westminster." Upstream from Warminster are the Deverills, five villages that have coalesced from the original nine listed in the Domesday Book: in order, Kingston Deverill, Monkton Deverill, Brixton Deverill, Hill Deverill, and Longbridge Deverill. Only minutes apart by car, it takes slightly more than forty-five minutes to walk through all five from Longbridge to Kingston, and although it looks perfectly rural, the consistent density of settlement in this valley cannot be exaggerated, surpassing the density of many U.S. suburbs. Today Longbridge is the largest of them all, and, in the mysterious way of English parishes, holds a population larger than seems possible, in this case, more than a thousand people.

Aside from the crossroads and residences of various size and character, the village today consists of one shop combined with a post office that also sells fresh, prepared, and packaged food; a petrol station and garage that also handles various dairy, grocery, and convenience items; a good pub, formerly a coaching inn, that does grills and sponsors occasional events; a house that sells free-range eggs; a handsome almshouse; a village hall, formerly a school, that is now used by the Women's Institute, by political parties, and for various events and extension classes; a handsome though not very special church; a policeman's residence and office; two bridges; and several large, very good, and well-run farms. For census and ecclesiastical purposes, the adjoining communities of Crockerton and Hill Deverill are now part of Longbridge Deverill, and they contain more houses and farms, plus a watercress farm, two churches, both mediocre and virtually disused, another pub (lunches only), and more shops, one of which began as a farm supply store and has slowly grown into a country version of an American department store or shopping center surrounded by an asphalt car park. The nearest market town is Warminster four miles away, an ancient borough with the amenities one expects: banks, fresh food and meat, specialty shops, clothing, movie theater, and today a seldom-used railway station. By the mid-seventies, it also had a perpetual traffic jam as through traffic contended with local and market traffic. Today a highway bypass takes the A350 around the town to the west, and the town has regained a fair amount of its dignity and character. Bus service, though regular, has a schedule both peculiar and awkward to use (let alone to understand and remember).

W. G. Hoskins, the dean of English landscape history, has said that we cannot *prove* the continuous occupation from Celtic times to the present day for any one site, many popular ones being abandoned and reoccupied subsequently, in some cases many times. Nevertheless, it would be true to say of Longbridge, as of many towns in Wiltshire, that there has been a long history of settlement and development beginning in Celtic times or before. Even in recent times this village has undergone remarkable fluctuations. Between 1861 and 1911, farming was economically depressed and the population plummeted more than 50 percent. Where ten public houses recently did business, now only two survive. Conversely, during the two world wars it was swollen by servicemen: more than five thou-

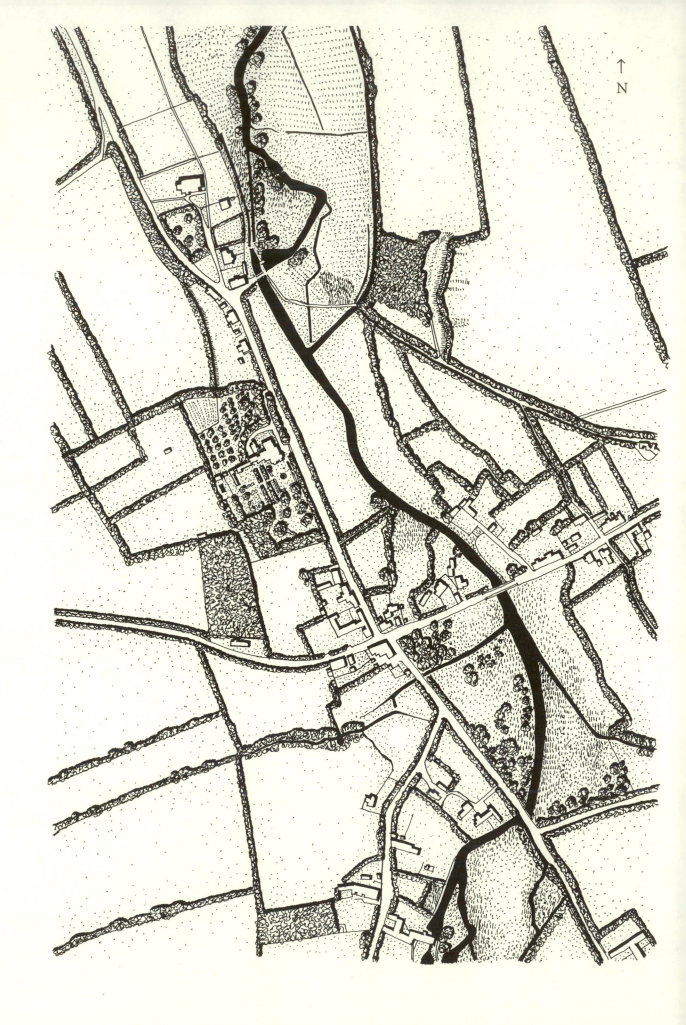

26. Plan of Longbridge Deverill village.

sand were encamped at Sand Hill farm during World War I and again one thousand men and their tanks during World War II. An elderly resident told me that between the retreat from Dunkirk and the invasion of Normandy the downs were covered with tents and you couldn't get into the pub for soldiers on Friday nights. Today, once again, it is a quiet, prosperous farming community. It has changed and it will change again.

BRONZE AND IRON AGE DEVELOPMENTS

Salisbury Plain is a great upland mass of chalk, hardly a plain by American standards but very much of one within the context of the fine-grain and intricate landscape of southern England. It is the setting for the great stone circles of Stonehenge and Avebury, and of Silbury Hill — the largest artificial mound in all of Europe — as well as numerous barrows, farmsteads, and causeway camps of an agricultural society that erected them. The magnitude and number of these remains, so avidly visited by tourists today, provide a clear indication of the numbers of people who successfully inhabited the region from very early times. The Romans found a widespread agricultural society when they arrived in 55 B.C. In the early years Vespasian had to ship grain in from Spain; by the time they left, England was regularly shipping some of its surplus to the legions stationed on the Rhine, and its wool was famous throughout the empire.

It used to be thought that the people of pre-Roman Britain lived exclusively on windy hilltops, in hill forts and huts, and that the river valleys below were choked with dense woods and fierce animals. It seemed to make some sense, especially since all the barrows, ditches, and primitive fields visible were on hilltops and in marginal or difficult areas for farming. In a pioneering work, *Air Survey and Archaeology*, O. G. S. Crawford wrote in 1923, "while an occasional Romano-British village occurs near a river valley, nearly all are situated on the uplands away from the streams, while with the exception of tiny groups in the south-east, not a single village of the Saxon kind occurs away from the immediate verge of a stream." In one breath he created a phantom dichotomy between early hilltop-centered civilization and later valley-oriented ones. In the scholarly warfare that followed, R. G. Collingwood, in his *Oxford History of Roman Britain*, ironically mistaking grain and working pits for huts at the Little Woodbury site, jumped to the correct solution about a native village tradition, which others were still at pains to disprove. Around Salisbury there were roughly five settlements to the square mile, and all were at or about the elevation of six hundred feet. The notion of widespread settlement in the uplands is now known to be correct for this region, but that of wild and uninhabited valleys is hopelessly wrong. As Bowen

27. *The remains of early settlement are found throughout southern Britain. This menhir, one of the many Bronze Age artifacts that include circles and barrows dotting the countryside, stands in the middle of an ancient farmstead in Cornwall. The Berryman family, who work the land today and have been in possession of it since the seventeenth century, grow much the same crops and raise the same animals as the "beaker people" who erected it. Porthmeor Farm, Cornwall.*

and Fowler wrote with unusual force for scholars in a field that is known for caution and tentative patience: "Almost certainly many other sites once existed, some beneath existing settlements . . . some blanketed beneath the water meadows, most perhaps lying within the areas of permanent arable in the valley and on the valley sides now totally obliterated by the more or less continuous plowing over the last millennium."

No one had thought of the obvious fact that what is the best farming land now was probably the best farming land then. No one had looked under or near the existing villages for early sites, and admittedly if they had it would have been difficult and confusing work, as it is today. But now, in case after case, archaeologists are able to document pre-Roman settlements under more recent or contemporary villages and fields, not only in the chalk lands of Wiltshire but also in East Anglia. By a quirk of scholarship, a great amount of time was spent proving something that hadn't been checked, namely, the supposed difficulties that Celtic man would have clearing the woods or plowing heavy clay soils, whereas every farmer knows that the reason the downs weren't more heavily plowed in the eighteenth and nineteenth centuries was how hard the chalk and flint were to plow, the thinness of the soil, and how easily it was exhausted and subject to erosion. Recent experiments in Denmark have shown that Neolithic stone axes were very efficient tools. Bronze and iron ones were even better, and the people using them were great consumers of wood. In an experiment carried out by archaeologists in Denmark, three men using a Neolithic flint axe, unsharpened in four thousand years, managed to clear six hundred square yards of silver birch forest in four hours. The drastic fall in pollen counts of large forest trees during this period point to the extent of clearing. Like the population throughout all of England at the time, the denizens of Longbridge Deverill used timber for their houses, fences, carts, chariots, looms, and fires. The decrease in forests and the sudden rise in grain tells us how effective they were. Furthermore, grazing by the increasing number of their animals prevented forests from regenerating, thus contributing to the gradual extinction of vast forest areas.

All around Longbridge lie remains from this period: crop marks, mounds, tumuli, ditches, and campsites. Every side hill in the valley has scraps of the early fields creeping up its sides, and the casual finds of artifacts never cease. Directly above and south of the village is a hill known as Cow Down, a clue that this has never been exclusively a sheep and corn-producing area, as the names of topographic landscape features tend to date from the earliest settlers around the world. There are similar sites on three of the neighboring hills, and fields of this period seem to have been nearly continuous along the valleys between them. We can see the edges of these early farms and roads on every side hill, peeping out from under the present ones like lettuce from beneath a piece of sandwich bread. It is a tantalizing albeit an increasingly faint sight. Modern agriculture and its methods have rendered many fields and earthworks recorded in the ordnance maps invisible on the ground except in unusual circumstances. Some can still be observed at certain times, however, from the air or with a particular low angle of light, during periods of drought or hard freezes. The second and third enclosures on Cow Down, no longer visible at all from the ground, have been thus revealed in aerial photos. Within the visible enclosure a large round house remains only partially explored. Although worthy of further study, it may wait indefinitely, as most of the digging in Britain today is done on a crisis basis, with archaeologists trying to stay ahead of various redevelopment and construction projects. The uncovering of human skeletons by a Longbridge farmer, Mr. Stratton, when he decided to plow up a portion of virgin downland in 1956, prompted this particular dig, lasting for several years. The large amount of irreparable damage done by recent deep plowing all over the chalk lands continues at a rapid pace, and, as had been remarked by many, most of our future knowledge is going to have to come from the sites saved in this generation. As in every region of the globe where archaeologists work, analysis and publication lags far behind, although it is miles ahead of any other country I can think of.

The settlements of the numerous farmers who worked these fields had to be somewhere, and since none are visible on the hills, they must lie lower down, under the present fields and villages along the riverbanks. At Longbridge there appear to have been at least two and probably three settlements around the marsh that by Saxon times could be called manors and later were taken over by the Normans with few changes.

The energetic farming people who built these early settlements were a tough horse-loving, hard-fighting lot, industrious and fiercely independent, as Caesar, Plautus, and Vespasian admit. While the tribes along the coast of Dorset and Hampshire who built the great hill forts at Maiden Castle and Cadbury were known as the Durotriges, those in Wiltshire were called Belgae by the Romans. Related to the inhabitants of the Thames Basin and East Anglia, as well as those across the channel in what are now Normandy and Brittany, they were one of the largest and more powerful forces in Britain and on the Continent, having been the only ones to resist the invasions of the Cimbri and Teutones into Gaul, and thereby came to play a major role in Rome's foreign policy and its eventual decision to become involved in the affairs of Britain. Despite recurring insular stereotypes, the concept of an isolated people clinging to bestial ways in the fog must be abandoned once and for all: England, even at this early time, was involved in European affairs. Roman writers have described Celtic Britons vividly, with their long hair, mustaches, wool plaid blankets, their large herds of ponies and thatched houses. We now also know that they rotated their crops, had better plows than the Romans, and fertilized their fields by running sheep and cattle out to graze upon the stubble after harvesting. They hunted and kept herds of pigs in the woods (as did the Romans in the Po River valley, among others — the beginning of Parma ham) and turned their long-legged sheep and short cattle up onto the downs to graze. The people living in the Wylye valley were clever and skilled at many crafts. Their dependence upon the downs for grazing, communication, and occasional sanctuary raised difficult and important problems. Water was everywhere and only too plentiful in the valleys below, but up on the well-drained chalk hilltops where they wished to graze their animals there was

*28. Corn: three of these grasses are carefully cultivated grains with an ancient pedigree —
wheat, barley, and oats — bred to produce large amounts of seed with a minimum amount
of stalk and leaf. All three and their wild relatives were picked on a walk over the Downs
from Brixton to Longbridge Deverill. From the left: oats, a wild grass, barley, and wheat.*

none to be found. The solution that they hit upon — dew ponds — was ingenious and is
still in use today. Gilbert White, the eighteenth-century vicar, in his *Natural History and
Antiquities of Selborne* described it thus in 1789:

To the thinking mind few phenomena are more strange than the state of little ponds on the summits
of chalk hills, many of which are never dry in the most trying draughts of summer. . . . No person
acquainted with chalky districts will allow that they ever saw springs in such a soil but in valleys and
bottoms, since the waters of so pervious a stratum as chalk all lie on one dead level, as well-diggers
have assured me again and again. Now we have such little round ponds in this district; and one in
particular on our sheep-down, three hundred feet above my house; which, though never above
three feet deep in the middle, and not more than thirty feet in diameter, and containing not more
than two or three hundred hogsheads of water, yet never is it known to fail, though it affords drink
for three hundred or four hundred sheep, and for at least twenty head of large cattle beside. . . . In
spite of evaporation from sun and wind, and perpetual consumption by cattle, yet constantly [they]
maintain a moderate share of water, without overflowing in the wettest seasons, as they would do if
supplied by springs.

How they hit upon dew ponds is unknown; possibly it came from the accidental creation of one or more of them by livestock in an occasional deposit of clay. To this day on
Cow Down, as on nearly every ridge in this region, there is a large version of one. In recent
times there still were men who knew how to build them and went about repairing these
ancient watering spots. Marjorie and C. H. B. Quennell describe the process: "A shallow
saucer-like depression is set out in the chalk and lined with straw. On this comes a layer of
puddled clay, with rims of chalk to protect the clay from the feet of cattle. Loose flints are
put in the bottom [to prevent cattle from wading out into the water and either poking
holes in the clay lining or excessively fouling the water] and the pond is started off with a
little water in it [carried up from below]. The straw and clay cut off the heat from the earth,
and when the moist mists drive over the Downs at night and come to the cooler pond, they
condense on its surface."

That the eighteenth century knew how they worked is clear from the further comments of Gilbert White, who tells us that it was his friend Dr. Hales in his *Vegetable Statistics* who worked out the principle of condensation over the cooler surface of water and clay
and says: "Persons that are much abroad, and travel early and late; such as shepherds,
fishermen, etc. can tell what prodigious fogs prevail in the night on elevated downs, even in

29. Up on the Downs: cows standing on banks thrown up from ditches of a large causeway camp on White Sheet Down above Stourhead; below, cows grazing the hillside below the large dew pond on Cow Down.

the hottest parts of summer; and how much the surface of things are drenched by those swimming vapours, though to the senses, all the while, little moisture seems to fall."

There are other pre-Roman facilities that have remained in use. In addition to the small tracks, paths, and lanes found around any farm or rural community in the world, a larger network of roads evolved in southern England. Known today as trackways, many of these are still easy to pick out on ordnance maps or in the field, curving along on ridges and hills with boundaries running up to but not across them, leading along, parallel to rivers below, and still in use, one way or another. The most famous pair, the Harrow Way and the Great Ridge Way, cross each other on the Downs about two miles south of Longbridge. Roughly north-south and east-west through routes, they connect Cornwall and Devon in the southwest to the Thames estuary and East Anglia as well as the area of the Southampton estuary and coast to the Cotswolds and the Midlands. Additional routes connecting to other regions tie into these and each other, providing an easy path for commerce and armies. Laid out with different criteria from Roman and modern roads, they usually climb a ridge and once at a fair height maintain a level path, going around valleys instead of across them whenever possible. Because much of their length is high and dry, running along chalk ridges, they require little or no maintenance and are never muddy or rutted, even in the wettest weather. Used largely by farmers today (except for several trunk roads that follow significant lengths, such as the A303 just south of Longbridge), and often still in use as boundaries, these wide and green highways were used to drive cattle to market until World War II since they could graze along the way and rarely have to cross other roads. The trackway on Whitesheet Down known as Hardway or Long Lane to the east of Longbridge, which I have walked many times, is still used by farmers to reach their livestock in fields on either side, the entire length of the down, most of which is still unplowed.

The Romans came to Britain to stabilize the political situation, to develop commerce and trade, and to exploit the abundant natural resources. For several hundred years they succeeded. Following the initial military phase came the creation of a physical and cultural infrastructure. In order to administer the territory under their control effectively, to dispatch communications, troops, or supplies, and to remove to their ships the minerals they were mining in various regions, they built a road system to their own specifications. These roads ran relatively straight over hills, valleys, and rivers, deviating only slightly to take advantage of occasional features like a ford or a better ascent of a ridge. Because they ignore the climate and terrain — unlike the Celtic high roads — it was necessary that they be carefully paved and drained, which explains why it is still fairly easy to find many of them, whether they run across fields or lie beneath modern highways.

Despite Roman technology and such elements as roads and aqueducts that formed part of the armature of the landscape (Sand Street, a Roman name for the oldest road leading to the bridge across the marsh at Longbridge, dates from this period), the basic fabric of settlements and farms continued to be that created by the earlier settlers. The Romans did exploit the Britons' agricultural system, however, largely by leaving it alone, and causing it to grow and expand by removing political and social insecurity, by extending roads into new territories, and through the creation of a market economy, thereby allowing the farmers to gain capital. Thus the Britons began to invest and expand their production, leasing or buying land, increasing their livestock, hiring more labor, further encouraging capital improvements in buildings and equipment. Roman bricks and flue tiles, numerous finds of which continue to occur throughout the Wylye valley, led to the introduction of corn-drying kilns, leading to further increases in productivity. In regard to the shape of fields, the manner of farming, or even the tenancy and subtenancy of the land, the Romans seem to have contributed very little. The families living at Longbridge would have kept to their native ways while keeping abreast of developments and trading in the nearby market centers of Bath (Aqua Sulis), Old Sarum near Salisbury (Sorviodunum), and Winchester (Venta Bulgarum).

Many scholars are convinced that the whole of Salisbury Plain along with most of the Cotswolds was transformed into a vast imperial sheep ranch. The reasons given to prove it are the apparent absence of major towns or villas in the area and the creation of weaving centers nearby. Another indication of this activity and its later development, the management of large herds, probably of cattle as well, is the construction of many large livestock enclosures on top of the earlier fields and settlement sites in widely scattered parts of the Downs, often of rectangular shape and including wood fences as well as ditches and mounds. Since this area was the largest corn-producing one at the time of the invasion, it is likely that the Romans would have wanted to secure it as a continued source of supply and therefore appropriated it. The farmers and their methods would have been unaffected in most respects. If, indeed, the Romans did introduce and encourage large flocks of sheep in this area, few if any people would have left; just as centuries later, during the great

30. Through route to the Mendip mines: above is the view looking straight along the path of a Roman road as it crests over a hill above Monkton Deverill and heads for a ford hidden in trees at Kingston Deverill on the Wylye (i.e., tricky) River, shown below. When crossed, the river is left behind as the road climbs the hill and passes out through the notch to the valley beyond. Fords, unlike bridges, are located where a river is wide, shallow, and without banks; where it has firm footing and where the animals or vehicles can go either upstream or downstream, not directly across. The river here bends obligingly twice to provide just such a safe and quiet spot for crossing even when it is unseasonably high.

medieval wool market, large cities and towns didn't evolve, even though everyone was kept very busy and the economy soared. This is because corn and sheep do well together. Arable crops needn't decrease as flocks increase; in fact, the two do best increasing together. This increase in livestock was a direct result of efforts to increase the arable acreage because of the dependency on stock for fertilizer.

The choice between sheep and cattle was tipped toward sheep by climate, terrain, and the recognition of the greater value of sheep dung. Columella, Varro, and Cato all list it as second only to pigeon dung, and much preferable to that of cattle or horses. The reason for this we now know is because of its higher nitrogen content. Sheep could also stand the open Downs for longer periods without watering — the dew ponds, then as now, were widely scattered — and they were better adapted to the treeless vegetation than either cattle or pigs, both of which were originally forest animals and were grazed in woods throughout the Middle Ages. It's more than likely that the Romano-Brits living in the Deverills ran large flocks of sheep on the Downs all summer, but they would also have folded them onto the rich cornfields of the bottomland after the harvest. Later the lush grass in the well-watered meadows fed them in the spring when the fields above were being plowed and sown. Summers the sheep spent up on the Downs while most of the villagers got on with the tilling, tending, and harvesting below. Farmers are famous for being conservative. Few agricultural changes happen overnight. The seeds for the Roman exploitation of Salisbury Plain as a sheep walk existed in the earlier practices of the Celts, just as medieval Saxon farming practices grew naturally out of theirs.

The end of Roman Britain is obscure. Whether abrupt or slow, large estates contracted and disintegrated. Towns were abandoned. Considerable fighting occurred. Ever more frequent and effective expeditions and adventurers from northern Europe passed along the coasts and ventured far inland. Nevertheless, as the era of Saxon England began, life went on — as it must — for as the wars of this century in Europe, Asia, the Middle East, and most recently in the Balkans have shown, as soon as the fighting stopped, men turned back to farming. So, too, for the Saxons and Celts, farming *was* their life. Then as now, the best farmland around Longbridge hadn't changed very much. Some fields were undoubtedly lost to weeds and scrub, some buildings were gone forever, and there were many new faces up on the Downs with the sheep, in the woods hunting and herding pigs, and following teams of yoked oxen in the back-breaking toil of getting in the crops.

MEDIEVAL LONGBRIDGE AND THE EMERGENCE OF WESSEX

Popular literature rarely discusses the remarkable Saxon achievement in the six hundred years between the depature of the Romans and the arrival of the Normans. Yet the lengthy lists in the Domesday Book of 1086 are just that — Saxon towns, mills, farms, abbeys, villages, churches and manors, burgesses, taxes and tithes, all recorded and taken over by the

Normans. These new conquerors contributed little to the general population or tenancy of the land they took over in 1066, though in manners of civil government and in the execution of William the Conqueror's policies, a small cadre of administrators played an important role. Plucking prime holdings for themselves, they paid a deep albeit rapacious compliment to the previous owners and managers of the land.

The Saxon arrival had caused considerable disruption and loss of arable land in Wiltshire, still heavily wooded and containing many wild areas. There is still some dispute as to the extent of the Saxon destruction of the Celtic population and culture; clearly Celtic strongholds or sanctuaries would have witnessed increased cultivation and inhabitation, and fighting continued in parts of central Wiltshire into the late sixth century, when in 550 the Celtic stronghold of Searo Byrg (Old Sarum) near Salisbury fell to the Saxons. But the old idea that farms and settlements were totally abandoned is challenged by the continuing discovery of Celtic settlements beneath Saxon ones. Although there must have been great damage, especially where the farming was highly specialized and complex, it is also clear that the Saxons returned it to levels achieved earlier by Roman administration, technology, and military manpower. Across England, the Saxons extended farms and communities into new lands.

I find it easier to conceive of this particular people's frame of mind at this particular time than at almost any other period of English history. They possessed what I would call a classical frontier mentality. As mentioned earlier, I spent the greater part of my childhood and young adult life in Alaska after World War II, when it was a vast wilderness with small clearings and a handful of settlements and towns. Because of the cold war with Russia, the military was always present, and one had a vague sense that if the bears, wolves, and the arctic weather didn't get you, the distant enemy might. The work involved in creating towns, roads, and military defenses and taming the wilderness was long and difficult, often with sudden or capricious hardships or disasters. Life was often short, with disease, accidents, floods, fires, and killings by animals and people. Nevertheless, there was an air of optimism. There seemed to be limitless space to move about in; the firewood would last a lifetime; the wildlife was endless. If the winters were long and hard, the summers were a great joy. More than anything else, there was a sense of common purpose in the work. The land was to be brought under control by man's labor. If enough trees were cut down, enough rivers controlled, enough roads built, and crops somehow established, then life would be perfect. The land and its activity, its energy and habits had to be domesticated or tamed at all costs. The people that my grandfather knew in the Klondike during the Gold Rush and that my parents and I knew in Alaska in 1946 were reenacting the story of our Anglo-Saxon ancestors as they labored to create the landscape of southern England.

Equally important during this period was the spread and growth in importance of Christianity. Six hundred years does not pass like a long, dark night. Near Longbridge Deverill, close to an abandoned villa two miles away, is a small community called Bishopstrow. Here a missionary bishop named Aldhelm preached to the Saxons. Whether this was beneath a well-known tree or a wooden cross is uncertain, because the Saxon word *treow* means both tree and cross. By the eighth century the entire region was thoroughly Christian, and large portions were owned and managed by the church. The two principal sources of information about Saxon life in this area are the Domesday Book, with its list of names and places, and the records that survive from the great abbey of Glastonbury twenty miles to the west in Somerset. This abbey, originally a hilltop sanctuary on an island in the middle of an extensive marsh, associated with both St. Patrick and King Arthur, grew to have tremendous secular and ecclesiastical power in southwestern England, owning vast tracts of land, including three of the most successful manors in the Deverills.

31. Not all medieval manors have evolved into villages or towns. At Hill Deverill only the old farm nucleus remains, a handsome cluster of sheds, barns, ditches, and fields.

I must confess that, until I had lived in Europe and visited remains of late medieval architecture, I had done the medieval church a great disservice in my imagination. I had often forgotten what a powerful institution and persuasive system of thought it was. It should not be confused with the many tepid and ineffectual organizations today, incapable of inspiring or reshaping our world, that survive with toleration but partial enthusiasm in a changed society, or the anti-intellectual, fundamentalist, or smarmy bourgeois sects of the Christian Right in the United States. Nor should it be considered comparable to the recently reinvigorated fundamentalist sects of the Middle East that eschew contemporary science, communications, and technology. To those who lived in England during the Middle Ages, it was a way of life, *the* way of life, and as credible and important to them in their daily lives as our science, bombs, medicine, automobiles, and highway engineers are to us. It wasn't merely fear, fable, and ignorance, as some today think. The clergy and their secular allies were the experts, the bureaucrats, promoters, and speculators of their time. They also were the literate, the intellectuals, the mathematicians, technicians, and artists. In one

year alone in the eleventh century there were two hundred thousand pilgrims to Canterbury in a land of only two million. That is, 10 percent of the population managed to travel to this one cathedral on foot or by horse, not to mention the pilgrims who would have journeyed to other holy sites in England and Wales, such as Glastonbury or Holywell, or even further to Rome or the Holy Land in the same year.

About the year 900 Alfred commissioned the first "Domesday" Book, now lost, which reckoned up the population, accumulated land development, property, mills, duties, and obligations of the land and manors in his kingdom. This inventory reaffirmed in terms of land-holdings and wealth the military control that his battles against the Danes had won for the Saxons. But it fails to make clear the dramatic changes effected by Saxon agricultural practices throughout the medieval landscape. Military success and the look and use of the land were intricately related: indeed, the plowshare followed the sword exactly.

From the mid-seventh century, two hundred years before the name of Wiltunshire is first recorded, Wiltshire had been politically and strategically crucial: as the base for attacks on Dorset and Somerset, providing men and supplies for Egbert's conquest of Mercia in the ninth century, the region had clearly recovered under the Saxons its agrarian vigor. It gave significant support to Alfred in his long struggles against the Danes (like George Washington centuries later, he managed over a ten-year period to combine hairbreadth escape, political maneuvering, and military skills in rallying a nascent society to common cause and extraordinary military accomplishment). In 871 at Uffington (near Buckland) and later, in 878, the Danish advances from the north and east deep inside Wiltshire were stopped dramatically: in the latter year, Alfred came out of winter quarters and marched with the men of Hampshire across Wiltshire, and, along the way calling in political debts of men and supplies, joined with a force of Dorset men and some from Somerset at a point immediately west of the Deverills called Ecghbrytes Stan (Egbert's Stone). Then marching along the trackway above the Deverills, Alfred's force took the northward route past Cow Down, camped for the night two miles east of Longbridge in the cover of Southleigh wood, crossed the Wylye the following morning, and defeated the Danes on the next range of hills to the north, near the modern village of Edington, just east of Westbury. This decisive victory insured that the West Saxon kings who followed Alfred, rather than Scandinavians, would be acknowledged as the legitimate rulers of a larger and larger area.

Thus it was that their form of agriculture and land tenure, recorded by Alfred's lost Domesday record, came to dominate southern and middle England. Their agrarian skills had modified earlier farm systems, but one strategy in particular had an enormous impact, completely changing the face of the medieval landscape. The Saxon farms increased the size and effectiveness of the plow team, so as to cope better with the heavier soils of the valleys and lower terraces; adding pairs of oxen, these longer teams of up to four pairs of animals, yoked in sequence, needed a lot more space to turn around. Out of this single maneuver, a wholly new medieval landscape was born.

Earlier boundaries of the small, square Celtic fields had to go, even on the side hills.

The furlongs that replaced them eventually covered most of the arable land in the lowland zone of England and lasted for centuries, in most places until the Enclosure Acts of the seventeenth and eighteenth centuries. In parts of the Midlands they survived until 1940. A system of continuous plowing with few turns led to long, narrow strips that were humped up along the middle owing to the continuous direction of the soil movement to the left, first from one direction and then the other, due to the shape of the plow and the concentric turns. The valleys of Wiltshire, including Longbridge and the Deverills, gradually converted to the new efficiency. In places these tremendously long fields run like giant stair treads on the side of the hills and are called "lynchets." One such remaining area frequently photographed by tourists and students of the landscape is to be seen just south of Kingston Deverill over the Down at Mere.

As in the previous period, the responsibility for the planning and organization of the labor and fields of each community was held by one man, a lord, and the area of his control was his manor. Most of what are now villages in southern England were once such manors and contained a mixed group of people in a hierarchy of freemen and tenants, bonded men, cottagers, laborers, and slaves. In Wiltshire, village and manor usually coincided, and only rarely was there more than one owner in a village. That there were many exceptions in this area — Kingston Deverill, two owners; Sutton Veney, two owners; Hill Deverill, three or four owners — shows what a rich and productive area, not to mention populous, it was. So productive were the Deverills that we find significantly more than the usual number of water mills for grinding corn, of which there were eight in the Deverills by 1086. Three of these were in Longbridge Deverill, which was growing in size and value. The church, rising in importance as a temporal power, steadily increased its holdings here. By the end of the eleventh century, religious institutions and clerics controlled as much property in the area as the king, his servants, and private individuals together. The abbot of Glastonbury owned two manors that were assessed at the same rate as the seven other Deverill manors put together. It is certain that there was a church in Longbridge at this time, very likely of stone as well as timber, and that the eponymous bridge across the marsh was complete. The separate earlier communities were by now linked together and surrounded by open fields. The medieval manor and landscape of Longbridge Deverill had emerged.

NORMAN PROSPERITY

The entry for Longbridge Deverill in the Domesday Book commissioned by William the Conqueror in 1086 translates from the medieval Latin thus:

The same church holds Deverel. It was assessed T.R.E. [*Tempore Regis Edwardi*, or "in the time of Edward the Confessor"] at ten hides. Five of these hides are in demesne, where are three plowlands

and two servants, fourteen villagers, twenty-four borders, and twelve cottagers occupy six plowlands. Three mills pay fourteen shillings and ten pence. Here are six acres of meadow. The pasture is three-quarters of a mile in length and a quarter mile broad. The wood is three miles long and three-quarters of a mile broad. A military man holds of the abbot one hide and one yard of land. Eisi who held them T.R.E. could not be separated from the church. The whole manor is worth ten pounds.

Taken item by item, a picture of the village as it was at the time emerges. The church that owned Longbridge was Glastonbury Abbey. Edward the Confessor was the last Anglo-Saxon king, dying with no heir and thus creating the struggle to claim the vacant throne between Harold, Tostig, and William. The phrase T.R.E. is used simply to mean "in the recent past" and to denote what taxes had been collected by the last stable government. *Hida*, a hide of land, was one hundred acres (one hundred twenty by recent English measure). Longbridge Manor, therefore, possessed approximately twelve thousand acres of cleared land suitable for arable farming, half of which was in demesne. Demesne lands were those cultivated directly for the owner of a manor by his men and animals. Plowlands (*carucata terrae*) are an estimate of the number of plow teams of eight oxen each that could be employed on the estate if it were to be exploited fully. This includes not only the land that they could till and plow, but also the required meadow, pasture, and houses needed to support them. Longbridge, like the majority of the manors in this area, was conceded to be already worked to capacity. The mills were water mills for grinding corn. Because of the large area of arable land listed, and the high crop yields indicated by the mills, we know that the numbers of livestock would have been high. There were probably between sixty and eighty oxen or cattle and between five hundred and eight hundred sheep — both to work the land and to manure it. Longbridge Deverill was a wealthy manor in every respect.

There were nine forests listed in Wiltshire in the thirteenth century, several of the largest dating from earlier times. Longbridge Deverill lay between two of these, Grovely Wood, the only forest mentioned by name in Domesday, and Selwood, which was ancient in the time of King Alfred. The woodland allotted to this manor and neighboring Sutton Veney was along the southern edge of Selwood. Although consisting today of recent planting, one portion of this allotment survives today and is called Southleigh (pronounced Suthee) Wood. At the time, this forest extended as a continuous mass immediately adjacent to and north of Longbridge manor. A folktale still told locally describes how Thomas à Becket, after consecrating the Longbridge church, "visited Crockerton Revel, coming through Southleigh wood dressed as a gentleman and going back as a beggar because he had spent all his money at the Revel." Because of the steady felling of trees, clearings had

32. Late medieval construction: Baggs's house at Fry Streams, Longbridge Deverill. Post and truss construction with a thatched roof of straw; the end wall of brick and the masonry infill were added considerably later.

appeared. One located halfway toward Warminster on the far side of this wood revealed a deposit of good workable clay. The production of rather coarse earthenware that resulted was to continue for centuries, contributing to Longbridge Manor's economy and the name of this satellite community, Crockerton.

Another thirteenth-century industry of Crockerton was the manufacture of whetstones, for there was also a deposit of gritty stone that even today the local residents look out for and use to sharpen their knives and tools. The water bailiff in Longbridge showed me one of these oval-shaped stones that look like a pumice and said that it was a "Crockerton burr." He'd found this one digging a trench to lay drain tile for a septic field in his backyard. Like his medieval ancestors, this individual and most of his neighbors can perform almost any task that exists locally. Neither having been trained for any particular task, nor feeling unqualified to do others, does he assume that many skills are beyond him, and he seems to be right. These people can garden, build houses, do their own plumbing, and mend autos or fences in much the same way that the medieval villagers had to fend for themselves and make the things they needed or wanted, whether it was clothes, houses, or tools. The not quite mythical stereotypes of the taciturn but able country man versus the specialized, verbal, and limited town dweller are rooted in this period of our society. Whether the stouthearted and skillful longbowmen at Crécy and Agincourt, or shrewd farmers solving a problem posed by taxes or foxes, the yeomen and peasants have contributed enormously to the growth of the country, and it was largely the debilitating effect on them brought about by urbanization and the industrialization of England that set off the reform movements and many of the social and political changes that are still in motion today.

Longbridge Deverill and its satellite, Crockerton, continued to grow. By the mid-thirteenth century, the population had doubled from that of Domesday. It was prosperous enough to have rebuilt the church in stone, to have rebuilt the mill at Crockerton, to have consumed large chunks of Southleigh Wood, and to have evolved a set of local traditions and festivals. Medieval farming was long and hard, and great emphasis was placed upon increasing production. This is shown in records that describe how the residents on the manor at Monkton Deverill had to pass fifteen times a day from farmyard to field carting dung, and indicate that plowing at Longbridge was increased from two times a year to three by 1262. This pressure, coupled with the fact that many payments — whether of rents, tithes, or wages — were made in goods or other kind, resulted in constant bickering over sizes and standards of measure, some of which ended in royal proclamations or edicts. At Longbridge, disputes over the proper size of a sheaf of grain were settled in an amusing and effective way. The sheaf in question was rolled in mud and passed through a hoop that was made by the hayward grasping his hair above the ear. If the muddy sheaf did not dirty his clothes or hair, it was too small. Perhaps one can draw two conclusions from this. First, that stewards or foremen were, as my own experience in construction and other manual work shows that they still are, often selected not only for their insight and ability to keep ahead of those working under them, but also for their size and strength: they must, if pushed, be tough enough to control physically any or all of their men. A man like this wouldn't take kindly to having to get muddy to keep people in line. Second, and more important then as now, one had to be willing to get his hands dirty in order to administer effectively (or to get ahead, become rich, etc.).

Two privileges that the abbot of Glastonbury and his tenants at Longbridge enjoyed during this period pertained to hunting and hanging. They were granted freedom from the penalty *de expeditatione canum* within the forest of Selwood. This was a penalty that the king's foresters were enjoined to inflict on all who presumed to hunt without privilege, which consisted in cutting out the ball, or soft part, of a dog's feet. Also Longbridge was granted a special situation in the Hundred Rolls and was what is known as a free manor, which made it not answerable to the normal administration, law, or jurisdiction of the sur-rounding area. The abbot possessed all authority of sheriff within the manor, including the rights of "pit and gallows." This meant the power to take, try, and execute offenders against his rule. Such matters are not taken lightly and were fought for on at least one occasion when the abbot's bailiff and tenants drove off the adjacent lord of Warminster's men who were attempting to use their gallows.

For the next four hundred years, with the exception of minor changes in skill or tech-nique and the gradual increased acreage of land under cultivation, there were few changes in agriculture until the seventeenth and eighteenth centuries. There was, however, a grad-ual and important rise in the number of sheep that coincided with the creation of an inter-national wool trade that changed life in many ways. Wiltshire was in the center of this surge, possessing enormous flocks of sheep. The abbeys of Glastonbury and Shaftesbury numbered their flocks in the tens of thousands. A clear indication that more than the vil-lage population was increasing at Longbridge is the steady increase in tax assessments and the transformation of the architecture.

ARCHITECTURE IN THE LANDSCAPE: THE GREAT REBUILDING

As the fifteenth century drew to a close, an increasing stream of money poured into the southwest of England from the great weaving, dyeing, and market centers of Antwerp, Malines, Bruges, Lille, and Delft. Sweeping social and physical changes began to take place, the most noticeable one of which was that of the Great Rebuilding. At first glance to an American walking about in England, the large number of old buildings — many of them hundreds of years old — gives an impression of almost complete and unbroken continuity with antiquity. It seems as if there must be representative buildings from every period.

101

More careful examination shows that this is not the case. There are very few buildings of any sort from earlier than the fourteenth century. What is more interesting is that there are no domestic buildings at all remaining intact from before the end of the fifteenth century. The reason is fairly simple. For centuries the most common building materials for rural domestic (even church) buildings had been unbaked earth, timber, and thatch. Then as today, not only was it easier and cheaper to build with wood and mud than with stone, but also every acre of woodland cleared was more land for crops and livestock. Naturally such buildings tend to disintegrate over time, a process that accelerates rapidly when they are not occupied or kept in constant repair. They were also easily destroyed by fire, which, because of the almost total absence of chimneys, was very common. A great change or "rebuilding" began to gather momentum, however, as the pressure for more dwellings to house the increasing population joined new concepts of privacy filtering down from the upper classes and was made economically possible by a steady flow of money into England for wool.

First came the churches. Many smaller structures, as well as great and large establishments, were to be rebuilt. In the region around Longbridge, religious orders at Bath, Wells, Glastonbury, Winchester, and Salisbury had been involved in great building programs for generations. These great cathedrals, like the ambitious wool churches in the parishes of East Anglia, were direct expressions of wealth and piety executed with large quantities of local stone, partly accounting for their diversity and richness. More important to the general appearance of the countryside, however, was the upsurge of secular construction that followed. While many older buildings, often of timber, were partially rebuilt or absorbed into new structures, it was the construction of thousands of new buildings in brick or stone, built for the lords of manors and the freeholders involved in the burgeoning agricultural and wool industry, that transformed nearly every village across the country. In rapid succession the men who had built up herds as tenants, buying land or long leases as they prospered, as well as for their merchant allies, began to build durable new structures for themselves. Along with this unprecedented construction boom came a great increase in furnishings, as well as an increase in personal property and privacy. Chairs, for example, instead of benches begin to show up in estate inventories. Life in the country was changing.

Although nationally the greatest period of this building boom appears to have been between 1575 and 1625, it came earlier to Wiltshire. The south arcade and tower of the church at Longbridge Deverill were built in stone about 1400. Another early work is a gate-

33. Products of the Great Rebuilding: the handsome sixteenth-century barn on the right contains fifteen bays. It exemplifies the great sweeping roof forms common to these structures. Shored up against collapse by German prisoners during World War I, it remains in need of repair. The adjacent house has been successively rebuilt. The present exterior dates from about 1700, while the interior was remodeled in 1973. Hill Deverill.

house to the old manor at nearby Hill Deverill that dates from 1470–1500. A large barn and some sheds from this same manor date from 1500–1530, and from that time on continuous building and rebuilding takes place at this manor, culminating in a major reconstruction of the house about 1700. The most important local building venture to affect Longbridge was related to the dissolution of the abbeys and the arrival of a new landlord.

The pressures leading up to the English Reformation, the break with Rome, the dissolution of the monasteries and abbeys, and the subsequent seizure and sale of all their property obviously went far beyond the personality of Henry VIII, his turbulent marriages, and

court intrigues. A large portion of the land and economy of England was involved. Ever since the crisis leading to Magna Carta when King John maneuvered the church (and the Pope) into siding with him against the barons, landowners, tenants, weavers, and workers, a general resentment and distrust of the church, its power, and its motives had been building throughout society. Even the earlier sentiment and support shown toward Thomas à Becket, a popular homegrown saint who'd stood up to a king, had soured, as is clearly indicated by a bitterly anticlerical folk rhyme of the period that was still sung by the children of Longbridge Deverill at the beginning of the twentieth century.

> Thomas-a-Bomas, a big-bellied man,
> He ate more meat than ten score men.
> He ate a cow, he ate a calf,
> He ate a butcher and a half.
> He ate the church, he ate the steeple,
> He ate the priest, and all the people.

It is hard to believe that, without major support from both nobles and commoners, any king, even Henry VIII, could have gotten away with seizing the holdings of all the religious orders. He would have been faced with a religious civil war. As it was, there was a certain amount of controversy and confusion, as many discovered what others had foreseen. It was largely a change in masters. Another local rhyme sums up tersely in a manner appropriate to country speech the developments of 1539 and the death of Abbot Whyting as they affected the Deverills:

> Horner and Thynne,
> When the monks went out
> They came in.

There is in Longbridge a very handsome seventeenth-century stone building known as the Almshouse (see fig. 37), which houses elderly pensioners for the parish. How did a building of such sophistication for such clientele come to be here of all places, I wondered? The answer lay in a sequence of ambitious destruction and construction projects related to the change of ownership of the parish. The monasteries that had been emptied out almost overnight offered a tremendous impetus to new construction, especially in stone. While some were converted directly to private residences, many became quarries, a fate that befell the once proud and magnificent abbey of Glastonbury. In 1547 Sir John Thynne purchased their former holdings at Longbridge from the Crown and moved into a house immediately adjacent to the church. Thynne was the protégé of Edward Seymour, duke of Somerset and lord protector of the realm, who had a house only four miles away in Maiden Bradley. Like some of the clients I have had the good fortune to know, Thynne was obviously a man who loved to build. The same year that construction began on Somerset House in London — one of the first and most influential Renaissance buildings in England, a project with which Thynne was intimately involved in both design and construction supervision — he purchased the defunct priory of St. Radgund adjacent to the western boundary of Longbridge Deverill. Between 1547 and 1553 he rebuilt the Longbridge rectory into a manor house for himself while pursuing his career in London, but the chilling effect of the execution of his patron in 1554 led him to withdraw to the country. There, with time on his hands and financial resources, he embarked upon a building project at his new property, now known as Longleat, that would have been a major Renaissance structure had it not accidentally burned to the ground in 1567. His fortunes under Elizabeth, unlike Seymour's, had improved, and he began to rebuild, if anything on a grander scale. This structure on the edge of the Downs in a remote corner of Wiltshire, unfinished at his death in 1580, went on under construction for another generation to become what is considered by some to be the greatest monument of Elizabethan architecture. Unquestionably it is enormous and very handsome. His earlier manor house in the village, still standing at the death of Thomas Thynne in 1639, was gone by the end of the century, and was almost certainly the source of building materials used in the construction of the nearby Almshouse, built in 1665, as well as for additional work done on the church in the early eighteenth century. Only an act of architectural cannibalism such as this could account for a home for elderly paupers possessing the superb drip moldings, mullions and window surrounds, and dressed quoins and jambs normally associated with the most expensive architecture in the realm.

Few fragments survive from this period of the more humble village structures. No doubt many were improved, enlarged, or rebuilt. The most common of the oldest survivors are the large timber frame barns, examples of which can be found in almost every small village of the region. The Deverills possess several fine barns of the early sixteenth century, the best of which is at Hill Deverill, mentioned above. Many of the houses have early portions and timber framing buried within later masonry structures, although only one in Longbridge is clearly recognizable from the exterior. Many of the oldest barns hide beneath black metal roofs. Considering the risk and current insurance rates for a large barn filled with expensive livestock, the gradual and widespread replacement of straw roofs on perfectly functional buildings is understandable. The barn at the manor farm in Longbridge, an enormous and handsome one, has had a succession of roofs. The present tile one was installed after a fire in the thatch. Likewise at White Cliff Farm a huge grain-drying machine sits inside a late medieval post and truss frame under a metal roof, and at Kingston Deverill Manor only one of the ancient barns has been completely torn down, while the others have constantly been modified and remain in use.

Buildings don't just grow. They are built. But there is a justification for sometimes thinking of preindustrial structures as organically related to their environment in a way that is rarely found in contemporary building. They were almost invariably made of local

34. Late medieval structure: a loafing shed for livestock in the farmyard at Hill Deverill. Although eroded from centuries of use — largely that of animals rubbing against them — the timber posts and trusses can clearly be seen in relationship to the limestone walls and thatched roof. The black drippings on the tie beams indicate the presence of barn owls, one of the farmer's great allies in the constant war against rats and mice.

materials: stone in regions like the Cotswolds, clay (in the form of bricks and tiles) in large river valleys like that of London, wood in forested areas, and so on. Their form was also related to the properties of the materials, climate, local sensibility, and taste. The process of material production or of building was nearly always a local phenomenon: logging, quarrying, brick making. It affected the affluence of local society and the look of the land. In Wiltshire the earliest buildings were of timber, cob, and thatch. Later these were replaced by stone and finally by brick. The great consumption of forests not only changed the character of the land visually and ecologically, but also gave rise to methods of framing structures that led to bay system concepts found in masonry construction, including the early Gothic cathedrals.

Wood Construction

From early times, oak was the favorite timber because of its structural properties. Fairly easy to work when it is green, it becomes harder and tougher as it seasons, and the heartwood is resistant to both fungus and beetles if kept dry. Nearly all wood-frame buildings were built of unseasoned oak as long as the supply lasted. As the wood aged and the structural loads settled, these timbers often sagged, taking on softer forms even as they became stronger. It was discovered that shrinkage and warpage could be greatly reduced by soaking the logs in fresh running water for a year or more before use. This is because the water gradually replaced the sap and acids in the wood and later could slowly evaporate over the years to be replaced by air. There was also a similar progression from the use of whole logs and poles through split logs and finally to shaped timbers and planks. Locally the use of carefully dressed timbers and sophisticated notched connection details goes at least as far back as the Roman occupation. Half timber construction, which supplanted earlier Saxon log structures, was not made of half timber and half something else such as plaster, as is commonly thought. Instead it refers to the use of halved or cleft, that is, dressed timbers. Pole barn construction, one of the earlier methods, where logs are set in holes in the earth, usually in several rows to form an aisled hall and roofed with poles, can still be found all over the United States. Half-timbered buildings are very different. They are framed structures with various fabricated members working together, not separately as in pole barn construction. The panels between the timbers can be filled with other materials or covered with a cladding. Of the various versions that evolved, nearly all of the surviving examples

35. Survival and transformation: this odd structure reveals the long succession of owners and their intentions at Hill Deverill Manor. Originally a gatehouse, with a coat of arms above the doorway, it incorporates stone, flint, timber, brick, and thatch. For at least the last century it served as a cow byre; today its stands as a garden shed and accessory.

in Wiltshire are of a particular type known as "post and truss." Two principal features of this system are that it allows large, open, rectangular wall panels and the distribution of the roof loads with additional roof members called purlins. This system is still frequently used in roof construction throughout the south of England, and it would be difficult to find examples of any other type in Longbridge that date from before World War II.

36. Stone bridge on the Wylye River at Hill Deverill. Unlike the two bridges in Longbridge Deverill, which have been rebuilt to accommodate modern highway traffic — one after it had been wrecked by a student tank driver during the last world war — this one retains its original form of the late sixteenth or early seventeenth century. As the drawing indicates, none of the arches is identical in shape or size.

By the mid-sixteenth century the dwindling supply of oak trees gave impetus to the rise of the coal and brick industries, and in the seventeenth the shortage was so acute that England began importing timber from the Continent. The need for timber was a major factor in the exploitation of America. By the nineteenth century vast shipments of timber came from Canada, which is the prime reason for the rapid deforestation of that country, whose population and industry were so small at the time.

A royal proclamation of 1604 said that "cutting of timber for firewood was to cease altogether." Not only was this ineffective, but even if it had been successful, the problem would have remained. The reason is not hard to find, for even after alternative fuel was developed and the major portion of structures became masonry, wood was still needed to frame roofs and floor structures, if not also used as a finish material. Clifton-Taylor points out that Georgian England was a great age of fine carpentry and joinery. One has only to think of the cornices, doors, and carvings on the exteriors, or of the casings, panels, stairs, and marquetry inside to realize the continuing dependence upon this warm and satisfying material.

Thatch

To the English, "thatch" originally meant any kind of roofing substance, just as "igloo" meant any dwelling to Eskimos. Their present connotation of a specific material is a result of the introduction of newer manufactured materials. It seems safe to say that almost all primitive roofs were of organic matter: straw, reed, heather, turves, even hides on small dwellings. The principal reason for this was the light weight, availability, and ease of replacement. Gradually straw and reed became the favorites and were used universally throughout northern Europe and England. The one drawback was that thatch burns readily. Early records and histories dwell upon its flammability and the sequence of disastrous fires that resulted, again and again, leading to its prohibition in towns and urban centers. Thatch, therefore, survives only in rural regions, and today isn't thought of as an urban material, although it once was. That it survives in quantity in some areas and has totally disappeared in others results from several factors. It won't necessarily survive even in an agricultural area unless several practical conditions can be met. The first is that there must be an adequate supply of quality thatch. Because of geology and agricultural patterns, some areas either can't supply enough thatch or have a more desirable alternative readily available. Examples of the latter are the easily split Cotswold stone and Welsh or Cornish slate.

Archaic thatching used straw gathered after the first frost. In medieval times only the ears or seeds of the grain were cut by the reapers with hand sickles, and the long stems were left standing in the field. Whatever wasn't used in crafts or construction provided fodder for animals pastured there later during the winter. This long, firm straw was gathered into small bundles and placed upon the roof frame beginning at the lower edge of the eaves, gradually working up to the ridge. Wet clay was daubed over this, partly as a deterrent to nesting birds and rodents of all kinds and partly as a fire retardant. One can see this clearly in the paintings of Pieter Brueghel and others. By our standards it must have looked untidy at best. Today the two main kinds of thatch are reed and straw. Reed, a water-loving plant, especially common in East Anglia and in Norfolk, has a stem without joints like those present in all of the grasses. Applied carefully it makes an unusually uniform surface texture of great beauty. Around Longbridge, however, as in most of England, the thatch is straw. Rye straw used to be considered the best for thatch because when properly applied it had an average life of about thirty years. Second best and probably more common was wheat straw, which could also last thirty years if the workmanship and the straw itself were of really superior quality. Less desirable and seldom used were oat and barley straw.

The problems facing a thatcher today almost guarantee that he can't make a traditional roof that will last twenty years (this is still pretty good, considering that in the United States it is hard to get a bonded roof of asphalt material, from even the most reputable contractor, to last more than ten or fifteen years). The reasons why even straw isn't what it used to be are many. Thatchers want long, strong, unbruised straw. Today the hybridized grains most common have been bred to produce a large nutritious seed head on a shorter, relatively weak stem. They are harvested by large combines that, even if prevented from baling the straw, certainly crush it. This means that if there is to be any thatching straw, it can't be a by-product of contemporary commercial farming but must be grown and hand harvested for that purpose. This the British government has been encouraging in a small way with grants to farmers for the production of high-quality straw for historic crafts.

About thirty years ago a technique originally confined to Devon and Cornwall has spread north and east, also with government assistance. Called "combed wheat reed," it combines the readily available straw of the area with an application technique similar to that used in Norfolk. It is especially beautiful, and a well-laid roof utilizing this technique should last for at least fifty years. The importance of such a method is clear when one discovers that a roof on a shed at nearby Hill Deverill done in the traditional local wheat straw technique and using modern agricultural straw was on the brink of needing to be replaced, black and rotting, after only nine years.

Undoubtedly much of the charm of thatch roofs is a result of their strong visual form, which in turn is a result of very pragmatic construction methods. Wiltshire lies in a great belt of rural country extending from Sussex to Devon, where thatching survives in considerable quantity. The weather is frequently very wet and windy. This plus the nature of the material have determined the forms. In order to shed water quickly and to keep it from sinking in, which prevents both leaks and eventual rotting, thatch needs to be on a fairly steep pitch, fifty degrees or more. This pitch plus the frequent sweeping around corners and over obstacles like dormers and gables gives it an aspect of swathing the building it protects. The importance of these soft forms, often quite large as in the great barns like the one at Tisbury, Wiltshire, has been commented upon often enough. Like hedgehogs and hedgerows, they are part of rural England. And like the speech of different regions in England, the variety of technique — of finial details, of trimming, binding, and edging — seems to have some local and historical pattern. Interestingly enough, except for the variation in materials mentioned above, almost all the variations seem to come about as a result of family traditions, individual thatchers, and personal styles, not from regional or local tradition. They are distributed by the thatcher's movements, which today can be wide ranging. This accounts for the distribution over several counties of distinctive characteristics or signatures and for the occasional occurrence of several styles in one village.

Despite the sometimes high fire insurance rates, there still are many good examples of thatching in the Deverills. This is almost entirely the work of a father-and-son team frequently employed by the most prominent local building firm. The son had gone through the rural industries program (a government project that finances young men through the lengthy apprenticeship periods of traditional crafts and arts). They have been able to find local wheat straw but have come upon yet another problem that may make continuity difficult in the future. Thatchers use a special nail with a curved hook on it to hold down hazel wands, which in turn hold the bundles, or yealms as they are called, in place. These flexible wands are key ingredients in both the decorative finish and structural integrity of the ridge and the eaves. The sequence of connections is designed for each element to hold the next one firmly in place without cutting or bruising it. This is vital if the roof is to work and last as long as it should (if water, rather than passing on, is held or let in, it begins the process of rotting at bruises or cuts in these organic materials). It turns out that these nails have to be made by hand by a smith, another vanishing craft, because so far machine-made ones have proved inadequate. Their current source of this small but important item is a man in southern Dorset. Likewise the right sort of young hazel branches are needed; these were once a common product of coppicing, another fading land use. And so it goes. Thatched roofs, like much of preindustrial construction, are part of a world of interrelated activities and their products. It is impossible to retain one part or element without sustaining a fair amount of a broader network.

Stone Construction

At the base of the several hills near Longbridge Deverill are abandoned chalk pits: at White Cliff Farm, Cold Kitchen Hill, and Cow Down. Easily quarried and in large sizes, it can take years to dry out. The whitest stone available, unadulterated chalk, consists of more than 95 percent calcium carbonate and is, therefore, a limestone of exceptional purity. Because of its texture and light weight, it was the natural choice of the Gothic masons for some of their most delicate and daring interior vaulting and tracery, and appears in Westminster Abbey and in Exeter, Ely, and Salisbury cathedrals. Even in a humbler church like the one at Longbridge, it lends a light touch and grace to the arcades of the nave. Here one can find two curious arcades made from cut chalk: that on the north is Norman in character: the other, later, appears to be probably of the fourteenth century.

Because this stone was so soft and too porous for exterior use, regions with no other local stone turned to the difficult and small flint nodules distributed throughout the top layers of chalk, in an attempt to fashion exterior facades that could take the weather and satisfy their sense of design and decorum. The results were ingenious. Flint nodules, only three to six inches in diameter, were usually split in half, revealing a hard, flat, shiny, black surface that was placed outward, roughly dressed on the sides to present a square. While easy to handle and transport, these napped flints were structurally problematic. An entire wall made up of only flints and mortar wouldn't hold together. Other larger elements had to be introduced at intervals to bond them to the interior structure and each other, as well as to reinforce edges at openings and corners. The Romans had used flat brick tiles. The Saxons and English later used stone. One such early and highly decorative structure of this sort, coming as it did just before the beginning of the great rebuilding period, prior to the use of large quantities of cut stone, is that of an old manor house gate at Hill Deverill.

Good building stone, although not immediately available in the Deverills, lay within easy reach in all directions. In fact, some of the most famous quarries in southern Britain were near: Bath fifteen miles away and Chilmark only eight miles to the south produced high-quality limestone. The major quarries at Chilmark operated until World War II. In 1996 I observed several small quarries still being worked for pavers, small-scale wall and fence material, and rubble. This fine-grained, sandy-textured stone as it was once supplied can be seen in the river facade at Wilton House, in Salisbury Cathedral, and in numerous buildings in the area. As the great rebuilding gathered momentum, stone came to be the most desirable building material. By the end of the seventeenth century, wherever it could be quarried locally it became the accepted building material, even for cottages. In the limestone belt, whole towns were built of stone: walls, roofs, fences, bridges, streets, walks, even minor sheds and outbuildings. Outside of regions with plentiful stone, this same period saw the development of equally total brick construction. So much so that even in a building of the importance of Hampton Court Palace, in all of its phases, stone is used only for the minimum of foundations and ornament. In Longbridge Deverill most of the stone construction is done with relatively small units of local varieties of oolite (limestone), usually from the Chilmark area. The most important stone buildings at Longbridge were those of the manor house and subsequent palace of Longleat built by John Thynne (see Chapter 4 below). Pevsner points out that in addition to the now vanished manor house there were masonry dovecotes, outbuildings, and a water mill north of the church. A portion of the wall that belonged to the manor complex still stands today. Local tradition holds that as long as it stands the Longleat estate will continue. To my amusement I noticed in the summer of 1972 that it had recently been carefully repaired, leading me to believe that at least one of the present members of the Thynne family was cognizant of the legend.

Many of the cottages from the seventeenth century on are built of small cobble-sized blocks of this stone and utilize bricks for the same through bonding and corner reinforcing techniques developed earlier with flint. The checker pattern, however, had passed from fashion, leaving horizontal banding as the most common such motif. This is most notice-

37. Stone walls, stone roof: the Almshouse roof at Longbridge Deverill and a typical tile. This one weighed five pounds and was similar to the smaller ones found high up on the roof near the ridge. The author found it about fifty yards upstream when the river was dredged by the Water Board in 1973. It was probably lost during the construction of this or another building. Notice how the tiles change direction at the valleys and dormers like feathers, making additional flashing unnecessary.

able on tall walls and end gables. Another striking feature of the period is the proliferation of stone roofs: not slate, not shingles, but roofs made of limestone tiles. Before 1300, stone roofs were a rarity, due to the great cost and weight; structures were too flimsy to hold them up. Because of the constant hazard of fire, chimneys and stone or tile roofs became two of the most sought-after improvements when the economy improved. From the fourteenth century on, both became more common. The earliest that can be dated in Longbridge with any certainty are from the early sixteenth century.

These roofs were expensive because of the labor involved in quarrying, splitting, shaping, drilling, transporting, and installing the tiles. A church at Potterne, when redone a few years ago, required ten thousand of them. Furthermore, their great weight requires a superb stout wood structure to hold them up. The small tiles along a ridge weigh between five and ten pounds each, while the larger ones along the eaves can weigh fifty pounds or more. Alec Clifton-Taylor estimated that one hundred square feet of stone roof weighs nearly a ton. Because of this load, and the unevenness of the tiles, these roofs work best at relatively steep pitches — never less than fifty degrees — which (like their predecessor, thatch roofs) gives them a striking and consistent visual form. Conversely, modern lightweight composition roofs are capable of working at lower, flatter slopes. While they may be efficient, such structures often look glaringly out of place when put into a context of these earlier buildings with their steeper pitch, shattering the visual harmony of entire ensembles and towns.

It is difficult at times for people today to appreciate how truly effective these buildings are, even from the perspective of cost-benefit analysis. We can hardly get past the seemingly slow and primitive techniques and tools used to build such a roof in the first place, let alone the unintended picturesque quality that has been bestowed upon them by time. But the fact that the tiles of a decent one should last for two hundred years without being replaced cannot be refuted. Nor can the conclusion that the beams should last indefinitely. This is a quality and value for money that we cannot match with any of our contemporary construction methods. There is no correlation with our mortgage and depreciation standards, which assume that buildings, furnishings, and equipment wear out and lose their value in relatively short periods of time. The cost of replacing the infrastructure of modern cities and towns is so staggering, especially in economies like those of England and the

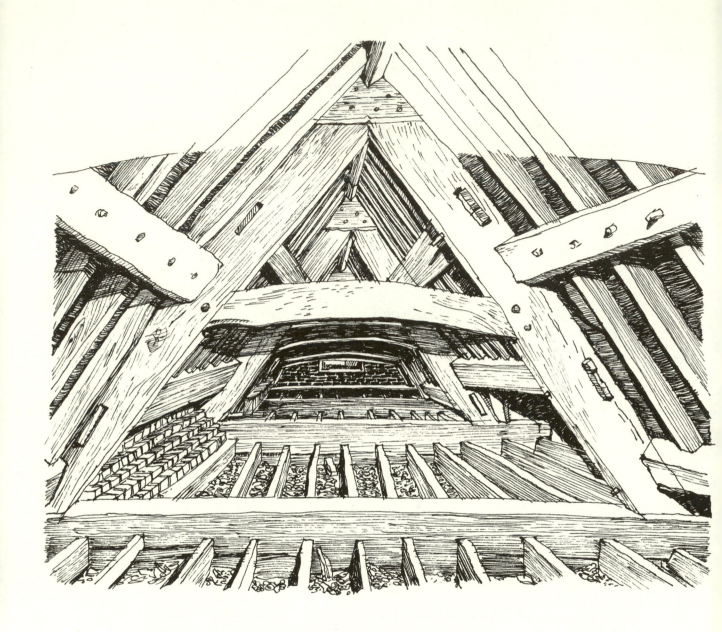

38. These stout oak trusses have stood beneath the stone roof of the almshouse at Longbridge for more than three hundred years and could easily do so for another three hundred. The purlins and rafters need attention from time to time, and the stone tiles seem to need looking at after they are two hundred years old. An interesting comparison could be made to modern methods if one were to assess the life cycle costs of each.

United States that are not expanding at the rate of the sixteenth or nineteenth century, that consideration of the merits of more permanent structures such as these seems more prudent than whimsical. Such buildings also pay great dividends in the landscape as well. The texture and size gradation of the tiles and the partial sagging of the timbers beneath their great weight give these roofs an unequaled strength and beauty. Like thatch, they literally come from the earth near where they are raised, and although manmade, they possess a consistency of color and form that is organically locked into the landscape where they occur. The older stone villages of Wiltshire, occurring as they do along watercourses and at the base of hills, interspersed with great trees — like the more famous Cotswold towns to the north — are invariably superb examples of architectural siting and the use of appropriate materials, achieved by a culture that even at the time was moving away from vernacular traditions toward an industrial economy and building methods.

Brick

The Romans introduced bricks on a wide scale to Britain. This industry ended with their departure, not to reappear until the pressure of the Great Rebuilding and a changing society could both produce and afford them. Baked bricks are fire resistant, unlike most stone, which usually contains some water and cracks or explodes when heated. The reappearance of brick and the gradual increase in its use came about almost solely for this reason. At first used for hearths, fireplaces, and chimneys, it was — like stone — much too expensive for all but the very rich to use in quantity. Before the Tudor period, small houses and cottages rarely had chimneys at all. By the beginning of the seventeenth century they were widespread. In regions where stone was a common building material, nearly every house had a brick chimney stack. The Almshouses at Longbridge are good examples of well-built stone houses of this era that still retain their original brick stacks. Widespread social acceptance of brick as a more common building material occurred during the reign of the Tudors, especially that of Henry VIII and Elizabeth I. The increasing scarcity and rising cost of timber, and a concerted effort to produce vast quantities of brick with a subsequent lowering of prices, combined with the immigration of Flemish craftsmen, many of whom were brickworkers, and the construction of large and prestigious buildings in the London area in this new material produced what has been called "the first great age of English brickwork." A century later this industry had penetrated the southwest, and brick began to appear in Wiltshire, replacing stone even for cottages and humble structures. Clay was plentiful throughout England. The ease with which bricks could be handled by workmen, the increase in availability, and subsequent cost advantages eventually led to their replacing all other building materials. Parallel with the development of bricks has been that of clay roof tiles.

In areas with a good supply and strong tradition of stone like the Cotswolds, this has happened only in the last few generations. Today many of these towns are aware that it is the homogeneity of building type and material that makes tourists find them so attractive. They either have banned bricks, tiles, and other modern building materials or are trying to establish methods and controls for new construction that will ensure that these inevitable changes will be positive additions to their small and complex environments.

Not only has brick come to appear in every possible environment, but there has been a steady evolution in both the bricks themselves and the way they are used. Originally handmade in molds from one of the many local varieties of clay, they were fired in small groups and at different temperatures. This produced a great variety in size, shape, and color, even from one small brickwork. Such bricks were laid up with relatively wide joints because of their unevenness, although often in decorative patterns. As manufacturing became more sophisticated, the bricks gradually became more uniform, and the craftsmen were able to lay them up with finer and finer joints. The subtle variations in color and texture that resulted, even in the very smooth and precise masonry of the eighteenth century, is extremely beautiful. Evolution continued, however, producing the recent great age of Victorian brickwork, and finally the present situation, which isn't quite as happy. Bricks are now produced under elaborate and careful factory conditions, extruded in an endless, uniform ribbon of clay. Sliced off identically with a smooth wire, they are continuously fired in a constant temperature for the same period of time. These limitless, identical objects are then laid up on oversize buildings by workers in a trade with steadily decreasing standards of performance. The joints are once again large and clumsy, while the bricks themselves are hideously boring to look at.

The current negative attitude of many people, including designers, toward brick has an antecedent. Even while it was becoming more affordable and common, a reaction set in among the upper class and their architects. This was not because of this new availability and popularity, as a cynic might suggest, but because the architects of both the baroque and Palladian camps in the late seventeenth and early eighteenth centuries developed a strong taste for stone. They had seen the Renaissance buildings of Italy and France and wanted the forms and details, the texture, and the solidity that only stone can give. Nevertheless, the need for economy, then as now, was overwhelming, and many of the major works of this period were built in brick. Mereworth by Colen Campbell, Chiswick by Lord Burlington, and Holkham by William Kent are all built of brick, although only the last wasn't rendered over with stucco from the start.

39. Changing materials and fashions of buildings in the landscape: above are the church, school, and Almshouse at Longbridge Deverill — referred to locally as Faith, Hope, and Charity. All three were built of limestone, while their respective dates range from the fifteenth to the nineteenth century. Below is Longbridge Deverill House, built for a well-to-do vicar, now a privately managed retirement home. The nostalgically Tudor brick facade dates from only the eighteenth and nineteenth centuries.

The most prominent brick building in Longbridge Deverill is located halfway between the church and the crossroads. It is also the largest house in the village, and with its twenty-nine flues and numerous gables it would dominate the village if it weren't partly hidden by its garden. Like the village to which it belongs, this structure has evolved through a process of growth by addition and absorption. The earliest dwelling one can identify within the present house is that of a cottage. Only eighteen feet wide by thirty-eight feet long, it has recently been used as a kitchen and scullery and may be thought of as the seed from which the entire house, outbuildings, and gardens eventually grew. This masonry building in all likelihood replaced an earlier timber- or earth-walled cottage on this or a nearby site, since the location, south facing and above the floodplain of the river, halfway between the bridge and the church, is a key one in the village. The house type, the stone, the location of the central hearth, the step up to the separated end room, and the few details all suggest that it was built between 1580 and 1640. The first addition was a second floor and a small cubic cellar. Sometime thereafter a wing was added at right angles, and by the mid-eighteenth century the house had become a two-story, L-shaped building. There were one and possibly two major renovations between 1750 and 1850 that completely demolished both of the north-south walls of the earlier addition; however, its ghost appears in a series of irregularities in both floor and ceiling — steps where none are now needed, redundant beams and framing.

The choice of warm red bricks and cream-colored stone for this transformation was a happy one, and was a device used by several generations of English architects, especially for rural domestic dwellings. Christopher Wren, who hailed from a small village seven miles south of Longbridge, was one of the first to seize upon this combination, raising it to a technique capable of a wide range of expression and high art, as can be seen at Hampton Court and Greenwich Observatory. One is a major formal statement, a distinguished addition to a great palace, the other a caprice that wittily refers to the sixteenth-century architectural treatise by Sebastiona Serlio and the homespun of Tudor pomp. This combination of red brick and crisp limestone was extremely rewarding for lesser architects as well. It guaranteed a richness of color and texture without requiring great imagination or invention. Like a large number of Queen Anne and Georgian buildings that survive in both England and in the United States, the 1837 renovation of Longbridge Deverill House was of this variety. It was built for Lord Charles Thynne, who had been given the post of vicar of Longbridge Deverill by his elder brother, the marquess of Bath, who lived nearby on the family estate of Longleat. One can tell something about this owner's nature from the building. Openly nostalgic on the exterior for earlier conservative English domestic architecture, but with a desire to impress, it has a handsome and effective facade toward the road and garden. Inside the public and formal rooms are large, sunny, and well proportioned in the manner of the eighteenth century. Elsewhere, abovestairs and down the back corridors, accidental and smaller spaces predominated.

Longbridge Deverill House physically dominated the village in the nineteenth century. So did the man who lived in it. One resident mentions in her memoirs, "He was an austere man and quite dominated the village so that the villagers were afraid of him." She said her grandmother "told me one Sunday she tied her little girl's hair with a blue ribbon when she went to church, and he took it off and told her she could not wear such profane things in church." During the Victorian period, extra stairs, cupboards, and partitions were added to the more utilitarian working wings; outbuildings proliferated and grew connections. Greenhouses appeared above the end of the garden. After 1920, during the residence of the Rev. J. W. R. Brocklebank, the garden also flourished and expanded. A pavilion and pool were built. For a time, there were five gardeners, bronze deer, urns, and statuary from Italy. Those who attended the large garden fetes given here in the 1930s agree that it was all very lovely indeed. But from this point until very recently, both the house and garden declined. The expense was too great. As with many another, the house was too large and remote from the life of the people of modern wealth. The society that had built such houses and had filled them with large families, friends, and household staff had all but disappeared. Short of physical collapse, however, such a house could not stand empty for long. Today again, places like this are being sought out by a new wave of people who strongly want to leave the enormous cities, whether only for weekends, for retirement, or simply to live well. After a period of ownership by a steamship magnate, followed by abandonment, it was purchased in the early 1970s by Baron Nugent and his wife, a retired judge from Wimbledon. Both house and garden were gradually repaired, restored, and inhabited, all to the relief and pleasure of many in the village. Their subsequent deaths and another period of limbo for the property has ended again with a period of occupation and renovation. Few people can muster the resources needed for such a task, especially in such a place. The house has now been taken over by a retirement home, a modern almshouse of sorts, which charges its residents for their assistance. A new, particularly ugly nursing home and a staff bungalow have been built just to the north of the house, where an ancient orchard and lane had stood. Like the large country houses that once provided employment for numerous souls in small villages throughout the countryside, this owner and transformation has undoubtedly been a boon to the economy and well-being of the village.

Few people would say that industrialization and the rise of industry are intrinsically bad. Some utopians even begin with the assumption that they are good per se. Many of the buildings spawned by this revolution have been undeniably ugly. Many others have been mediocre, or merely boring or dull. Some have been very good, and not just highly refined skyscrapers and the exquisitely crafted villas of the early years of twentieth-century modernism. Take greenhouses as a case — whether of wood or metal frame — consider how they represent a whole range from artlessness, as in most nurseries, to the extraordinary grace of the great structures erected in Hyde Park and Kew Gardens by their designers, Joseph Paxton and Decimus Burton. Many industrial structures are merely innocuous, like the innumerable black sheet metal hay barns and stock sheds that now pepper the countryside. These buildings, with their pole or metal frame structures, are remarkably similar

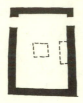

Before 1500

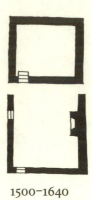

1500–1640

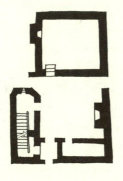

1640–1700

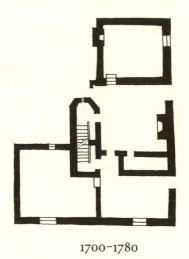

1700–1780

0 5 10 20 30 40

40. The evolving ground floor plan of Longbridge Deverill House.

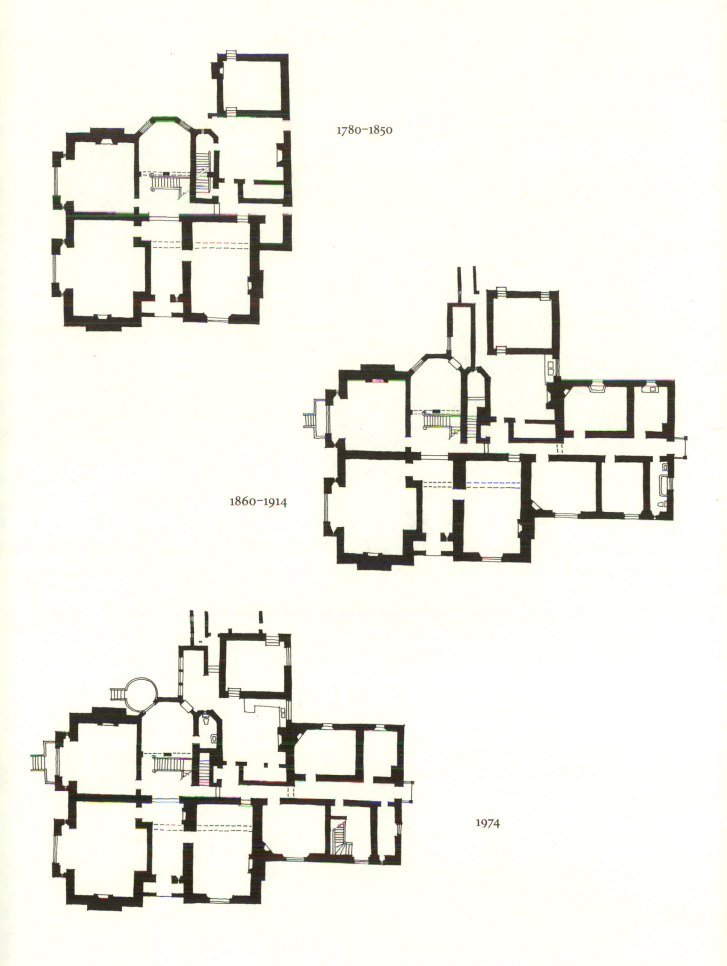

1780–1850

1860–1914

1974

41. *Garden facade, Longbridge Deverill House: local red brick and tiles with Bath stone for sills, quoins, and coping produce a warm and richly textured surface. Behind the studied asymmetry and eclectic facade are generous eighteenth-century rooms with high plasterwork ceilings, Adam fireplaces, and a delicate stair hall.*

42. *Organic growth, Longbridge Deverill House. Here seen from the back, the steady expansion and numerous changes of use and occupants are clearly expressed. At the core of this crystalline growth is the original seed, a cottage. Now used as a kitchen, it is located in the center of the drawing, surrounded by dairies, stables, and pantries and overgrown with the numerous specialized rooms of later inhabitants.*

to earlier medieval prototypes. Also, black is a good color to paint them, and not just because it was traditionally used on wood buildings of the same general configuration and use. Originally, black was used because tar was painted on the wood to keep it from rotting and from being devoured by animals, especially insects. The visual merits of this color became obvious later. Black absorbs rather than reflects light. In a small, mixed landscape like that of England, this is extremely important because it tends to make objects appear smaller or farther away and keeps them from visually leaping at one, from making a discordant and unsociable shout.

Sir Peter Shepheard has pointed out that a lot of nonsense is talked about building materials. "A good architect can make asbestos look elegant; a bad one can make marble look cheap." He maintains, and rightly so, that the outline of the building, its position, and general color have more to do with how we perceive a building in a landscape than anything to do with materials, workmanship, or details except as these latter affect the other more important factors. Modern farm buildings, as modern farms in general, tend to be larger, more homogeneous, and machinelike. The question we should ask is not should we have them (without them the cost of food would rise even more than it already has with them), but just what can they look like, what forms can and should they take, and how much and from what distances do we want to see them? The large number of discordant, ugly, and poorly sited buildings that have been built across England in modern times is a matter of public knowledge and constant outrage. If powerful landowners and factory managers, together with subservient government corporations, were guilty of creating the grim bylaw towns and the industrial assault on established patterns of city and country in the nineteenth and early twentieth centuries, it is probably fair to say that county councils, planners, and architects have been responsible for most of the recent blunders. One might say that many of the people doing the most damage are the same people as before but with different titles.

Colin and Rose Bell in *City Fathers* have written a good survey of both tied towns and transport towns like Crewe, Swindon, and Middlesborough. In addition to this discussion of what Americans would call "company towns," those tied to oppressive industries and their owners, a scathing attack upon English council housing directed toward the failures of social planning, physical function, and design may be found in Martin Pawley's *Architecture versus Housing*. Like the Bells, he gives a short summary of the forces leading toward the garden city movement and the mushrooming of suburbia and of the flirtation of modern architects with industrial processes. The poor quality of several generations of design and planning has led to a backlash wherein citizen groups are constantly at loggerheads with government, and groups such as English Heritage, the Royal Institute of British Architects, and the Council for the Protection of Rural England oppose one plan after another put forward by the planning authorities. My own experience of working on redevelopment schemes for the abandoned Kings Cross railroad yards and Canary Wharf dock during the robust economic decade of the 1980s, wherein fierce opposition from a wide cross section of the community — laymen, professionals, the press — broke out to each and every proposal, convinced me that the local authorities and design professionals had completely lost the trust of the citizenry. While they could vote out the legislative members, the planners and staff were protected by civil service and had become untouchable and unresponsive.

In all fairness it must also be pointed out that most of the construction throughout history has not been great or distinguished. Even so, there are important differences between the buildings of periods before our own and those of today. In the past, as every village along the Wylye River attests, buildings represented major commitments of time, effort, and expense on the part of the builder, who in many cases was also the owner and occupant. The structure's position, orientation, and appearance were not arrived at lightly. They were both individual and social gestures. Durability and permanence — such investment must have a long-term payback — were essential. The high environmental quality of the result, or to use a term with biological connotations, their "fitness," is neither an accident nor a romantic notion. It is genuine. They are good, functioning structures in close harmony with each other, the landscape, and human use.

In hindsight the events of history often seem logically linked together, even inevitable, although almost never is this true. A perfect example is that of the industrial revolution and the various directions it has taken. Whatever reasons one wants to give for the fact that the Chinese didn't develop firearms or internal combustion engines, even though they had many of the elements necessary for their assembly and evolution centuries before Western Europe, it is no easier to demonstrate just why these events happened exactly as they finally did in the West. These are only two examples of how noninevitable (or indeterminant) evolutionary processes are. Recent studies in biological evolution suggest that both chance and intention are extremely important. The intentions and ambitions of the people involved have largely determined what use is made of chance discoveries. In England the decline of vernacular building and the rise of industrialized materials, methods, and forms are the result of a concentrated effort — at a time when many of the eventual effects were not foreseen or understood — and not one of haphazard or natural selection. Just as railroads didn't just happen, but were carefully planned, willed, and forced into reality, so has it been with the history of building.

CLIMATE, ECOLOGY, AND THE LANDSCAPE

Although only a large island off the coast of Europe, a fragment once broadly connected to it, in fact, England behaves more like a miniature continent. There are a remarkable diversity of geological formations and many ecological communities. Within a generally mild climate there is a myriad of exceptions and variations, some extreme—from subarctic in Scotland and the Peak district, through (temperate) boreal forests and grasslands of the Midlands and the south, to subtropical conditions in parts of Cornwall and the offshore islands of the southwest. There are great receding ocean cliffs on the west, the weather side, and enormous estuaries and low-lying beaches where the land slides off into the sea to the east, the lee side. While the Wiltshire landscape I describe here is largely one situated upon the great chalk plains and ridges, there are also major landscapes to be found upon other geological formations: peat, limestone, granite, basalt, clay, and sand, each with its appropriate soils, flora, and fauna. While it is as difficult to generalize about England as it is about North America, some generalizations are useful.

Physiographically England can be divided into two zones, highland and lowland, by a line running generally from the southwest to the northeast. The land and history of these two areas are markedly different. The highland zone, with its hills, mountains, small farms, and poor soils and mineral reserves, time after time received the people who had been pushed out of the farmland to the south and east by new invaders. Conversely, the lowland zone, which encompassed the lands around Buckland and Longbridge, was left unglaciated during the last Ice Age, thereby acting as a sanctuary for plants, animals, and people, and, with its low hills and open beaches in easy reach of the French coast, has evolved into the most complex part of the English landscape.

The highest point on the English chalk is Walbury Hill in the southwestern tip of Berkshire. It is only 975 feet above sea level. The highest in Wiltshire is Brims Down at 912 feet, a part of the ridge that also contains Cold Kitchen Hill — of which more later — above Kingston Deverill. Chalk is a comparatively soft rock, very porous, and nearly all the rain that falls on chalk sinks below the surface, contributing to a vast reservoir of groundwater. As a result, there is little surface water or river erosion in southern England at present. The name *bourne* encountered often in the chalk country refers to a stream that disappears in the drier months of the year. This groundwater is held from sinking further by impervious rock below, producing a layer of water-bearing rock that can often be hundreds of feet thick. Within it the water flows in whichever direction there is an outlet, emerging as springs, at times surprisingly part of the way up a dry hillside. The top level of the saturated rock, below which all of the pores between the rock crystals are wet, is called the water table. This level varies, depending upon the water entering the system either vertically from rain or horizontally from underground flow (which ultimately depends upon rain for its volume), and in turn causes changes in the flow and volume of water in streams, rivers, lakes, and wells. Another notable feature of chalkland is the presence of flints. This material occurs in nodules wherever chalk is found and has played a major part in the early history of this region. Because of a dependency upon flint for tools for thousands of years, the flint mines in this region were very important. It is not surprising to find that in Neolithic times the chalk ridges provided natural causeways for the movement of people and animals — high and dry as they were with lighter vegetation when compared to the overmoist bottomlands with their vast oak forests. The trackways of Bronze and Iron Age man radiate in all directions from Salisbury Plain.

In trying to explain some of the physics and thermodynamics of meteorology and the statistical basis for generalizing and predicting microclimate, one of my professors once remarked that "climate is what you expect and weather is what you get." Everyone talks about the weather in England, as much or probably more than anywhere else in the world. This isn't just a recent phenomenon derived from the invention of pubs and television reports. As far back as the Roman occupation, there are recorded comments about the climate. Julius Caesar remarked, "The climate is more temperate than in Gaul, the cold seasons more moderate"; while Tacitus elaborated that "the soil, except for the olive and vine and other fruits usual in warmer lands, permits and is even prolific in crops: they ripen slowly, but are quick to sprout — in each case for the same reason, the abundant moisture of the soil and sky." It really does rain a lot in Britain, although not as much as in the Pacific Northwest of the United States. London has more rainy days than either Seattle or Portland, but a lower annual rainfall. The absence of severe cold, especially in the western half of the island, is due to the Gulf stream, a large, warm current of water that passes nearby in the Atlantic to the west. Warming part of the ocean at times when the air is very cool, this current provides England with a climate that is not only wetter and more changeable than that of most continents, but also one that is warmer in winter and cooler in summer. This moderate, nearly uniform, moist atmosphere sounds rather like the description of life in a greenhouse, and the effect is similar. The size and lush quality of the vegetation in summer can be overwhelming. Climatically England can be divided into east and west, instead of north and south, despite the great range and number of exceptions. The southwest is even milder and wetter than the rest. Ireland, Wales, and the south and west of England are famous for the intensity and extent of their green hills and valleys, and nowhere else in the world do such great green billowing clumps of trees stand about in so many tranquil landscape parks.

The climate hasn't always been thus, and as it has changed, so have the plant communities. Before the mixed beech and oak forests of today, great oak forests and grasslands were dominant from 5000 to 400 B.C., a long period during which the climate was more continental: colder in the winter and hotter in the summer. Before that were three thousand years of pine and birch forests. And before that a longer period of arctic and subarctic climates of the last Ice Age with its tundra and smaller scrubbier plants. As the plant communities have changed, so have the animals. This has had as much to do with man, however, as with the climate. For at least four thousand of the seventeen thousand years since the last Ice Age, humans have been clearing forests, burning grass, draining marshes, and cultivating crops in southern Britain, while new plants and animals have been introduced continuously, with about half of the species of deer and rodents in England intro-duced whether consciously or not by man.

Only recently have the mechanisms of natural communities come under careful and systematic study. When I began this work many of the pioneers of ecology were still living and at work but already a general picture and some important principles have emerged. The first and most obvious principle is that every plant and animal is closely linked with others living around it. These relationships, whether those of cooperation, competition, predator, prey, host, and so on, can be studied and expressed in many ways; examples of this are energy flow, behavior, physical dispersal, or the number and structure (fluctua-tions) of populations. The next principles are not as obvious as the first: natural commu-nities tend to evolve from simpler states to more complex ones; and the more complex a community becomes, the more tendency it has toward stability. One after another, various researchers have converged upon the principle of instability as a result of simplified or lim-ited populations. Conversely no system ever does, in fact, reach or maintain stability, no matter how large or complex. As a general rule, however, it can be stated emphatically that those landscapes that are the most evolved have the most diverse, complex, and layered populations; they are the most productive and likely to remain so.

For a very long time people have been aware that there is some relationship between the populations of various living organisms, especially of animals and plants. There have been numerous instances of generally sound environmental policies developed empirical-ly ages before nineteenth-century biologists such as Charles Darwin or Alfred Russel Wal-lace began their work. Examples abound from the ancient Mediterranean to American native peoples on both continents. England in the seventeenth century provides the fol-lowing:

In the peaceful reign of King James I the Parliament made an act for the provision of rooke-nests and catching crows to be given in charge of court-barons, which is by stewards observed, but I nev-er knew the execution of it. I have heard knowing country-men affirm that rooke-worms, which the crowes and rookes doe devour at sowing time, do turn to chafers, which I think are our English locusts: and some yeares wee have such fearfull armies of them that they devour all manner of green things; and if the crowes did not destroy these wormes, it would often times happen. Parliaments are not infallible, and some think that they were out in this bill.

A contemporary of John Aubrey, Dr. Woodward, concerned with replanting and con-servation, rebuked the residents of Great Horwood, Buckinghamshire, for their attitude toward the woodland in their trust, stating that "they beat down the acorns for their hogs before they are ripe and so leave no acorns to fall and scatter on the ground for the increase of young trees." He rigidly implemented the forest laws of Henry VIII and Elizabeth I, commanding that a certain number of trees should be grown to the acre, a law that was prompted by the needs of the navy. On November 15, 1664, he quoted a statute of Henry VIII to the people of Colerne, Wiltshire, "against putting cattell into coppices newly cutt until after six years," and warned them that they would be subpoenaed "3s 4p every month for every rod or pole so violated."

The number of creatures and relationships involved in these complex communities often seems more staggering to people working in this field of study than to laymen, largely because of our almost total unawareness of their existence and activity. Take, for example, an area of Berkshire near Oxford of less than two square miles. Charles Elton has described it thus: "the country is quite an ordinary representative of English Midlands — woodlands and fields, streams and marshes, a few patches of limestone grass on the top, and the River Thames flowing round two sides of it. We already know that in this ordinary (and quite beautiful) bit of English countryside, only moderately spoiled so far by the progress of twentieth century forestry and agriculture, something like twenty-five hundred species of animals exist, and that there must be more than this to still be observed. The number of individual animals on the whole area undoubtedly runs into thousands of millions." These animals are arranged in a hierarchy of habitats, which themselves are composed of fragments or groups of complex plant communities. Plants, although generally fixed in one place in the soil, are both gregarious and extremely diverse in many ways. They possess motion (of various kinds) and, most important, in one way or another support all animal life on this planet, including ourselves.

A common term used in ecology is that of *succession*. It refers to the process of plant invasion and evolution that occurs when a barren site gradually goes from open land, through grasses, to meadow, scrub, young woodland, forest, and finally to whatever might be the maximum possible climax situation in such a bioclimatic region. Often such a progression is interrupted by natural phenomena — floods, fires, landslides — or human intervention — forest clearing, the grazing of livestock, or the growing of crops. Each clearly defined stage in natural succession is called a *sere*; arrested or artificially deflected stages are called *plagioseres*. Most heaths in England are temporary subclimaxes in succession caused by man. As soon as the management, burning, or grazing is removed, they return to evolution and disappear into scrub or forest. Some forms of agriculture (forestry is a form of farming) and some crops and methods are plagioseres. Coppicing is an example where the hazel and underbrush are disproportionately encouraged as a crop. Of such interactions between humans, livestock, and the natural world, one of the more dramatic examples is the wonderful, springy, dense, and multiflowered turf on the chalk downs. Although it corresponds to a stage in the evolution from open ground to beech woods, there is no such natural community. It could not have come into being without the persistent close cropping of sheep, and when they are removed it disappears, as many farmers, hunters, and picnicking urban dwellers have sadly found out in recent years.

While it is common for alien, foreign, or exotic plants to be introduced into gardens, or for them to escape and colonize open and barren ground — witness the ailanthus and paulownia that have spread through U.S. cities and along railroad and highway embankments — only rarely are alien plants truly able to invade a natural system, and the chance of their success decreases as the complexity of the community increases. Of all the plants introduced into England since careful records have been kept, none seem to have established a niche in the natural forest community, only in open country or in agricultural settings, along roads, ditches, and so on, and even these are eventually checked and limited, not by man, but by some kind of natural resistance.

As implied, the agricultural landscapes created over the past two thousand years consist largely of interrupted successions, artificial or deflected seres, and highly simplified monocultures. Some of these have great beauty and are highly rewarding materially; others reveal meanness, poverty, and gradual decline. Nearly all definitely tend toward instability and are vulnerable to accident or invasion. Natural systems, also, are dynamic rather than static, as one conference paper and article after another have shown. While many ecologists still believe that somewhat more stable states can evolve in relationship to greater complexity, nearly all agree that increased simplicity leads to greater instability, to wilder population swings and crashes, and vice versa. A. G. Tansley puts it succinctly: "Nothing could be more certain that that vegetation, like all life, is dynamic and kinetic, and not static, and that it can only be understood by considering each plant community we observe in nature as something which has had an origin and will have a fate. Climax communities are relatively permanent because they are in approximate equilibrium with all the conditions in which they exist. When these conditions change, they too will give place to something else."

Happily, Longbridge Deverill still has many of the habitats possible in southern England. A list of the major ones within a one-mile radius of the village includes: oak, beech, mixed deciduous, and conifer plantations, all in various stages of maturity; arable farms, ley pasturage; traditional (plagiosere) chalk pasture downlands and valley meadows plus examples of both returning to scrub; countless variations of roadside, path, and field hedgerows; and a series of riparian or water-related traditional zones in and along the Wylye River ranging from marsh to stream bank, floodplain, and water meadow. The particular richness offered by this diversity of habitats is explained by another principle of ecology, the importance of which is hard to overemphasize. This is that of the "ecotone," the edge condition where two different habitats abut each other, especially where one of them is woodland or scrub. Such edge formations are almost invariably richer in the number and diversity of species of both plants and animals than the heart of either adjoining formation. Curiously enough, this kind of interface commonly found between higher and lower formations of vegetation is something that is often created by human activity, in vast quantities, and usually as a by-product of efforts to do something else. The most important and impressive example of this is the network of thousands of miles of hedgerows throughout England largely resulting from the Enclosure Acts discussed below.

Forest and Woodland

The patches of forest that exist in the vicinity of Longbridge Deverill are relict fragments of the ancient forest of Selwood, itself a fragment of the greater expanse of vegetation that had sprung up as the last glacier retreated at the end of the Pleistocene. William Camden, in his atlas *Britannia* of 1607, says that *Sel* means "great" in Saxon, and that an earlier historian Asserius Menevensis had earlier interpreted the Saxon word *Selwode* as Sylva Magna, the great wood or forest. It seems an apt name, judging by the widely separated fragments of wood that have all been identified as portions of this ancient forest. Both neighboring parishes of Hill Deverill and Brixton Deverill were within this forest. Encroached upon and broken up through time (like nearly all others), its surviving portions were fenced with wooden palings called "pens," which in themselves devoured great quantities of timber. Many such pens are shown by Christopher Saxon on his county maps (ca. 1574–79) as ovals or circular enclosures with trees and walls. This convention is repeated by Camden in *Britannia* and his map of Wiltshire, where he shows fragments or pennings of Selwood at Corsley, Longleat, and Stourton. These fences were made of stout oak pales, more than six feet high, often on earth banks with ditches and kept in good repair. To Americans they are clearly recognizable as models for the stockades built by English settlers on the frontier from Roanoke onward.

Although felling and dismemberment were to continue (and still do), the rate at which the forests were decreasing eventually began to slow down. This was partly because of the wide-scale planting that began at the end of the seventeenth century (which continues today) and increasing pressure to conserve such an important and dwindling resource. The pattern of land use by then was relatively fixed, and tight controls existed at every level because nearly every manor and community had expanded its sphere of activity until it met those adjacent in all directions. Industries that consumed large quantities of timber were developing. Reckless felling — similar to the headlong use of petrochemicals in recent times — inevitably led to a crisis and shortages, primarily of oak, by the latter part of the seventeenth century. At Longbridge, this is revealed by the use of elm and other less desirable wood for the repairs and replacement of parts in timber construction from about 1700 on. This is also noticeable in buildings nearby at Hill Deverill. Then as now, the vast amounts of material involved make it difficult to comprehend the situation. Gregory King published a study of the problem in 1688. He estimated that the acreage of woods and coppices was approximately three million acres at the time, and that the combined total of forest, parks, and commons (some of which were heavily or partially wooded) ran to another three million acres. Although this may seem like a lot, both he and subsequent historians like W. G. Hoskins believe that this represented a drop of more than a million acres of wood in less than two hundred years.

As frequently happens, many people independently came to the same conclusion about what to do, but it is John Evelyn, one of the founders of the Royal Society, who is given the most credit for initiating a nationwide movement of planting and reforestation that followed the publication of his book *Sylva, or a Discourse of Forest Trees* in 1664.

At the same time his contemporary, Samuel Pepys, who had been unpopular and vocal in the Navy office on this subject, was in part responsible for the request sent to the Royal Society for ideas and remedies for the shortage of shipbuilding timber. In *Sylva* Evelyn catches both the mood and many of the motives of the time. Here are selections from the opening discourse:

Since there is nothing which seems more fatally to threaten a *Weakening*, if not a *Dissolution* of the strength of their famous and flourishing *Nation*, than the sensible and notorious Decay of her *Wooden Walls*, when either through *Time, Negligence*, or some other *Accident*, the present *Navy* shall be worn out and impair'd . . .

. . . For it has not been the late Increase of *Shipping* alone, the Multiplication of *Glassworks, Iron-Furnaces*, and the like, from whence this impolitick Diminution of our Timber has proceeded; but from the disproportionate spreading of *Tillage*. . . . It is in the meantime the propagation of these large spreading *Oaks*, which is especially recommended for the excellency of the *Timber*, and that his Majesty's forests were well and plentifully stored with them; because they require *Room* and space to amplifie and expand themselves, and would therefore be planted at more remote Distances, and free from all Incumbrances: and their Consideration, how *Speedily* they spread, and dilate themselves to all *Quarters*, by Dressing and due Culture; so as above *forty years* Advance is to be gain'd by this only industry: And if thus his *Majesty's* Forests and Chases were stored, viz. with this *spreading tree* at handsome *intervals*, by which *Grazing* might be improved for the feeding of *Deer Cattle* under them (for such was the old Saltus) benignly visited with the *Gleams* of the Sun, and adorned with the distant *Landskips* appearing through the Glades and frequent Valleys;

> (. . . betwixt whose Rows the azure sky is seen
> immix'd with *Hillocks, Vales* and
> *Fields*, as now we see Distinguish'd
> in a sweet Variety;
> Such Places which wild *Apple-trees*
> throughout Adorn, and happy *Shrubs*
> grow all about. . . .)
> Lucretius l.v.

As the *Poet* describes his *Olive-Groves*, nothing could be more ravishing, for so we might also sprinkle *Fruit-trees* amongst them (of which hereafter) for Cyder, and many singular Uses, and should find such goodly *Plantations* the boast of our *Rangers*, and *Forests*, infinitely preferable to anything we have yet beheld, *rude* and *neglected* as they are: I say, when his Majesty shall proceed (as he hath designed) to animate this laudable Pride into Fashion, *Forests* and *Woods* (as well as *Fields* and *Enclosures*) will present us with another face than they now do.

Even so, probably nothing significant would have happened if there had not been such a rewarding market for timber. It was a foolproof investment. The rush to plant hardwoods was on, especially oaks in coppices, which Evelyn recommends as of the first priority. Similarly, his hopes for the widespread planting of trees in hedgerows for utility and decorum of the farm scene would never have come about if it hadn't coincided with the Enclosure Acts, a wholesale carving up of the old open fields and commons, and the financial interests of the gentry and Parliament.

Coppicing, a common plantation technique, had been used in England since early in the Middle Ages. Later called "coppice with standards," it consists of oak trees spaced far enough apart to encourage them to spread laterally and to grow a full crown. This method not only provides a general type and quantity of timber, but also the specific curved sections for ribs, connections, and knees then in demand for shipbuilding, just as they had provided the timber and shapes for timber building frames earlier. Between the oaks were planted shrubbier plants like hazel, which were cut back at frequent intervals — every six to eight years — allowing the oaks above to keep growing up and out without any interference. From these periodic harvests came poles, branches, and twigs for hurdles (wattle), fences, firewood, baskets, brooms, bean and hop poles, and other domestic implements. One of the last of these at Longbridge was Crickett's Coppice, today only a place-name on the ordnance map, for not a bush remains. No longer considered an economical form of forestry, coppicing is not yet in total danger of extinction because from earliest times it has been recognized as a good environment for raising wildlife, especially game birds and foxes. Today various combinations of hunters, conservationists, farmers, and landowners are actively trying to continue this relict form of forest management.

The most impressive result of this replanting effort was in the number and size of the hardwood plantations created by major landowners. For some country folk this development was an attack upon the wide-open spaces of the ancient field system and a disaster. For others like John Britton, writing at the end of the eighteenth century, it was a triumph. He describes the zeal of the third Lord Weymouth at nearby Longleat in his *Beauties of Wiltshire*, "during which time [the forty years between 1755 and 1796] he planted, without intermission at least fifty thousand trees, on an average annually, which are now [1801] in the most flourishing state."

Today only fragments and patches of this outburst remain. There are two forest plantations in the Longbridge parish, and with a few minor exceptions they have the same physical size and shape as the pieces of the ancient forest of Selwood that remained at the end of the Middle Ages. There is, however, one big difference. Except for small segments of

Southleigh Wood, these plantations are now nearly all evergreens and larches. The exceptions are of mixed deciduous/conifer and several handsome stands of oak. Since all are part of the forestry division of the Thynne family's Longleat estate and are of uniform age and species, someday soon local residents will be as horrified to see most of them cut down and the land open as they were years ago when the trees were first planted.

Forestry policy, like many other environmental affairs, has become controversial partly because many people in government and outside the actual business of forestry management are no longer convinced that those supposed to be experts really know best. While some argue the pros and cons of clear-cutting or of mixed species plantations, the biggest debate stems from the use of soft woods (conifers, often species originally from America or Scandinavia) for the use of the enormous postwar reforestation schemes. This strategy was only a public extension of a movement that began with experiments in private arboreta and park plantations in the last century. One reason for the intensity of the discussion is the importance of these plantations in the appearance and ecology of the countryside. At the beginning of this century England was among the least wooded countries in Europe. Even after fifty years of government-sponsored reforestation ventures, public and private, and an increase of several million acres, the percentage of the total landscape forested is only eight percent. Any change in the population of trees in England, whether of health, age, kind, or location, is bound to have an enormous impact not just upon how the country looks and feels, but also on how it works.

Among those in the most immediate past generation who have sensed this and tried to direct the energy and form these changes were taking were Roger Miles and Sylvia Crowe. Generally they follow Evelyn's lead. Both believe that visual methods and goals should be extremely high priorities and that they can be achieved with no loss of utility. While one could argue that ecological considerations should carry more weight, interest-

43. Southleigh Wood's canopy of young oak trees. Except when young or when grown close together, these trees do not cast a very deep shade and so help to produce a rich layer of shrubs and smaller plants below. The total number of associate plants both in number of species and quantity exceeds that of any other kind of woodland in Britain. Here, unfortunately, rhododendrons have become one of the major shrubs. Undoubtedly planted by the previous owner as a decorative touch along the rides and glades, they now are feral. In the Orient, rhododendrons are part of a sere and occur as a second growth jungle. In portions of the American Pacific Northwest and Southeast, they occur as part of a different community, providing habitats for indigenous animals and functioning as working members of the ecosystem. Here in England, they choke out all the field layer plants below them and have little or no related animal life. In the background, across a small clearing can be seen a stand of pines. Although a quick cash crop, they provide a less rich community of related plants or animals than any deciduous stand of equal size.

ingly enough, the hardwood forests that are aesthetically favored by Miles, Crowe, and a large number of the citizenry excel in this matter also, for the richest terrestrial community of flora and fauna possible in temperate climates exists within and on the margins of the climax deciduous forest.

Farming and Enclosure

The largest living elements in the landscape produced by natural processes are climax forests. The largest elements produced by society are farms, which throughout Western Europe have replaced the forests. In England today less than three percent of the working population may actually work on them, but everyone depends on them. It has only been very recently in the history of civilization, and only in the most industrialized countries, that the vast majority of society has not been directly related to farming in some way. Across Europe and North America, industry, mines, towns, and forests have traditionally occurred as events in a continuous pattern of agriculture. The new phenomenon of a seemingly continuous pattern of urban development like that of Manchester-Birmingham or of London and the southeast can only replace this pattern except at its own peril, for people must eat.

In the United States, the largest urban regions have also coalesced into twelve major city-regions or megalopoli, as they have been called. This has tended to depopulate further vast rural areas that once had a fairly even distribution of farming communities and market towns. In England by the 1990s a similar pattern had developed, with six such city-regions reaching out toward each other along major transportation routes (the M1, M4, M6, and A1, for example); however, in such a small country, the formerly open countryside is neither as depopulated nor as large in extent as in America, but smaller and more fragile, as reports by the Council for the Protection of Rural England and the Secretary of State for the Environment, John Gummer, published in the autumn of 1995, made clear.

Although Wiltshire was involved in the early stages of the industrial revolution, it has always been a farming region. Even the industry here was related to agriculture, predominantly wool and grain. The villages, towns, and a few cities were primarily market centers. Buyers came from London and Bristol to purchase butter and cheese. Numerous local markets for cloth, corn, and livestock were famous throughout the country. The farm landscape of the Deverills in the middle of the seventeenth century was relatively unchanged from that of several centuries before. The long ridge and furrow strips of the open field system were still cropped in rotation, grazed over and manured by livestock. Draft horses had begun to replace oxen, but tilling (weeding) was still done by men and women with hand-held hoes, and seed was sown as it had been in Roman times. The weary and awkward walk of the peasants who toiled in these fields still lingers in our epithets "clodhopper" and "clod." From that moment to today there has been a continuous intensification and mechanization of farming methods with a steady increase in production. In at least one way this has been essential, because as the population has increased, the acreage of land available for agriculture has become limited and is now steadily decreasing in England, as elsewhere in the West, as other land uses, especially urban ones, expand.

At Longbridge, as in many parishes in Wiltshire, the open fields survived nearly until the end of the eighteenth century, when three developments led to the complete rearrangement of the pattern of agriculture, changing the appearance of every valley and in some cases even that of the Downs. These were the introduction of horse-drawn cultivating and drilling, the development of water meadows, and the Enclosure Acts. The first followed the publication of *Horse Hoeing Husbandry* in 1762 by a gentleman farmer named Jethro Tull. It consisted of a method for controlling the sowing of seeds in long, straight rows (called drills) using a horse-drawn rig, and then, as soon as the grain came up, passing down the rows with a horse-drawn cultivator (in effect, hoeing weeds). Even though this method was effective on the old furlong strips, it also worked well on wider fields since the smaller four- and two-horse teams and the light rigs they pulled could turn with relative ease compared to the older teams of oxen. While preliminary plowing to break up the soil and turn under the previous stubble was still needed, this could also now be done with smaller horse teams and improved plows. Tull's optimism that he had found the ultimate cure for weeds sounds familiar to those who have lived through the wave of short-lived chemical wonder sprays of recent years: "The new Hoeing husbandry in time will probably make such an utter riddance of all sorts of weeds that as long as this management is properly continued there is no danger to be apprehended from them."

A second factor in any attempt to raise the acreage or yield of arable land was the need for fertilizer that came from animal manure, and was therefore limited by the amount of livestock that could be supported. The evolution of water meadows in the river valleys finally overcame a long-standing shortage of fodder for this stock. Discussed later, these were a sophisticated exploitation of a natural phenomenon, transforming the formerly boggy bottomlands of chalk streams into long, winding corridors of lush meadows.

Finally, there were the Enclosure Acts. "Enclosure," R. E. Sandell writes in *Abstracts of Wiltshire Enclosure Awards and Agreements*, "is the process by which land that has formerly been owned and exploited collectively is divided into separate parcels, each owner exchanging his share of the common rights over the wider area for exclusive rights in part of it." The motive behind this was a desire to allow landowners and commoners to rationalize the portions of land they were working. In the medieval system a man invariably ended up with several separate parcels of land only one or two strips wide and distributed throughout the entire field system surrounding the manor. While it isn't clear just how much of England was tilled and harvested in common, we do know about grazing. Land that was tilled and harvested part of the year by several individuals was then grazed commonly after the harvest. In addition to this there were permanent pastures. The first type of land was called "common fields" and "common meadows," the second type was usually called "commons" and "wastes" or more specifically "greens, pastures, leasows, marshes, moors, and downs." This meant that while cultivated land was under common use, animals had to be allowed to graze over it unrestricted, except by means of movable hurdles, which meant that there could be no fences except for an overall boundary of the entire group of fields.

Under earlier farming methods and truly communal situations, or alternatively even under a powerful lord with a predominately subservient workforce, this didn't matter too much. The fields had to be worked methodically and in sequence anyway, no matter what the ownership or division of the yield at harvest time. With the rise of self-enterprising and free men, whether owners or tenants, whose success in the emerging capitalist economy depended on their own efficiency and not that of the group, the medieval layout of fields was inappropriate. Everyone was spending too much time moving about between the various portions of their land, which no longer conformed to the newer tools and methods, plus there now was a need for boundaries to separate the increasing numbers of competing private flocks and herds. Reform of some sort was appropriate. Free men began making private arrangements with each other. Individuals began to trade and redivide land, placing equivalent areas to those of the previous arrangement into new combined areas, so that all of each person's holdings were contiguous in one or more larger, squarish fields. Unlike the older fields, these had to be enclosed with some sort of boundaries to keep the private herds separate or from violating a neighbor's crops. The majority of these fences in the lowland zone were made of quickset hawthorn hedges, often planted, as Evelyn had hoped, with trees like elms. As this practice grew and abuses by the powerful became more common, Parliament intervened, eventually administering the restructuring of nearly the entire country through a series of laws known as Enclosure Acts.

In Wiltshire all of the early parliamentary acts affect the north and northwest dairying region, the "cheese." The chalk grasslands of the south were enclosed later. Here local farmers were partly spurred on by the argument that they should convert the large sheep walks to cereal farming using the new methods. The wool market had been declining in profitability for a number of reasons and grain prices were rising. As one slogan of the time put it, "down horn, up corn."

The scene in which this struggle was taking place was one of unique and genuine quality. John Britton (in *Beauties of Wiltshire*, 1801) wrote of the Wiltshire downs near Longbridge: "In summer season the air teems with the rich fragrance that arises from the wild thyme and various herbs and flowers, which blossom and dispense their balmy sweets through every part of these extensive plains."

44. Sheep turned out into a field of stubble above Longbridge Deverill. Nearby on the ridges of the Downs, once again there are large flocks of sheep as well as large herds of beef cattle, a recent phenomenon. Dairy cattle are still pastured on lower slopes and in the valleys.

The beauty of this aromatic sheep-maintained grassland was no deterrent. If anything, it confirmed the logic that it would be highly profitable if enclosed. One manmade landscape was to be replaced with another. The areas eventually enclosed here in the south were larger than those in the north, partly because of the numbers of sheep that were still present. Sometimes in the middle of the enclosures of this period one finds an area not included or mentioned in the award. Usually this was where the lord of the manor had previously enclosed an area for his own use, generally called "the farm." Enclosure began at Longbridge in 1795. Of the 3,811 acres of land covered by these acts, 2,140 were owned by Bath and included important and still recognizable portions of the parish. At Hill Deverill adjacent to Longbridge no parliamentary enclosure act exists, as it had already been done. The village had disappeared. It was privately enclosed earlier in the seventeenth century by Edmund Ludlow, when "it was credibly testified that 'whereas the ancient tenants kept ploughs . . . the new cottagers do live but barely, only by their day labour.' Some of the cottagers, together with the servants in husbandry, who were quartered in a converted farm house, were engaged in ploughing for Ludlow himself, but some may have been reduced to beggary." This village, which had dwindled to a few cottages in 1650, was only a series of grass-covered mounds by 1800 and is recorded as an ancient site by Richard Colt Hoare in his history of Wiltshire. Today a row of drab council houses again face the manor and nondescript church.

If urban poverty produces crime, cunning, and relentless pressure for upward mobility at its worst, yoking productivity with cynicism, rural poverty has traditionally produced bestiality, ignorance, and stagnation. John Britton, writing in the *Beauties of Wiltshire* at the turn of the nineteenth century, pauses in his account of scenery and agricultural progress to quote from an address on farm labor conditions given to the Bath and West Society by a Mr. Davis, a portion of which says:

Humanity shudders at the idea of an industrious labourer, with a wife, and perhaps five or six children, being *obliged* to live, or rather *exist,* in a wretched, damp, gloomy room, of ten or twelve feet square, and that room without a floor; but common decency must revolt at considering that over this wretched apartment there is only *one* chamber, (sometimes not *one*) to hold all the miserable beds of this miserable family. And yet instances of this kind (to our shame be it spoken) occur in every country village. How can we expect our labourers to be healthy; or that their daughters, from whom we take our future female domestics, should be *cleanly, modest,* or even *decent,* in such wretched habitation?

Britton goes on to say: "this picture is very gloomy, but very true, as far as it is finished; but I could put in some touches, and introduce a few additional figures, which were copied from life among the cottagers of Salisbury Plain, that would render the picture too painful for sensibility to contemplate."

From today's vantage point it seems clear that the rural poor in the nineteenth centu-

45. *There are things that don't survive: clever, useful things can have a life and then be finished, can have a beginning, a run of success — importance even — and then come to an end. This humble forerunner of today's leisure caravans (remember Toad's gypsy caravan?) and sport utility recreation vehicles is an abandoned shepherd's wagon, a relic from the once common days of shepherds, of men living alone with enormous flocks out on the Downs. Buckland, Oxfordshire.*

46. *There are things that do survive: for instance, designer animals. Unlike the shepherd's wagon, these dogs have been carefully bred over a long period of time for their intelligence, work habits (a transformation of their hunting methods when wild), and devotion to humans. Border collies retain their utility and survive as extremely useful members of the agricultural workforce as well as in the lives and affections of many families today around the world. This is Jess, thirteen years old, deaf, retired, and the grandmother of many working dogs.*

ry, although engaged in healthier occupations, lived in a desperate state compared to their fellows in the factory towns. The social classes were as far apart as ever, with perhaps more ignorance, less competence, and less well founded arrogance on the part of the aristocracy than in the centuries before. It was also a question of opportunity as well as desperation. Today's sociologists, who, unlike Oliver Goldsmith, see deserted villages not so much as the result of an arrogant and irresponsible aristocracy, an altered economy, or failed farms, but more as settlements left behind by people who have moved to town and raised their standard of living, actually have a point. The bitter view of pastoral servitude with its squalid lives and ugly people seen in *The Village* by George Crabbe, or the unromantic roughness and toil that shows through the lively hedgerows of John Clare's un-self-conscious and often lyrical portrait of this period, especially in his *Shepherd's Calendar*, contrast sharply with Virgilian views in the parks discussed in the next section. The anger in Thomas Hardy and D. H. Lawrence is authentic and well founded. They loved the land and hated ignorance. Not only was the land in the grips of a social and economic system that seemed disastrous, but both it and the people were being destroyed. William Blake's *Jerusalem* had not come to pass; something much worse, and nearly the opposite, had.

I would not like to pass too swiftly over consideration of the work of these writers, for in many ways they are one of the few contacts we have with the emotional lives of the people who inhabited this landscape. John Clare is a prime example. A gifted poet who at the same time was genuinely unsophisticated — his spelling is often as imaginative as it is unique or naïve — he was truly outraged and despondent over the helpless plight of the rural workers and the changes sweeping across their landscape; as can be seen in this typical passage from one of the many verses he wrote in the first two decades of the nineteenth century:

> Now this sweet vision of my boyish hours
> Free as spring clouds and wild as summer flowers
> Is faded all — a hope that blossomed free
> And hath been no more shall ever be
> Inclosure came and trampled on the grave
> of labours rights and left the poor a slave.

Clare's complaints ring true, and like the cowboy artists of America a century later, who saw the open range fenced and plowed, he didn't live long enough to see a new beauty evolve. For him and the villagers of his generation, the old ways were gone, the wide-open spaces — their plants, animals, and life — vanished forever. Later, looking back, W. H. Hudson was to offer a glimpse into what the earlier landscape had been like, writing about this corner of Wiltshire in *A Shepherd's Life*, *An Old Thorn*, and several of the essays from *Afoot in England*. In these he describes this other, earlier England, which still survived in fragments within the new landscape, with the eye of one who grew up accustomed to the new pattern. It is right to call Clare a peasant, not only because of his birth and social position, but also because of his relationship to the land, his attitude toward it, and his command of husbandry. For him, to live and to work were identical. The concepts of leisure and limited work were alien to his thought. Like all peasants, he felt a direct responsibility toward the land as part of the duties bestowed upon him by both his earthly and heavenly lords. But Clare was oddly able to articulate his thought and feeling. He is unusual partly because we have so few direct expressions from this long succession of weather-beaten humanity so well described in the paintings of Millet and Van Gogh and in the *Hunting Sketches* of Turgenev. Clare at his best gives us a glimpse into the thoughts of the lonely woodsmen and gaping farmworkers as they appraised the world.

The new pattern of hedgerows laid upon the earlier landscape continued to mature with little interference for a hundred and fifty years as Longbridge, as all of southern Wiltshire, continued to experience economic difficulties and falling population. The census report of 1831 reveals that the situation was desperate, noting "Longbridge Deverill, over 100 persons had emigrated to America since 1821." The population fell steadily from 1,228 in 1801 to 562 in 1931. Contributing factors were steam power and machinery, plus the railroad bypass of Warminster in preference to Westbury. When the change in fortunes caused by wartime reorganization and methods came, the population increased rapidly. By 1951 the population of the parish was back over a thousand and today it is over fifteen hundred. This pattern, not always so dramatic, was common throughout the entire region. This was finally arrested and reversed only with the onset of World War II. Expanding use of motorized machinery and chemicals, the introduction of tractors, deep plowing, combine-harvesting, packaged fertilizers, herbicides, and insecticides has radically changed agriculture again as an occupation and as a business. The number of people employed has again decreased, and the amount of foodstuffs produced has significantly increased. The investment in heavy machinery, chemicals, and physical plant has also increased in a series of leaps related to the overall economy as the sums involved in sales and the average size of each working farm have shot up. The technical and business knowledge required of successful farmers today, although possibly no more difficult or complex than that of their predecessors (in relation to that of general society), certainly has greatly increased from only a generation ago. In the late 1950s, more than fifty thousand farmers were engaged in dairy farming in England. Today the number is only thirty thousand. Yet despite the loss of twenty thousand, or 40 percent, of all such farming businesses, Britain was heavily fined by the European Community for overproduction of dairy goods in 1994.

In 1996 "the chickens came home to roost," to use an old agricultural saying. A panic stemming from "mad cow" disease swept England and the Continent. This affair, a direct result of applying intense industrial practices and ever sharper profit margin decisions to vast aggregations of formerly disparate but now interrelated phenomena, created such havoc with English farming in the spring and summer of 1996 that the national economy, the government, and the fate of tens of thousands of workers, as well as the confidence of the public in government and the safety of the entire food supply system, were severely shaken. The European Union imposed a worldwide ban on the export of British beef products, tens of thousands of cattle were slaughtered, and beef sales fell by more than 25 percent in some countries, with the European Union committing three billion dollars in aid to the farmers. The outlook for the future is still unclear. One thing, however, is certain. The industrialization of agriculture is a permanent feature of society and the landscape.

47. *A windrow of beech trees along a medieval boundary line. Beeches, once native to the chalky terrain of Wiltshire, had disappeared by the time of Aubrey and Britton, who only reported them on the Hampshire border. Undoubtedly planted, these elephantine trunks and great leafy crowns, a benefit to crops and livestock alike, will not live much longer, for even if spared from the woodsman's saw, they are entering old age.*

As with the cumbersome oxen teams in medieval times, today's machinery for all of its sophistication is most efficient when worked in large open fields with gentle grades. Farmers, having entered the computer era in business, are keen to eliminate any and every irregularity that might introduce a loss in their yield. The stakes are high. In the past few years British farmers have been encouraged by government and the economy to restructure their holdings and to tear out hedgerows, spinneys, walls, and ditches. Throughout the country, the average size of both farms and fields has been steadily increasing. As a result of the evolving international commodity situation and membership in the European Community, there has been a marked simplification in crops grown and livestock raised. Countries and regions have virtually been told to specialize. Because of this, barley is now the main crop grown in southern Wiltshire, and over the last twenty years there have been incentives to increase the numbers of livestock on what remains of the Downs. In doing so the natural meadows, grasslands of the past, and sheep-altered turf have generally given way to cultivated grass (leys, i.e., planted through disking and seeding). Only on the steepest side hills can one find surviving fragments of the earlier chalkland flora in anything larger than a hedge or a verge. The scale and detail, the form and content of the largest component of the English landscape have been changing again. Only this time there may not be so many happy accidents as from the Enclosures.

Twenty years ago when I first wandered about the broad valleys and open Downs planted in barley as far as the eye could see, I was reminded of parts of the American West. The rolling wheat country of eastern Washington and Oregon is one of the most beautiful places I know, but the weather, geology, history, ecology, and population of Walla Walla and Pendelton are very different from those of Wiltshire. There are countless differences between life in the Columbia River basin and the network of roads, settlements, clearings, and plantations in the Wylye River valley that are common to large sections of southern England. For one thing there is the difference in the size of the population of each. While both are attractive, thousands of people live in relatively close quarters in one and not in the other. However, just as the eastern portion of North America was largely settled by English farmers during the period of the Enclosures, which led to a residential pattern of scattered, isolated farmsteads rather than villages, so, too, the farms and ranches of the West were developed during a period of agricultural industrialization that led to vast holdings worked by small numbers of workers; thus it somewhat resembles many of the characteristics of the more recent southern English landscape exemplified by that of the Deverills. Odd as it seems, my experience up on the Downs has on numerous occasions been uncannily similar to that which I've had before in America. Whether in Wiltshire or the lands of Chief Joseph and the Nez Percé, in the golden sun of late afternoon with the constant wind moving the grass and barley and unrestricted views for miles in all directions, it feels like one is on top of the world and that it is the grand curve of the globe itself that one is standing upon and seeing. It is hard not to repeat to anyone standing nearby the old cliché of the similarity to being out on the ocean.

Today many of the hedges have gone. The system of rotation used at Manor Farm now includes a large herd of dairy cattle on the lower slopes and plowing to the top of Cow Down. The lynchets on Lord's Hill have been plowed smooth. With few exceptions the grass has the telltale too green color of the uniform crop that it is. Nevertheless, the land introduces irregularities where natural and more complex communities persist, and people go about their business below along paths that were old when the Saxons arrived.

I remember the last summer I was at Longbridge Deverill; it was nearly July and harvest time as it had been for centuries. I walked up the valley to Kingston Deverill and started along a footpath beside a field. A sparrow hawk came out of a spinney at the top of the vanished medieval village, mewed at me, and disappeared in a looping arc behind a hedgerow. Grouse started up ahead of me and moved off toward Brim's Down. Earlier in the summer I had a conversation here. As I crossed the second field, a farmer spraying nearby had timed his return to meet me just as I had come up to the corner gate. He had shut down the engine for a cigarette and a few words. I asked him if he was spraying pesticide, but it turned out to be an herbicide with which he was hoping to keep down the weeds. He told me that pesticides were hardly used in this area, partly because they have little need for them and partly because the cost is enormous in one way or another. I asked him about rust — I had read that it was the worst barley pest. He responded, "only a little recently, but in East Anglia this year they are hit bad with rust already." He looked around nervously as he spoke, adding that he sure hoped it wouldn't spread to Wiltshire because he had a lot of barley planted this year. As it turned out, the predictions were for a bad year, but at Longbridge the weather was even more of a problem. He told me that the cost of the spray alone is normally higher than the loss to the rust, scales, and insects, and that it is made worse by the time and equipment it takes, not to mention the crop lost to tractor tires when he drives through the crops to spray, nearly one-eighth of every field. "Airplanes?" I asked, thinking of crop dusting in America. "Well," he said, grinning at me in the cunning way farmers have sized up urban folk for centuries, "they cost more really, don't they?" In the Fens, the Midlands, or on Salisbury Plain it might not be so, but here, for now these men were picking and choosing with great discrimination those portions of modern technology that worked best for them.

I continued on up the valley past his barley, now ready for harvest. There really is nothing else like it, the color and shimmer of the long-haired ears rustling in the wind with a scattering of scarlet poppies along the edges that somehow evaded his spray. On Brim's Down I walked up a shady lane between two hedgerows that predate the Enclosure period and heard a cock pheasant bark. Butterflies were gathered around a few moist spots in the shade at the end of the lane just before one bursts out into the sun again below the crest of the hill. Here to my surprise I found a new wire fence where only recently there had been a hawthorn hedge, now vanished. I admired the view of the valley below and followed the wire around the side of the hill until I was above Brixton Deverill. Going down on a farm road, I passed two men on ladders rethatching the roof of a cottage and entered the village

48. A busy fragment of an unmowed headland of a barley field. I wrote in my notebook while drawing: "2 Sept. 1972, the richness possible in a few square yards of earth is hard to believe until you sit down and stare at it for a while. In this drawing there are four species of flower and at least twice as many grasses. All the flowers were being visited by various insects continuously, and I could hear mice somewhere beneath in the grass. Birds overhead. It is unfortunate I can't show the colors. An orange fly of some kind probing about in the scabeous, itself a delicate mauve. Several wasps came and inspected the small blue rosette on the end of my fountain pen."

to the barking of its entire population of dogs. I left town wondering which dog had first given the alarm and feeling very much the power and atavistic sensation that a stranger can still be made to feel when approaching a village, even a familiar one, on foot to the barking of dogs.

I walked along noticing that another community was revealed by the large number of small creatures that had been crushed on the road: hedgehogs, mice, birds, and frogs. Between Brixton and Monkton Deverill a tractor pulling a wagon, also heading for the harvesting above Kingston, passed me. The boys on it had just finished lunch and were hurrying back so that someone else could stop to eat. The combines had to keep going. In Monkton I encountered another farmer, this one on foot coming out of his gate from lunch. "Good afternoon," I said. "Quite warm now," he replied, as if we had been having a conversation that extended in both directions from his remark. He climbed into his car and headed for Kingston Deverill. A few minutes later in Kingston I stood on the steps of the store watching the machines on the hill west of town. Large red combines moved down the hill. Blue tractors and trailers moved up to them for their grain in turns. The sun really *was* warm, despite the wind that never seems completely to die down in the region. I waited for the store to reopen at 2 P.M. and listened to the birds chattering in the trees and hedgerow, the humming of the tractors, and the baaing of the sheep and lambs above the chalk pit on the hill. A cow coughed behind a hedge. The man in the store told me that the two combines were harvesting forty acres a day, and as I ate my cheese in the churchyard, the carts kept passing with corn for the drying sheds of the manor farm. I looked at the lichens on the headstones and smelled the air. Despite the many changes I knew were taking place and had been documenting, it couldn't have seemed more timeless.

Even so, there can be a cold sun in Wiltshire and a difficult time of it, farming. A week later I was on top of Cold Kitchen Hill with John Latham, the owner of the George Inn in Longbridge. We had gone up in his Land Rover to the triangulation marker placed at elevation 845 feet by an ordnance survey crew. I was hoping to see the ocean and the Isle of Wight to the southeast or at least a glint of the Severn estuary in the west, but it was too hazy from burning stubble to see either. Nearby two men were baling and loading hay. Below to the north a combine and two wagons were working a small patch of barley. We went down and talked to the farmer, Mike Allard. He said he was doing badly that year and probably wouldn't make cost. He told me he had started out here eight years before and that this small valley, called Bush Combe Bottom, couldn't even support fourteen cattle at the time. Now he has barley on the top and more than fifty head of cattle in the bottom grazing the side hills (bought for £50 apiece in Ireland, they were already worth £140 each and were what he would have to fall back on if his prediction about his barley crop proved correct). At the time he had increased his operations to seven hundred acres with four men all year and the addition of two, usually students or laborers, at harvest time.

On the way back we watched a pair of peregrine falcons hovering over a field on the ridge. I watched them through the field glasses for a time, a great treat that not many people in this generation have had. While we watched, the male — considerably smaller than the female — dropped twice, probably onto voles in the stubble. These rare birds are now heavily protected, and the local people had been hoping for several years that this pair might breed. To our delight about two minutes later we found another, a younger one, hunting alone over the crest toward Boar's Bottom. This was good news. As recently as 1968 there were only forty pairs of peregrines in the country, and many of these had become infertile or were ailing, nearly all as a result of chemical poisoning through the food chain. Five years later, as a result of voluntary bans on the part of some farmers, stricter governmental controls in particular areas, and luck, they had begun a comeback, but one that was too small to withstand any further setback. The British Trust for Ornithology reported that by 1972 approximately three hundred young peregrines flew, but when this number was set against the high adult mortality rate, it was still a fragile population. Descriptions of the infertile and broken eggs of these poisoned birds, or worse, of the suicide smashups at speeds of more than a hundred miles an hour that occurred when their nervous-muscular coordination was impaired by a steady diet of the organochlorides their prey had loaded up on by feeding on precoated seeds made one's hair stand on end. Twenty years later the situation has greatly improved, and the peregrine is now a common occurrence once again throughout much of the countryside and is described as such in

49. A small death: the harvester harvested. I found this dead mole on top of a beam in a farm shed in Hill Deverill Manor, where it had been left for some reason by an owl. Barn owls, considered the most beautiful and beneficial birds in Britain by some naturalists like Garth Christian, have been steadily declining, as are all British birds of prey. One pair hunting over grassland and mixed woods in Wiltshire was bringing home an average of 104 small creatures a night — mostly voles, rats, and mice — or approximately 3,800 per year. Because of this farmers are now less hostile toward them, but new hazards, such as rodents that have been poisoned or contain a high amount of chemicals derived from sprays used on grain crops or as seed dressings, keep their population from improving.

guidebooks. One could hardly ask for a clearer example of the ability of society to alter the environment or to take corrective action when it sees fit to do so.

Latham and I went back down the hill, stopping on the way to chat about this with the men baling hay. They were from Warminster and were working on a contract basis. When I asked why they burned off the hay in one field and were carefully baling the next, they explained that they didn't burn it unless they had to, especially because they knew it was disastrous for wildlife. There are several reasons, however, why they do resort to it frequently. One is if couch grass has moved into a field that is to be used for arable crops. Burning seems to kill it off. Another is if a cereal crop has been underplanted with grass and they want to remove the straw in a hurry to speed up and fertilize the grass. And, most commonly, many farmers burn off straw because they have more than they need for their stock and can't afford to pick it up or dispose of it in any other way. The resulting waste, frequency of mistakes and fires out of control that damage trees, hedgerows, and valuable plant communities used to be accepted by farmers and ignored by others. Now, like spraying and hedgerow destruction, this has become a public issue. Indeed, many farmers often feel the public and planners are telling them too much about how to farm without knowing the issues at firsthand, while the public often feels that farmers acting independently without coordination or control are cutting down and poisoning everyone's national heritage for short-term profits. Both seem to be right at times and to varying degrees.

The conditions and problems of the farming landscape affect us all, whether we live in city or country. Arthur Hollins of Fordhall Farm, noted for his application of organic principles to commercial agriculture, stated the issues as he saw them on BBC Radio 4 broadcast as early as 1973:

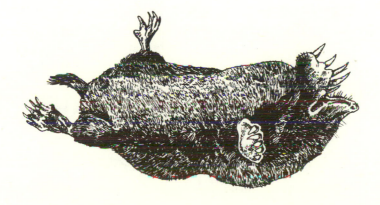

There is . . . a sinister process at work at this time in Western society, one that governments should take a look at: the enormous flow of energy from those slender few inches of soil into our seas, to be lost for ever. The modern one-way farming system depends on an excessive use of fertilizers and sprays, and on putting our animals in factories, and with the washing away of farm sludge, and the emptying of waste into sewage systems of our cities, rivers and seas are becoming choked with squandered energy. Rain and river may steal away our soil without our realizing it.

The fault lies in our desire for cheap food. Given the huge increase in human population and the decrease in animals, the surpluses from food processing and sewage must find their way back into our soil, or there will be a disaster. And western society cannot live on cheap food from developing countries facing a similar situation. Time is not on our side. Half of the soil energy at Fordhall was washed into the River Tern during the 15 years my father farmed it. The greatest civic service a city-dweller could perform would be to hand back his waste to the farmers, composted, and free from any toxic residues. This is the way to subsidize farming.

Land is the real capital of civilization. This complex of microbes, animals, and minerals that is easily destroyed and exhausted can only be built up slowly by decomposition, a process of nature and an activity for which modern factory farming has little interest or patience. An inevitable smash must come if we continue to farm as we now do because one can measure the slow and steady sloughing away of the precious few inches of land that feed us. All the artificial fertilizers in the world cannot finally support, replace, or rebuild this resource at the scale it is needed when it is gone, witness Africa and the American Southwest.

Hedgerows, Verges, and the Conservation of Variety

No other country in the world looks like England. From the ground, and especially in the valleys, it often appears to be covered with a nearly continuous wood that begins somewhere in the middle distance, just beyond the nearby fields. As one approaches this forest, however, it seems always to recede, maintaining its distance. It is an illusion. Seen from above, whether a hilltop or airplane, the reason becomes clear. Nearly the entire countryside is one vast patchwork of fields, connected and separated by a network of hedges, windrows, and spinneys. It is these thin bands and clumps of trees that, viewed horizontally, give England its intimate, informal, and verdant appearance. The fields at first appear to be an infinite series varying in size, color, slope, and most generally square or rectangular in shape. The mixture and layers of hedgerow and fields present a landscape of great beauty, care, and order, but the remark of the chess grand master Mikhail Tal "that few people are aware of the disorder of the squares" could also apply to this peaceful scene.

In the forty years since the publication of Rachel Carson's *Silent Spring*, people in the West have become aware of the enormity of the problems facing society regarding ecological disruption. These aren't just problems of heavy industry, motorways, and oil spills, but also of the domestic scene and ordinary life, of steadily deteriorating communities of flora and fauna everywhere that there is chemical pollution. As it turns out, the farmers of Europe and America have been among the largest distributors of deadly chemicals. At the same time farmers in England were dumping hundreds of tons of poisons, defoliants, and chemical fertilizers in the landscape, they have been eliminating the habitats of the largest system of plant and animal communities that remain in the country, the hedgerows. While the size of this network is impressive, the rate of its destruction is even more so. In 1968 the amount of hedgerows remaining was estimated at six hundred thousand miles, and the rate of loss was estimated at between four thousand and seven thousand miles per year. By 1973 studies showed that it was even worse than feared, and that only about four hundred six thousand miles of hedgerow remained and that the estimated loss was approximately five thousand miles per year, and this loss was concentrated primarily in the lowland farming region. Nearly one-third of England's hedgerows have disappeared within the lifetime of the current adult population. In some areas, particularly in East Anglia, nearly seventy percent have disappeared. The area around Longbridge, while still provided with many hedgerows, has also lost miles of them. One has only to set out on foot with an ordnance map to discover how hopelessly out of date even recent editions are and how the character of the landscape continues to change.

Things that work well develop their own continuity. Most people think of English hedgerows as a product of the parliamentary Enclosure Acts of the eighteenth and nineteenth centuries, but they were already in use on countless homesteads when the Romans arrived. Like ditches and banks (also used to a great extent in Bronze and Iron Age Britain), hedgerows were a fairly universal kind of fence throughout the western world. The treatise of the Roman agronomist Varro lists it along with other kinds of walls, and there is no doubt that it was frequently used as one of the elements in Bronze Age fortifications. As such ancient devices, they would be an interesting part of the history of the landscape, even if they weren't visually and biologically important. They possess two qualities so beneficial that they have ensured their continuous planting by farmers from Roman times until the beginning of this century. One is their effectiveness as boundaries, whether for administrative purposes, defense, or the control of livestock. The other is that they can provide a source of valuable commodities — fodder and wood. In the oldest known surviving Latin text, Cato the Censor says: "Around the borders of the farm and along the roads plant elms and some poplars, so that you have leaves for the sheep and cattle; and the timber will be available if you need it. Wherever there is a riverbank or wet ground, plant poplar cuttings, and a reed thicket . . . plant Greek willows along the border of the thicket, so that you may have withes for tying up the vines."

Because grass becomes burned out in central Italy in the summer and is green in part of the winter, Roman habits of feeding stock reflect this. Elsewhere he says: "Feed the cattle

50. Fences, dead and alive: typical of hundreds of miles of local roads in this region is this approach into Longbridge Deverill along the still used Romano-British Sand Street. The "laid" hedges are of hawthorn and date from the end of the eighteenth century. The wattle fence shown below is made of hazel, which was commonly coppiced with oak. This one was used to fold sheep on a field at Longbridge. An ancient technique, wattle could be used for portable and temporary fencing, as in this case, to shift and secure flocks within portions of large open fields, or when inserted into the frame of a medieval structure and plastered over, it could become part of a permanent structure. Today netting or electrically charged single-strand wires are replacing it for livestock management, and cinder block has replaced it in buildings.

elm, poplar, oak, and fig leaves as long as you have them. Fold sheep on the land which you intend to plant; and feed them leaves there until the forage is full grown. Save as carefully as possible the dry fodder which you have stored against the winter and remember how long it lasts." In August 1973, while living in Italy, I found farmers in the Tiber valley of Umbria north of Rome standing in the shade during the hottest part of the day patiently stripping leaves from oak and willow branches into large wicker baskets to be put away in storage for feed for their oxen. The bare branches went into piles graded by size, destined for various tasks: wythes, baskets, brooms, fuel, and so on. As they had for centuries, they fed the oxen leaves and a slurry called *amurca* made of grape skins, pips, the watery liquid left after pressing and removing olive oil, and soft olive pits.

About fifty years after Cato's essay, Varro went further in his specifications of the kinds of enclosure possible and wrote: "the first type, the natural, is a hedge, usually plant-ed with brush or thorn, having roots and being alive, and so having nothing to fear from the mischievous passerby."

Seventeen hundred years later when John Evelyn was exhorting his peers to reforest England, we find him recommending hawthorn hedges to protect these new plantations, using quotations from Virgil and Old English rhymes for added emphasis and authority. He described the best hedges he had seen (in the Netherlands) and gave technical advice, pointing out that after planting, one must tend new hedges like any other crop, weeding them constantly for two or three years, especially of brambles, thistles, and dock. After this period they must be cut and laid, "plashed," which makes them shoot out, thicken, and accelerates their growth; after another three years they are plashed again, and so on until they are self-sustaining and function as desired. It took effort, but the cost was largely one of labor, and the barrier that resulted was so effective that even rabbits could be enclosed effectively. Evelyn goes on to point out that in some areas, like Herefordshire, fruit trees, most often crabapples, were introduced into hedgerows, making them additional food sources. He also recommended liberal planting of trees for shade and timber along these hedges: elms, oaks, and beeches. His wish came true. Throughout southern England the

51. *While there is great variability in the composition of hedgerows in different regions, they can be admirably adapted to climate and terrain. This field pattern in Devon, largely Celtic, had become ossified as early as medieval times. The small fields and enormous hedge-banks are laced together by ancient droveways and lanes, as here beneath Kes Tor on the edge of Dartmoor. Chagford, Devon.*

52. Hedges can be made with many kinds of plants. This one had only recently been started by a gardener at Hill Deverill. The ground was too boggy for thorn, so he had shoved in a row of small willow cuttings, and as they'd begun to grow, he just poked the shoots behind each other.

Enclosure Acts were accomplished almost entirely with hawthorn hedges, often planted with hardwood trees, mostly elms.

As recently as 1955, hedgerows still produced one-fifth of the annual production of hardwood for the country. With steady felling, Dutch elm disease, and the failure to plant new hardwoods in hedgerows or forest plantations, this figure has since plummeted. Dutch elm disease, although a natural disaster with more than three and a half million trees dead and dying in southern England and spreading without any apparent real resistance from man or nature, isn't the only such threat to hardwoods. Recently there has been a sharp increase in other sylvatic maladies. Plane trees are under attack from the gnomia canker and anthracnose, beeches are suffering from a bacteria called nectria, and an epidemic of massonina is killing off weeping willows in large numbers. In the United States the same holds true with gypsy moths wiping out whole forests on both coasts, Australian beetles ravaging the eucalyptus of southern California, live oaks in decline throughout the entire Gulf Coast from an unknown cause, and American elms and chestnuts reduced to extinction in this century. All of which brings one back to Evelyn's plea that during a period of known decimation of a valuable resource and amenity there is an increased need for large-scale thinking and action, in this case massive replanting as well as research and disease combat.

It is noteworthy that these hedges normally contained only one species (usually hawthorn) when planted and that they were carefully weeded for some years. Few hedges today contain only a single species. Dr. Hooper, at the Monks Wood research center, after considerable study concluded that the number of species present in a hedgerow can be of great use in helping to date it. Roughly, it takes about a century for each additional species to invade successfully and win a place in the hedgerow itself. The greater the variety of plants in the hedge, the older it will be: one with eight species in a proper sample length would be approximately eight hundred years old, one with five species, five hundred, and so on. In the hands of skillful historians like W. G. Hoskins, this is valuable, indeed, because information about ancient boundaries and community development for which no documents exist can now be extracted from the land itself. But this is only, of course, if the hedges aren't removed.

Almost as unknown as the history of hedges is what goes on in them, even though they are teeming with life and in plain sight. The thesis that farming is directly related to

53. Hedgerows in various states of development at Longbridge Deverill House: one is very ancient, having run along the inside edge of the western open field system of the manor, and has developed into a row of enormous trees, the tallest of which contains a rookery. There is a diverse series of shrubs and a crumbling mound of vanished plants beneath it. The other, a thriving community of hawthorn, has been successfully invaded by other trees and shrubs, showing a well-developed transitional edge to the adjacent pastureland.

ecological forces needs no more explanation or defense than to point out the eternal battle farmers have fought against weeds, animals, insects, fungi, and bacteria. Charles Elton has written about what happens when, for one reason or another, an ecological imbalance or vulnerability exists within an area. In *The Ecology of Invasions by Animals and Plants*, he points out that complex ecological systems tend to be more resistant to instability or biological invasions, and that radically simpler communities like modern farms are inherently susceptible to sudden invasions of both plants and animals. He remarks: "If the wilderness is in retreat, we ought to learn how to introduce some of its own stability and richness into the landscape from which we grow our natural resources." In England, such a reservoir of plants and animals already does exist, stretching for hundreds of thousands of miles in every direction — the hedgerows. Providing food, cover, refuge, and channels of communication and movement for perhaps as many as half the plant and animal species in Britain, they are extremely important. Elton goes on to say: "the hedge and road meadow verge are extraordinarily variable in structure and communities. No stretch of roadside is quite like another. But nearly all are ecologically rich, usually stable. . . . I cannot think of any ecological system in Britain that so clearly has all the virtues inherent in the conservation of variety . . . small nesting birds, and abundant insect populations, not only on the leaves and twigs, but visiting flowers early in the summer. A great many of the species are ones that also live at the edge of a wood or woodland glade."

A traditional assumption has been that this is where all the insects come from that prey on crops. Some do, but most recent studies show that without the hedges it would be far worse. They are also loaded with predators working on the farmers' side. Ladybirds (called ladybugs in America), for example, produce larvae that can eat up to five hundred aphids each in the course of three weeks. Hoverflies, one of the most common creatures of hedge and verge, are even better. Their maggots can eat twenty aphids in twenty minutes. Many of the most common birds with large populations have what has been called "a definite relationship to the large weed population of historical agriculture." Examples of this are goldfinches with their fondness for thistle seeds, or partridge with their dependence on chickweed and other broad-leaved pests. That hedgerows form a reservoir for the enemies and parasites of insect pests of crops is now known to be more than a theory. The main reason that hedgerows contain so many useful animals is that they provide a wide variety of habitats. These range from small-scale meadow plants like grasses, herbs, and flowers to taller broad-leaved plants like hogweed and nettles and the larger, denser, and woody shrubs and trees. They produce a range of different heights, temperatures, structures, light, and matter that renders them effectively representative of scrub or woodland edge communities, the richest habitat zones available on land in England. This is especially true if they possess a characteristic A-shaped cross section with a broad base, for it is on the leaves of many of the lower plants in its verge — nettles, for instance — growing in the sheltered microclimate of the hedge that many insects, including the most colorful butterflies, place their larvae.

54. *Life within the hedgerows: it is hard to conceive how any other kind of barrier could support as much life as a hedge. These two nests are examples taken from a hornbeam hedge at Longbridge. Both were built by fairly common birds. One, the long-tailed tit, generally nests in small-scale shrubs and trees; the other, a mistle thrush, builds its nests higher in larger and older trees (below). Just as hedges have their bird and insect populations, so do these nests have their own little communities of plants and animals. Some, like the tit's nest(above), which, cunningly felted together from moss, lichens, wool, and spiders' webs and lined with feathers and down, are taken over by mice when they are abandoned.*

Hedges help farmers in another way also, by altering the climate. Hedgerows, especially older ones, or ones with trees at frequent intervals, change the wind conditions, humidity, and temperature of the adjacent land. This comes about in many ways. First, hedgerows or any kind of vegetation increase the roughness of the landscape and cause a decrease in the wind speed near the earth (compared to what it would be over smooth terrain and above the hedgerows at slightly higher elevations). Second, downwind and extending for a considerable distance from a hedgerow there can be a shadow where the wind is greatly reduced or absent. This reduces the chill factor and decreases evaporation, that is, has a warming effect and the equivalent of increasing rainfall. Third, meteorologists refer to air sheds, which like watersheds obey certain rules having to do with the movement of air, slope, weight, temperature, and so on. One of their discoveries has been that at certain times of day cool air flows downhill and tends to form ponds like water behind barriers, one of which can be several degrees warmer on one side of a hedge than another. In one way or another these facts were intuited centuries ago by farmers watching their animals bunch up near them in cold weather and noticing patches of frost or wind damage in their crops. This last item is very important, for hedgerows, windrows, and shelter belts are the best defense the farmer has against one of the largest potential agents of soil erosion, wind. In a hedgeless and treeless landscape at those periods after plowing and before the crops are up, there is nothing to prevent the soil from drying out and blowing away. Widespread removal of hedgerows in southeast England between 1950 and 1970 created potential dust bowl conditions similar to those that overtook the American Southwest in the 1920s and 1930s, with serious damage. Large quantities of soil blew into the North Sea and English Channel before action was taken to stop and reverse the trend.

For Longbridge Deverill, as for most of the Midlands and south-central England, the basic pattern of fields and lanes established by the Enclosure awards survives to this day. A few roads have been straightened and widened, boundaries adjusted, and many of the hedges, which were gradually added to subdivide further the enclosure parcels, have recently been removed. The biggest difference in the pattern of the hedges today from that of 1800 is largely one of maturity. The enormous full-blown trees of field and hedgerow that we know today are a relatively recent phenomenon. As on the Continent, these trees and their predecessors had been systematically pruned and pollarded for centuries. Topographical drawings, paintings, and engravings reveal this to have been common practice until well into the nineteenth century. One of many such examples is William Holman Hunt's painting *The Hireling Shepherd*, where in the middle distance a row of tassel-topped and heavily limbed elms are depicted along the edge of a field. The tall, limbless elms and short, hacked-off willows, hazels, and plane trees prompted significant protests from supporters of the picturesque landscape movement. The landscape designer Humphry Repton remarked in his influential treatise, *Observations on the Theory and Practice of Landscape Gardening* of 1803:

The browse line of about six feet above the ground gives to trees a measure of relative scale so that we can tell how large they are, how far away, and if untrimmed generally what kind, but that if they are trimmed by man above this line all is lost. . . . The last tree in the foregoing example is supposed to be one of those tall elms which, in particular counties, so much disfigure the landscape. . . . I am sorry, to have observed that when trees have long been used to this unsightly mode of pruning, it is difficult, or indeed impossible, to restore their natural shapes. . . . Single trees, or open groups, are objects of great beauty when scattered on the side of a steep hill, because they may be made to mark the degree of its declivity, and the shadows of the trees are very conspicuous; but on a plain the shadows are little seen, and therefore single trees are of less use.

One of my favorite hedgerows at Longbridge successfully masks the busy road from Shaftesbury to Warminster (now the A350), giving peace and a sense of isolation to the garden of Longbridge Deverill House; another is older and more decrepit, with a row of tall — one might even say painterly — elms, which offered the song of the first cuckoo I ever heard. The northern end of this hedgerow I later learned has been called "cuckoo corner" for generations. Its survival is due to the action of a former owner of Longbridge House named Huffman. A retired Canadian banker, he was generous and well liked in the community. He loved trees with a passion and apparently more wisdom than his widow, who later nearly wrecked the garden.

One day the tenant at Home Farm across the river began cutting down elms in this hedgerow, which runs along the water meadow. He had cut about halfway toward cuckoo corner before anyone paid attention. Huffman, shocked, sprang into action and asked him to explain his actions. The answer was simply that he intended to sell the timber and needed the money it would fetch. Huffman gave him the sum he expected to make for the remaining trees, and they were saved. As well as providing a fence for cattle in the water meadow, this particular row of trees is a key element of the view and shape of the Wylye valley for a large part of the village. Adjacent to it is also a path between two old banks from which the shrubs and trees have grown together overhead, making a shady circular tunnel that locals call the "rabbit hole." Whether it is the tender budding and twittering of spring, the ravishing smell and abundance of hawthorn blossoms in May, or the profusion of butterflies in July and August, the life of every one of these hedgerows is enough to lift one's spirit.

Nan Fairbrother once remarked that hedges could only be defended strongly on visual grounds, that it was "useless trying to justify trees in terms of farming." I think she would be happy to know that this is not so. She was right, though, that they are an intrinsic part of what everyone thinks of as the English landscape. They would be worth keeping in quantity for that reason alone, for in a country as gently undulating as England they provide not only an extraordinary visual amenity — color, texture, pattern, open and closed

55. Functionally layered landscape. In the foreground is the clipped hornbeam hedge of a garden that hides a busy highway; beyond, on the curve of a hill, are a series of pastures and hedgerows. These also conceal another road, a neighboring house, and a large farm complex.

spaces — but also an extremely practical method of dealing with visual clutter. They reduce the potential visual conflicts and chaos of a country that is very small and extremely crowded, and help to make it seem vast, green, and ordered. This is more important than most people realize. Also this landscape fabric, deceptively simple and carefully made over a very long period of time, is easily unraveled. When such a screening device is shattered or eliminated, whether as a result of a natural disaster such as the hurricanes of the 1980s or human folly as in East Anglia in the 1960s, the resultant scene is often small, cluttered, tawdry, and oppressive or worse. A lot of nonsense has been written about the wonderful wide-open spaces that can be had in England if only people would stop fighting the future. While it is true that many people originally opposed Enclosure on visual and aesthetic grounds, England is not Montana, and one can't go back to the supposedly halcyon days of John Clare's open fields.

The sense of incipient disorder and of a world coming apart was to last for some time. Like Clare before him, Thomas Hardy also gives vent to a sense of loss precipitated by these sweeping changes in ownership, farming methods, social upheaval, and the look and feel of the land. While his writing focuses on the human impact, the wreckage and survivors, the new style of owner and manager, it is pickled in the weather and moods of the landscape between Shaftesbury and Salisbury, the area that surrounds and includes Longbridge. His woodmen who see the end of their forests coming closer and the tired cottagers who are about to be thrown out of work by the new threshing machines could as well have resided in the Deverills as just over the downs in Dorset. But change it did. The Enclosure Acts and its hedgerows altered everything, and, oddly enough, if they hadn't happened it would be hard to imagine how the land could have absorbed the next developments. Today there are many millions more people living in the south of England than in the time of Clare or Hardy and at close quarters. No other device offers the flexibility of hedgerows, nor provides so many positive features with a minimum of means — from the conservation of ecological variety to screening the rapidly proliferating number of highways and buildings, whether handsome or ugly.

Footpaths

In England the notion of trespass as applied to land has long had the connotation of being a wrongful entry upon the land of another combined with damage, however slight, to real property. It is not merely being upon, or passing across, another's property. The actual laws, rights, or privileges for any particular place in England are often complicated and ancient. Generally, in practice many more people have access to or the use of a remarkable amount of other people's property, whether physical or merely visual. Most common is the use by villagers or tenants of portions of parks or estates of major landowners in their area. The strict sense and elaborate code of social behavior, so often remarked on by visitors, has given the English a method to express this phenomenon. In Britain everyone seems to know that one shouldn't walk across a field of barley, knocking down the stalks — instead, one should walk along the headlands or fence where there is inevitably a tractor rut or an unseeded strip — and that it is discourteous and dangerous (not to say a crime) to leave a gate open in a field, whether there is livestock present or not. Off and on over the past twenty years I have walked about the English countryside pretty much anywhere I pleased, almost always on someone's private property, always conscious of their rights and my debt to their courtesy, and I have never yet encountered difficulty. More often than not I have been offered help in navigation or conversation regarding the surroundings, the season, or my projects. How impossible this would be in America, Italy, or France! As cities increase in size, and as more urban folk move out either to suburban homes and summer cottages or on day trips to the country for recreation, conflicts between them and the rural population are increasing. These include traffic congestion and accidents, competition for resources such as water and real estate, strangers wandering about in the middle of agricultural operations interfering with crops and livestock, and protests and legal challenges against various forms of hunting, cultivation, and animal husbandry, to name some of the most vexing. This is partly because these city folk do not understand farming and its practices and partly because of their numbers. It is also because modern farming in some instances has been as ecologically damaging and socially destructive as other industries. There are dozens of amenity groups, the most remarkable of which is the Ramblers, who purposefully walk footpaths and attend hearings to maintain traditional rights of the people to have access to the land. In the past twenty years the situation of a rising tide of urban-bred nouveau-riche landowners, steeped in Thatcherite values, faced with greater

56. A young swallow, which, like the lark, sings as it flies over the fields, often used as a symbol of individual freedom in English folk songs and literature; and a stile, a symbol of public access. This device allows a footpath to cross a fence or barrier, avoiding the problem of gates that can be locked or left open. There are dozens of designs (styles!) for stiles in different materials, which vary with the locale. Buckland, Oxfordshire.

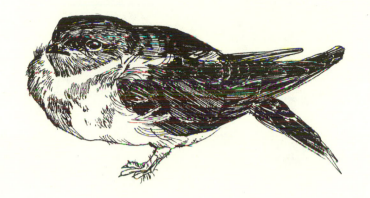

and greater waves of vacationers and ecologically devoted activists has led to increasing conflict and litigation.

Gardens and Parks

One particular social institution, that of primogeniture, has contributed significantly to the pattern of landholding and the remarkable creation of England's many private parks. This device was used to keep the great estates intact, insuring that they would be economically strong and could continue to supply a guaranteed amount of military service to each lord. In this system all property was inherited by the eldest son (or daughter if there were no sons), and none went to the younger ones, who were forced to go off into the world. In continental Europe, on the other hand, estates were often divided among heirs, leading inevitably to fragmentation of ownership, often related to the subsequent outbreak of anarchy in economics and power. The effect of primogeniture on English history cannot be overestimated. It provided men of the highest classes for the clergy, professions, and government. It prevented the upper class from becoming a closed caste as on the Continent and kept the land in large holdings managed by people who had the time and power to become great innovators and managers of agriculture. This system created a pattern of land parcels, villages, and park lands that can still be seen clearly over vast portions of southern England today. Examples of the numerous parks are discussed in the next section.

In addition to their obvious social and aesthetic contribution to the landscape, the many parks and gardens of southern England also contribute to the ecology, providing plant and animal habitat. Varying considerably in size and purpose from enormous landscape parks to small allotment gardens, they contain many of the elements and problems found in the three topics discussed above: cultivation, arrested or diverted natural-succession communities, numerous edges, variety of species and structure, and large monocultures. Examples of many garden forms and styles are numerous throughout southern England. The range around Longbridge Deverill, again, is surprisingly complete. On one boundary of the parish is Longleat, one of the largest and most important private country parks to survive in England, with thousands of acres, artificial lakes, forest plantations, for-

57. An ornamental garden within an agricultural landscape: looking from what was once a parterre into an irregular portion of the garden at Longbridge Deverill House. Beyond are the mixed trees and underbrush of peripheral planting that encloses it. This garden, small and quite undistinguished compared with thousands in England, functions as a minor bird sanctuary in its setting. Surrounded by open downs and vast expanses of barley fields, it provides a great variety of food and shelter for many species that otherwise would not be present in the vicinity, both seasonally and all year.

mal and informal gardens, and a vast deer park, part of which has been converted to a public display of African animals. A few miles away is Stourhead, one of the most heavily visited, visually attractive, and certainly among the most intellectual and artistic of the eighteenth-century landscape garden movement, set within a working estate. Adjacent to Kingston Deverill is Maiden Bradley, the remains of a park and house built by Thynne's benefactor, the duke of Somerset, and in Sutton Veney on the eastern boundary of the parish is another tree-girdled park and late Palladian house. Farther down the Wylye toward Salisbury is the earl of Pembroke's great creation at Wilton. Within all of the Deverills are kitchen gardens and modest houses with gardens of varying size and ambition. Of these, the largest was at Longbridge Deverill House.

Parks and gardens, discussed as artistic creations briefly below, have been an integral part of England and this landscape for centuries. But, just as they have evolved from fenced hunting preserves to open grounds with artistic as well as recreational intentions, so too they have shifted from physical isolation until today, as part of a seminatural ecology, they have become inextricably involved in the farming landscape. Like hedgerows, they too have become reservoirs of animal and plant life, enriching the farm landscape ecologically, visually, and culturally. For many people their environmental role is secondary. More important, parks and gardens are a major topographical element in the history of English social and artistic life that fortunately cannot be packed off to museums or abroad. Even so, particular and priceless as they may be, like all architecture they can be vandalized or deprived of their context, meaning, and life. Too often this possibility has been realized. No longer deeply involved at the center of social and cultural activity, they are increasingly less understood or carefully considered. The ambivalent attitude toward these parks that I have frequently encountered must in part be connected with the ongoing debate about how to produce a society that is more equitable.

There is no doubt that for many people these parks and houses are symbols of aristocracy and inequality. They represent power, whether in fact it is present any longer or not. The desire to smash inherited privilege is as strong in England today as it has ever been. Nevertheless, the obvious beauty and accomplishment of these parks evoke a response in many of those in the working and urban middle classes who flock to the more famous country parks that have been opened to them by their owners who need the revenue for income and upkeep, or that are now in the hands of the government or foundations like the National Trust. Frequently dismissed as ornamental, many people regard private parks as offering little to modern society or ecology. In my experience this is not true at all. They are important for the contribution of habitats they offer, which add considerably to the ecology of the simplified farm landscape. Fortunately, this has recently begun to be documented and understood within the preservation community. For a great many animals the particular species of the vast majority of plants are not as important as the combined structure and cover that they provide. The more variety, however, and the more highly developed the layers, especially the field layer, the more animals will be present. As noted earlier, the richest habitat zone is usually a well-developed edge condition. This is a particular situation that many parks excel at as a result of artistic conventions that produced undulating meadows and plantations, screens of trees, peripheral enclosures, lakes, serpentines, picturesque islands, and fragments of deciduous woodland and forest plantations as backgrounds. What they may lose in complexity from any compulsion for tidiness or lawns, they often make up in variety of species, structure, and decay. Further ecological richness is added by the frequent inclusion of bodies of water, usually accomplished by damming a stream. Stocked with fish, eels, and birds, many have evolved into natural systems. If not overly manicured, these ponds, with their varied plants and edge conditions, add a substantial number of animals and birds to their vicinity.

Ironic as it may seem, the difficulties many landowners have today maintaining inherited parks contribute greatly to their increased value to the countryside. An inability to maintain parks and gardens on the same scale as previously has been caused partly by the rising cost of labor and materials, partly by a shortage of people trained or willing to do the work, partly by the financial situation of owners facing sharply increased taxes and death duties, and partly by the increasing age and physical state of the parks themselves. The most important reason that such parks are richer in fauna than well-manicured ones or the surrounding farms is that they contain a large quantity of fallen organic material in shade or within a well-developed field layer of plants. No one would recommend that more formal, lovely gardens be let go to seed, but it is needless tidying up, especially in landscape parks, that is so detrimental to wildlife. Fallen logs, branches, and leaves on bare or open ground that is exposed to the sun are virtually sterilized and ecologically unimportant, whereas those that have some cover can be utilized by a myriad of creatures. The difference is that between a soft, rotten log and a dead, dry branch that snaps with a crack. The first is teeming with life, bacteria, fungi, and invertebrates that feed birds and small mammals; the second is not.

While this is all to the good, the situation isn't static. The rich contribution of their present decay will come to an end as these parks vanish. The present trend is for their steady breakup and disappearance or their absorption into the tourist and recreation industry. Laboriously built over long periods of time and at great expense, English parks and gardens are not creatures that can regenerate themselves. Any balanced landscape-planning policy, therefore, must develop mechanisms to conserve, restore, replace, or expand them — most likely as publicly held estates, that is, "commons," albeit in a different form and purpose than those of the Middle Ages.

River and Water Meadow

The most important body of water in the parish is the River Wylye, which rises between Kingston Deverill and Maiden Bradley. Fed by numerous springs, it winds between chalk hills, passing down through the Deverills, first headed east, then north, and finally passing

58. Forest floor: here is the richest layer of the environment, containing more varieties of plants and animals than any other. Nearly all plants pass through it. Birds, insects, and animals of all kind feed, walk, or live here. This is where the dead and dying are broken up to feed the living, harvested by both plants and animals. Although hard to locate, there is a small tit standing on the fallen log (follow the top line), one of many animals that came to visit the temporary puddles that had formed in the valleys of bark. There were dozens of these small bodies of water — the two largest are on the left — and all had developed populations of insects and larvae in their brief history. This drawing was made in the boundary planting of Longbridge House garden and shows the potential ecological contribution such gardens can make.

Warminster, it rounds Southleigh Wood and heads southeast for Salisbury down a lovely open valley. Like all of the other chalk streams and rivers, it has been managed and altered by human activity for centuries but is now in great danger. Today its upper reaches, formerly called the Deverill, have been irreversibly changed. Even so, diminished in size and in constant need of attention, it is still a lovely chalk stream. In most essentials it fits the description of what has been called the "ideal" river, one that is richest in plant and animal life, is silted a bit, but not excessively, and particularly not with silt that is preponderantly organic, since the layer above thick organic silt becomes deoxygenated.

In the stretch of the river between Brixton Deverill and Warminster — Longbridge is halfway between them — there are numerous birds, including herons, bittern, rails, coots, moorhens, ducks, swans, and a large variety of songbirds. There is at least one known family of otters, as well as eels, numerous fish, especially brown trout, and a large community of insects and invertebrates. Compared to many other rivers, the extension into the late twentieth century of the same fauna that was present in the seventeenth century is something of a miracle. Of the Wiltshire rivers John Aubrey specifically wrote, "In wiley river are otters, and perhaps in others." Discussing fish he doesn't mention the Wylye, but it is obvious that it abounded with them (or else no otters), as it still does. The commonest fish he mentions are "trowte," "umbers" (a form of grayling), eels, crayfish, and carp. Farther downstream (below Salisbury) were to be found perch, salmon, tench, pike, roach, and dace, several of which surely found their way up a river such as the Wylye to spawn.

This spectrum of animals can exist only if a large variety and extent of suitable habitats are present, and these are only possible so long as the quality of the water is kept at a relatively high level. Rivers in totally natural systems are dynamic and, like lakes, tend to evolve and change. Unlike lakes (especially shallow ones), which normally are shrinking, silting up, and gradually in the act of disappearing, rivers move about as they silt up and become choked with plants. This can occur steadily and gradually or suddenly and violently. In natural systems this means that, as long as a river is allowed to move about, it will probably continue to maintain most of its plant and animal communities and cycles, although not always in the same location. Unfortunately, wandering rivers do not work well with the obligations and habits of farmers and people investing in properties along

their banks and their attempts to maintain the size and shape of parcels of land or buildings they don't want to be flooded frequently. Thus for centuries around the world people have been trying to channel and control streams and rivers. But in rivers not allowed a natural renewal process, the death of their populations of animals and plant habitats is nearly inevitable as they are choked out by invasive plants, silt, and pollution. This is why most rivers today, constrained and constantly threatened with imbalance and one-way evolution toward simplification, need constant maintenance and help.

In an effort to harness and control the Deverill, which is what the upper Wylye is still

59. Towering over river and meadow, this enormous poplar is the lone survivor of a group planted early in the nineteenth century. A hybrid called black poplar (Populus italica nigra), it was developed in France around 1750 and has been planted extensively along canals, streams, roads, and boundaries, where most frequently it is seen heavily pollarded, producing the familiar stumpy tree with a thick head of small branches. Recent plantings of Lombardy poplars occur both up- and downstream from this location, which has been done solely to keep up the quality of the Wylye as a trout stream. The trees are part of a system that provides an optimum of light, shade, plants, and animals — insects are blown off the trees onto the river, for example — which guarantees the fish food and cover.

called by some, the villagers had created an elaborate set of ditches, dikes, mills, races, ponds, weirs, and hatches by the seventeenth century that define the river within its present course. Even so, a tendency for great volumes of water periodically to overwhelm this system and flood the surrounding fields led to the development of what one historian has called "technically the crowning glory of English Agriculture." This was the floating of water meadows. Most scholars point to the seventeenth century as the time of their appearance, but like many other things it seems that the agronomists of the time were well aware of ancient precedents, if not of specific techniques. In his *Natural History of Wiltshire*, John Aubrey wrote: "The improvement of watering meadows began at Wylye, about 1635, about which time, I remember we began to use them at Chalke. Watering of meadows about Marlborough and so to Hungerford was, I remember, about 1646, and Mr. John Bayly, of Bishop's Down, near Salisbury, about the same time made his great improvements there by St. Thomas' Bridge, This is as old as the Romans; e.g. Virgil, 'Clandite jam rivos, pueri, sat prata biberant.' Mr. John Evelyn told me that out of Varro, Cato and Columella are to be extracted all good rules of husbandry; and he wishes that a good collection or extraction were made out of them."

The method was simple in principle but required great effort and skill to execute. A system of ditches and hatches was constructed in conjunction with a careful regrading of entire river valleys into extremely shallow and subtle ridge and furrow systems. Water was then diverted from the river and run out into this system, eventually passing back into the river. When floated the meadow was covered by an evenly distributed, almost unbroken sheet of flowing water only about one inch deep. This thin sheet of water, often much warmer than the surrounding air in late winter and early spring, deposited chalky pebbles and organic sediment among the blades of grass growing there, fertilizing and helping to produce an unusually luxuriant crop. This technique (thought of as irrigation in more arid climates) is in widespread use today throughout the vast agricultural territories of California's San Joaquin and Central valleys and in the regions around Yuma and Phoenix, Arizona, where the leveling is done by enormous machines known as land-planes that shave the land flat and employ lasers to measure the gradients. Here, in Wiltshire where it began, the work was done by hand and with animals and early surveying instruments. In essence, what was being done was to turn the natural cycles of flood and siltation into a predictable agricultural event, tantamount to fertilization and irrigation, something the Egyptians had earlier capitalized on.

Locally the most famous example was to be found twelve miles east of Longbridge in the parish of Orcheston. John Britton tells us that his friend Thomas Davis, curious about a seemingly miraculous grass, went there in 1794 to see for himself and reported: "Its extraordinary length is only produced by the overflowing of the river on the warm gravelly bed, which when it happens at the proper seasons, disposes the grass to take root and shoot out from the joints, and then root again and again. . . . so that it is frequently of the length of ten or twelve feet and the quantity on the land immense, although it does not stand above two feet high from the ground."

The result *was* remarkable. Two and a half acres at Orcheston in a favorable year were able to produce "upwards of twelve tons of hay in one season." No wonder that the technique spread to the other chalk river valleys until by the beginning of the nineteenth century it was estimated that between fifteen and twenty thousand acres had been placed under this system. These water meadows greatly increased the amount of fodder available for sheep and cattle, especially in the difficult months toward the end of winter, and they have often been credited with being the single most important factor responsible for the large increase in the numbers of livestock on the Wiltshire Downs in the eighteenth century. This in turn led to increased yields of corn, estimated to be as high as 25 percent per acre. At Longbridge there was usually at least eighteen inches of grass in the meadows by April, and often it was possible to get a cutting as early as March. For all its intricacy, extensive area, and value, once this system was completed the water meadows of an entire parish could be operated by a single man employed full-time, keeping the ditches and canals clear, working and operating the hatches. Their importance is shown by the shape of many of the parishes along the Wylye, where fragmented, detached, and greatly elongated parts of parishes give evidence of the need to share these precious meadows. Additional support for this fact is the frequency with which they are mentioned and the regulations regarding their use and maintenance (especially of ditches and hatches) in the enclosure awards for the region.

With the onset of World War II, the water meadows began to fall into disrepair. In the changed pattern of agriculture that emerged after the war, they had no place and were gradually added into the arable crop rotation system, except in areas that are still subject to repeated flooding. Examples of the former are to be found between Brixton and Hill Deverill, where the ridges in the meadows alongside the road were plowed away with the introduction of barley crops in 1970. Examples of the latter can be found immediately upstream from Hill Deverill Manor in a long, heavily furrowed rough meadow and below Longbridge Church toward Crockerton. There also exists in Longbridge one particularly ancient meadow that has been grazed and mown continuously since Domesday but has never been plowed or graded. It exhibits a particularly luxuriant and archaic succession of flowering plants, many of which are considered weeds and pests by farmers (e.g., several kinds of buttercups and mustard), that were once common to the entire region and country, as well as a large variety of tall and wild grasses. This meadow still floods frequently and was under water several times the last winter I stayed in the village. Although it is not hard to understand the passing of these floated fields, one can only regret never having seen them in use. Looking at photographs and walking among them, I can only think that, like windmills, they were a remarkably apt method of utilizing natural energy in a pleasing and environmentally productive way.

60. *Beyond this wall along the former site of Sir John Thynne's manor house, one can still see the pattern of the water meadow circulation system delineated by different shades and species of grass. The Wylye River, maintained in its present course for centuries through constant attention, winds past the western edge of Southleigh Wood.*

River Conservation

Every morning at 5 A.M. before most of the village is up, a man and a dog walk across the river meadow adjacent to Longbridge Deverill House. Wearing gum boots and carrying a shotgun and game bag he heads north along the river. Fred, a black Labrador, leads until they disappear from sight beyond the church. Between 12:30 and 1:00 P.M. he reappears and goes in to lunch. Some days in the afternoons the man can be seen along the riverbank with odd and ancient-looking tools. His name is Richards, or Mr. Richards, or Ted, depending on how one fits into the social structure of the village. He is the keeper of the river, the water bailiff. This portion of the Wylye River is his world. The West Wiltshire Water board, which answers to the Avon and Dorset River Authority, may have the power to divert or pump water and to monitor flow; the marquess of Bath (one of the Thynnes) may actually own the land that the water flows through and may control the rights to fish and take game; he may have posted the paths "Private," and be Richard's employer; the villagers may take it for granted that they can walk on the posted paths as they have for centuries; but everyone knows that it is Richards who knows the river. It is his judgment and work that maintain the variety of life to be found in the miles of it under his care.

During the years I lived in Longbridge Deverill, the marquess of Bath (or simply Bath, as he was known and signed papers) still employed two water keepers, Richards, who lived in Longbridge, and another man named Bucket, who lived and worked near Longleat House. Among their many duties, they also helped to set out pheasants and with the shoots. Years ago Richards used to help out in the annual thinning of the deer herd at Longleat Park, but now that was done on contract by an outside firm. The keeper staff has dwindled to two, although the entire staff was around one hundred thirty in 1972. This included foresters, gardeners, restaurant and lion park employees. Bucket at the time was more than eighty, and Richards, who was a grandfather, must have been in his sixties at the time of my initial studies. Richards had an obvious love for his work and a great respect for his employer, who until 1948 owned nearly everything in the entire valley. He smiled and told me slyly in his soft accent, "Lord Bath says he isn't making any money and that he's broke, but I notice that if he wants anything he always gets it." Nonetheless, the pattern of aristocratic land ownership, employment, and wealth had largely been broken in the region.

As bailiffs these two men could (and did) arrest poachers and looked after life in the water and along the banks, deciding where and when to cut the weeds in order to keep an optimum habitat for trout. If they cut too much, the fish would have no shade or cover, and too many would be taken by herons, kingfishers, and others. Also when there are too few plants the river becomes more turbulent, and the ensuing cloud of silt in the water suffocates the fish. Richards told me of an incident where more than a hundred trout were found dead in Longleat Park after the cutting of a large portion of watercress in 1972. On the other hand, if no weed is cut the plants gradually extend their range into the water,

61. The Willy-beds: located in the middle of Longbridge Deverill, this portion of the Wylye River, now a carefully maintained spawning area for trout, is all that remains of a once extensive marsh. In the distance is Manor Farm, the descendant of Upinton, one of the early Celtic settlements on the edge of this marsh. The drained meadow in between was a common from medieval times until 1795 when it was enclosed.

slowing down the current and warming it, trapping silt and causing the bottom to become muddier. In addition to this, more organic matter is deposited on the bottom, which as it decays uses up more and more of the oxygen available in the water. The result is a river growing stagnant that begins to shift its location and to flood frequently. So Richards watched and guessed what to try as the situation constantly changed. I asked him if the herons and others didn't eat a lot of fish. He said that they did, but pointed out that this is good, for a stream with no predators soon becomes overstocked with small fish. There isn't enough feed in a stream for an unlimited number of trout. He tried to keep a balance, so that there were always some big ones and the stream didn't have to be stocked, which so far had never been necessary.

He was also well aware of the endangered situation of most of Britain's predators and had a deep belief in their conservation. An example of his wisdom and real authority over this two-and-a-half-mile stretch of river (not always made known to his employer) is indicated by the following incident. One day I was talking with him about otters. Richards remarked that he had watched one for about fifteen minutes the day before. It sat on the bankside grooming itself with its tongue and forepaws. Finally it slipped into the river, "but they never make a splash, you know." I asked him how it managed to survive unnoticed in this busy valley. He told me that word had got out that there were otters on his stretch of the river and that Bath had offered him £100 if he would trap a pair to put in the zoo at Longleat. Although that was a lot of money to Richards, he feigned that he had no luck in his attempts to comply with this wish. "My predecessor trapped several," he said. "They're quite easy to trap in certain places." Part of his reluctance was because the animals were frequently drowned when caught in these traps, like beaver. Bath finally gave up and ordered others from India, and Richards then happily trapped eels, which are relatively plentiful, to feed them.

Fishing rights on the river are as exclusive (and as expensive) as elsewhere in Britain. There are only thirteen rods regularly allowed to fish here, although I have never seen more than two or three present at any one time and rarely that. Given the frequency and variety of skill displayed, these fishermen are no match for the population of fish. Roy Beddington has pointed out that many trout in the Trent and Itchen rivers to the east of the Wylye valley swim upstream to spawn. This is equally true of the Wylye. When the fry hatch out, they find the clear water, clean gravel, and beds of ranunculus, watercress, and water celery so congenial that they tend to remain there and don't move back downstream. If predators have been removed and fishermen only take large fish — throwing back the small ones in the mistaken belief that it is somehow more fair to the fish — a crisis can develop, and the overcrowding of small starving fish must then be relieved by netting them in sufficient quantities to allow the remainder to thrive and grow.

The river above Longbridge and parts in the center of the village are spawning grounds for brown trout. One particularly good area known as the Willy-beds is a surviving fragment of the large marsh of Celtic times. Downstream from the Willy-beds and running north to Warminster is a stretch of river that is an ideal trout stream. Here it has gradually developed a series of bends, holes, fast and slow, sheltered and open portions with plenty of feed. One hot day in July, I found Richards and Bucket working along the river meadow, cutting weeds. Like most river keepers, Richards prefers to work alone and with a hand scythe, often wading in the river for hours at a time. This is difficult, but the results are generally more exact than the method they were now resorting to. On this occasion, the situation had become so severe that broader measures were required. It was the middle of a hot spell, the river was very low and slow, and the weeds had spread dramatically. The river was running only at three million gallons per day at the time, compared to fourteen million gallons per day, which is normal in late winter. In an effort to keep the river from falling too low, the speed of the water behind the weir was drastically slowed down. This, combined with the heat and long hours of daylight, caused the algae and weeds suddenly to grow at an alarming rate. One reason the river was so low in volume was the pumping of large quantities from the aquifer upstream from bore holes used by the water board to supply urban areas and industry elsewhere in the region.

Using an old underwater cutting tool made of links, they stood on opposite banks tugging in unison at an especially luxuriant growth of weeds. This cutter was only twelve links long, but devices of up to twenty links have been used by water keepers for some wider stretches further downriver. These jointed saws have short lengths of chain and rope on each end and are difficult to operate because of the coordination required between the two men working against or with the current of the river. He showed me one of the older ones they used to use that was much heavier. Some were so awkward they took four men to operate. Even the lighter ones used today have a tendency to dig into the mud on the bottom, to "dive," as he put it, and a hook has to be kept on one end with which it can be twisted back into a flat position. After several days of this selective cutting and ponding (he had all but shut the gates when he began cutting), Richards, using a long pole and a scythe, floated the cuttings over the remaining desired plants, now under high water, downstream to hatches at the weir by the church. Here he shut off the downstream hatches and opened one leading to the old water meadows where he diverted the cuttings. With the cut weeds spread out in the field he restored the normal flow to the river, which now had a suitable amount of plants for the volume of water and the rate of flow. While keepers like Richards and Bucket can keep up with and adjust the ratio of plants, water, and animal life, sedimentation — the inevitable and continuous siltation of riverbeds — is a more difficult matter to handle.

In an attempt to counteract this phenomenon, the River Authority, as a matter of routine every eight to ten years, dredges out particular stretches of the river with large machinery. I witnessed such an instance in the winter of 1974. A drag line worked its way along the river, scooping yard after yard of topsoil and chalk particles from the bottom of the channel, along with whatever plants happened to be there, spreading them along the river bank and meadow. It was January, cold and bleak. I was horrified to see this mechanical behemoth crawling alongside what I by then considered my precious meadow and stream. Returning in late June I found the meadow gloriously ablaze with plants and the river purring between its banks, trout playing among the weeds and darting into shadows beneath the banks, as if nothing had ever happened. The realization that what I had witnessed was gardening or husbandry on a larger scale than usual, that entire valleys were being managed with the same will and understanding that one can tend a back garden, was a shock, even though it shouldn't have been by then. What had seemed to me a brutal and clumsy technique a few months before, I now saw was actually in scale with the problem, rather like prairie fires in the United States that restore and replenish the great grasslands, or even the controlled burns that help forests. As the U.S. Department of the Interior demonstrated in 1995 with its dramatic scouring and revitalization of river life in the middle and lower reaches of the Colorado River, such drastic and crude interventions can effectively replicate natural events. The devastation of floods and the instant erosion and renewal they bring is efficiently reproduced here along stretches of the Wylye by local authorities on a regular basis. This is gardening on a large scale. Walpole's remark regarding William Kent and the early landscape garden movement, that "all of Nature was a garden," had come true in ways he had not imagined.

The quality of water doesn't affect just snails and trout. Eventually it affects us all in one way or another. By now nearly everyone understands the issues of sewage, groundwater, and health. John Aubrey tells us that the beverages brewed in Salisbury were among the best in England because of the fine water in the rivers that came together there, one of which is the Wylye. Certainly English beer and ale have been a triumph for centuries, are identified with the British way of life, and today contribute significantly to its foreign exports while remaining a pillar of the national economy. It is equally as difficult to imagine England without watercress sandwiches as it is to think of doing away with the pubs. But, like all other aspects of the business of modern food production, the business of supplying the ingredients for both has changed considerably from that of only a generation ago. Just as small local breweries have given way to large corporations, many of which in turn have been swallowed up in mergers, so too have the independent seasonal watercress picker and vendor disappeared. One of the new year-round, large-scale watercress farms has been growing steadily since the early 1970s at Longbridge. It is an interesting venture, and one that, like the fish farms to the north, can work only if the quality of the surrounding environment, especially of the river, is kept high. Located in relatively open portions of the marsh that separates Longbridge from adjacent Hill Deverill, a series of interconnected

paddies have been constructed. Fresh running water is diverted from the river, moved through the beds, and returned to the river. In long, shallow beds the tasty aquatic plant is carefully grown in great quantity. Like all agriculture, it encourages some forms of wildlife and discourages others. In this case these plants would normally be part of a freshwater edge successional stage, one that is highly favorable to small aquatic animals, especially fingerling fish. The location of these beds within portions of the river traditionally used as spawning grounds perpetuates a supply of trout and the quality of life while adding another layer of human productivity. The intense activity of insects, invertebrates, frogs, fish, and birds within this working setting is remarkable. I have never gone to visit the beds of the watercress farm when I haven't surprised herons and ducks. This indeed is agriculture in harmony with natural processes.

LONGBRIDGE AT THE CROSSROADS

Changes in transportation, more than any other single factor, have wreaked havoc with the villages, towns, and cities of the Western world in this century. Longbridge Deverill is no exception. Located on early trade routes, partially formed by a crossroads since at least early Roman times, it has witnessed the characteristic phases of roadway evolution in Britain: Celtic trackways, Roman roads, Saxon and medieval English lanes and paths. By the beginning of the eighteenth century, there was intense pressure for the creation of new and improved routes to help speed the flow of people and goods throughout southern England. References to the condition and character of roads become more common in letters, journals, and books at the time. These frequently come in the form of complaints resulting from the standards or expectations of an increasing number of sophisticated people from one region traveling to others. Arthur Young's description of the road from Tetford to Oxford, which he remarked was "called by vile prostitution of language, a turnpike, but christened, I apprehended by people who know not what a road is: it is all chalk-stone, of which loose ones are everywhere rolling about to lame horses. It is full of holes, and the

62. Watercress and fingerling trout: as difficult to convey in words as in pictures are the multiple worlds and activities in these shallow and lively beds. Plants and animals above the water, shadows, reflections, and movement on the surface, and more lives and motion beneath. While drawing one afternoon I observed and noted down the following: in the air above were three species of butterfly and numerous species of flies visiting the flowers, including a small dragonfly; in and on the water were fish fry and small minnows, snails, swimming beetles, surface insects like boatmen and striders, shrimp, ducks, mostly moorhens, a heron, small finches, and various songbirds visiting the water and catching insects.

rutts very deep; and withall, so narrow, that I with great difficulty got my chair out of the way of the Witney waggons. . . . The tolls are very dear, and considering the badness of the roads, vilely unreasonable." By 1750 the north-south road between Warminster and Long-bridge had been upgraded to become a turnpike. This improvement had been extended as far south as Shaftesbury by 1775 as part of what eventually became a nationwide system of toll roads. The east-west road (the Romano-British Sand Street) was converted to a turn-pike in 1752, the period from which the George Inn dates. Like many country pubs, it was built as a coaching stop at a crossroads along with the necessary stables, yard, and out-buildings, including a malt house where it brewed its own ales. This inn at the meeting of two modern highways became the physical center of the village, which it still is two centuries later.

With the exception of one road, there have been no new roads in the area since 1750, only improvements to ancient ones. This accounts for the extremely narrow roadways one encounters in this parish. The exception, however, is interesting because it sheds light on what was once a common practice: in the open field landscape before enclosure, the grassy headlands along the ends of the plowed strips and fields were used not only as footpaths, as the edges of many fields throughout England still are today, but also as roads. One could wind about through the parishes and counties between the field systems in almost any direction on foot, on horseback, or by cart. Omnidirectional like the walls of a honeycomb, it guaranteed universal freedom of movement, even if forcing constant changes of direction. The reorganization of property by enclosure ended this. Many small communities were casualties and found their access curtailed or cut off completely. Locally this happened in the early private enclosure of Hill Deverill. Direct access up the Deverill valley to Brixton and Monkton Deverill from Longbridge ceased. One now had to go west toward Rye Farm and then back again around or over Brim's Down or Cold Kitchen Hill to reach these upper villages. This led to the local habit of riding by horse or cart right up the streambed of the Wylye River itself. A retired East India merchant residing in Brixton Dev-erill, who undoubtedly thought this was deplorably backward, finally at his own expense had an improved road built alongside the water meadows between Hill Deverill and Brixton at the beginning of the nineteenth century. Motive is important in any form of evolution. Chance and physical laws alone rarely determine the course of human events.

As with many communities and transportation bypasses of one sort or another, Monkton Deverill has suffered and dwindled. A pub, long since failed, has now been converted into a house with the inappropriate and pretentious name "Saxonburg" tacked on its gate. There is no store. The school and church no longer function. The first has been converted to a cottage; the second is steadily deteriorating from the assaults of vandals, animals, and the elements. This hamlet, once called Over Deverill and given to the bishop of Glastonbury in 930, today is engulfed in unsympathetic modern buildings. A crop of California-style bungalows with carports, ugly council houses, and the usual proliferation of signs and public utility vandalism are the twentieth century's contribution to its long history.

Longbridge has also suffered. Today, although possessing the size and ingredients of a village, it lacks definite form or the cohesion we usually associate with a village. Ironically enough, it once very nearly had such form and community focus. The long process toward

63. Monkton Deverill church, access cut off from every street, deteriorates surrounded by new building. These transplanted American ranch-burger houses clearly represent a dream of a world of comfort, central heating, appliances, and modernity to an enormous number of people in Europe and the rest of the world. Although it is self-evident that the desire to have the benefits these houses represent is in conflict with the desire to remain within or adjacent to traditional villages and to retain familiar landscapes, this has not yet been realized by many people. The inability of many with the authority to control or redirect this desire, energy, and investment into forms more particularly suited for the situation is only one aspect of the larger inability of most governments in the Western world to either provide or allow the development of sufficient housing in general.

cohesion of the hamlets around Longbridge marsh had very nearly succeeded. Recent public constructions (ironically referred to as improvements) have now seriously thwarted this. A tightly knit central connection has been torn down and traffic blasted through in its stead. New housing construction, which offered the opportunity of dozens of new buildings to strengthen and reinforce the structure of the village, has been brainlessly squandered, leaving the community more diffuse and formless than ever. In 1940 the village existed as shown in figure 64. On the corner opposite the pub at the crossroads stood the village store. Next, to the east along Sand Street, stood a garage owned by a former blacksmith; this was followed by the post office. Opposite these were a row of allotment gardens and ditches draining to the marsh and Willy-beds adjacent on the east. Important meadows stretched both ways from this spine along with two other important elements of the village. In one direction to the north lay Longbridge House, the church, and school; in the other to the south was Manor Farm and its satellites. The nexus of all this was the crossroads with an important building on axis at the end of the road when approached from either the north or south. Automobile drivers and traffic engineers were not so charmed as annoyed by this, however. They had to stop and proceed cautiously, changing direction at the offset intersection. Complaints mounted. The village became known as a bottleneck on the increasingly heavily trafficked road from Warminster to Shaftesbury. It was considered backward by planners and villagers alike. Having been skipped by two national transportation systems that had been laid over the earlier landscape — the canals and railways — this corner of Wiltshire was now proving difficult even for vehicular traffic. Economic oblivion loomed.

Times were changing in other ways, too. The Labour governments that took office after World War II instituted many changes, one of which was an economic assault on the surviving aristocracy. A series of new laws aimed at breaking up the old pattern of real estate ownership, wealth, and power were passed from that time into the late 1970s. As recently as the election that brought John Major, Margaret Thatcher's successor, into No. 10 Downing Street, people have continued to argue in public whether these efforts have been effective or not. Locally in Longbridge they did succeed. The pressure of sharply increased death duties, taxes, new governmental programs and controls, changing economic and farming situations, and rising costs for nearly everything, combined with various emotions, not the least of which was an optimism and wish for a new and more open society, led to the abdication of the hereditary owner and lord of Longbridge Deverill. In 1948 the marquess of Bath, in a series of historic and exciting auctions, sold most of the homes, farms, fields, and shops he had owned in the Wylye valley.

Everyone present at these auctions remembers them vividly. In many cases, the property was sold to the people who had lived on and worked it for years or generations. As I learned from local residents, some of whom were involved, although Bath sold some of the portions at decent prices, the object really was to divest himself of the region and burden. The prices seem ridiculously low today, but even then they were low, for otherwise many of

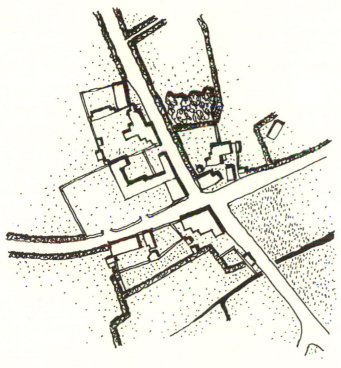

64. *Plans of the Longbridge crossroad before and after the straightening of the A350. Note the former jog in this north-south road from Shaftesbury to Warminster versus the straight course of the Romano-British east-west route of Sand Street, which passes over the River Wylye and its former medieval bridge.*

Before

↑
N

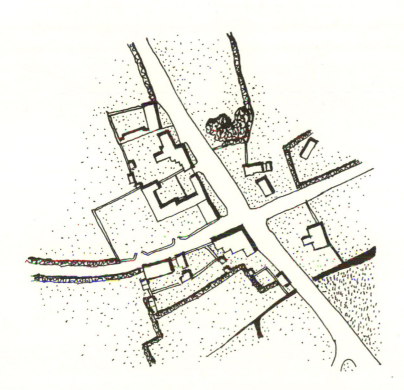

After

the people would not have been able to stay and would have been turned out, or the land and cottages would have gone without buyers. For his family he kept the Renaissance palace and grounds at Longleat, the timber plantations, some revenue-producing sites and farms, a mill house (which the last marquess lived in) at Crockerton, and several miles of the river for fishing. Since then additional property has been let go at higher market prices, and slowly the land he released in the late 1940s and 1950s has been turned over at increasingly dear rates as pressure for country retreats and profitable farmland has increased. The old authority was gone, and along with its social and economic abuses went the patronage, responsibility, and benefits of having one man's taste and judgment exercise control over landscape planning for the region. The era of committee power, planning, and patronage is firmly in control now everywhere in the Western world. With it have come new abuses, benefits, and mistakes. Many of the results of large-scale private planning were neither beneficial nor successful, and, so far, the same can be said of the new order. Again, events at Longbridge provide a good example.

Among the first and still most powerful of the new planning agencies to emerge were those of highway and traffic engineers. On their decision the offending village store was pulled down in 1964, and the roadway was straightened. The grade and curve by the church were rebuilt with a hedgerow and trees knocked down. A petrol station was built on the site of the central allotments. A new village store and post office concocted by the county council of ersatz stone (cinder) block eventually appeared but was set far back from the road, and traffic was free to roar by. It certainly did and still does. A drawing of this scene (fig. 24) before the late 1980s expansion of the petrol station appears at the beginning of this section. The heart of the village was hopelessly smashed, and the crossroads, which had been a bottleneck before, became the most dangerous corner for miles around. I can remember when, in one week alone in the first summer I visited, there were three collisions here, two of them serious. The same week a car also went off the curve near the almshouse and church, plowed through a fence, and ended up in the water meadow below. Pensioners from the almshouse have been hit by speeding cars, one woman twice. One day I asked Richards if there had been many accidents before the road was straightened, considering the poor visibility. "Oh, no," he said, "there never was an accident there." I was astonished and quizzed him closely, but he was adamant. The old road was annoying to everyone. No one could see very far. Everyone had to stop. People did have to be careful stepping out of the pub because the road was so close, but *no one ever had a collision or was hit*. The reason is obvious, of course: everyone had to stop and look about before proceeding. Today the beguilingly straight road is an invitation to speed. The village becomes unreal and unimportant to those in cars as it blurs past. A pedestrian or even another motorist on the crossroads can hardly cope with the sudden appearance of several rushing vehicles, irrationally passing each other heedless of the intersection and their limited vision or understanding of the situation.

Later in the week after my conversation with Richards, a motor coach collided with a farmer's tractor, cutting it in half, and there was a nasty two-car accident that spun one car more than a hundred feet into the layby near Richards' house, flinging a girl out by the store. Today, twenty years later, there is no letup in sight. Indeed, prospects seem quite to the contrary. The volume of traffic is increasing, especially that of the large freight haulers. This has been accentuated by the recent flood of vehicles from European Community countries, which are considerably larger in dimension and weight from those that used to pass through. Also a considerable portion of summer and weekend traffic heading for the amusement and entertainment areas of Longleat and the south coast is drawn through this crossroads. By the summer of 1973 the situation was so extreme that a warning was broadcast over national radio for motorists to avoid the area if possible, as one road of which (the Corsley road from Warminster) had become completely clogged and was motionless for a length of six miles. The daily situation in Warminster had become desperate also, prompting a study, *Warminster Traffic and Environment*, sponsored by the Warminster Outer By-Pass Associations. This report documented the increased medical problems, including a large rise in sleeping pills consumed by the residents as a result of the increase in traffic. Eventually in the 1980s such efforts were successful, a bypass was built, the town is now spared the deluge of traffic that nearly destroyed it, and the high street once again has life and humanity. Longbridge Deverill, however, has had no such luck, organization, or solution and suffers ever-increasing traffic and its effects. When I visited in 1995 and 1996, the unremitting pressure of traffic continued to plague the village and region. In the summer of 1996 attempts to relieve the situation had traffic tied up due to road-widening construction on the A30, the former trackway, south of the village at Mere; this had also led to a national controversy over a bypass proposal for traffic on its continuation, the A30 at Salisbury, to build a highway through a former water meadow recorded by Constable in one of his most famous paintings of the cathedral. The geographical situation that placed these communities at the center of national commerce and events for centuries, when coupled with new recreation and tourism activity, now forces unprecedented vehicular traffic through them.

The villagers were as ill prepared to envision the issues involved in the changes wrought in their lives by such traffic changes as they were impotent to do anything about them if they had. Nor could they control the new housing scattered about on the periphery of the village. Instinctively shying away from the hostile center they had created, the council planners and architects abandoned the opportunity of helping or reshaping the village with this mass of new building. Instead, they have encroached on the surrounding farms and countryside, worsening the situation of the older houses that now confront a miniature form of suburban tract housing sprawl. It is honestly hard to imagine what else could have gone wrong architecturally, except perhaps the destruction of the pub. This sole survivor of the old heart of the village, much as I like it and the people within it, isn't very special by national or historic standards, but if it went, the village would truly become uninhabitable. As it is, the school has been closed, and the children are bused elsewhere to

consolidated schools as in rural settlements in the United States. The church, although not yet declared redundant like several other neighboring ones (Crockerton and Monkton Deverill), has services, but only on a rotational basis with others in the region.

Given the thousands of years of continuity and the present size of the community, there is little chance that Longbridge Deverill will disappear. Almost certainly it will grow. Since 1945 agriculture in Wiltshire has expanded again: cattle, sheep, acres of arable, and population — almost the exact opposite of the previous one hundred years. But, like the rest of southern England, which it represents in so many ways, the quality of its future is uncertain. If Lewis Mumford is correct that one of the fundamental differences between a city and a village is their relationship to the natural world, that the village maintains ties with the natural world, whereas a city tends to transform, eliminate, or replace its earthbound aspects, then Longbridge Deverill is on the brink of losing not only its form but also its ethos and reason for being. Clearly it is not on its way toward becoming a town or city, far from it. Longbridge Deverill has entered a new phase of development, like vast sections of England, Europe, and the United States. It is time to consider what that phase could and should be. It is no more inevitable that this village should become a characterless suburb of Warminster than it would be desirable for either community. Today only the people who live there can successfully husband their future. I have learned to love the valley and this village and wish them well. I fear the worst, yet I also realize how hardworking and resourceful its residents have been in the past and see what great beauty they have made in their landscape, making and remaking it, over and over, layer upon layer.

To the English who know their land — and few countries in the world have a population so conscious of their inherited environment, so fierce in the defense of their amenities — the new motorways, suburbs, airports, and power stations that have appeared and are spreading from every population center seem about to engulf the entire island. To them the extent of the rupture and discontinuity is overwhelming. They may be right, but the network of fields, hedges, parks, woods, lanes, villages, and streams that still remains — as I hope I have demonstrated — is more than impressive. Today two counterdevelopments seem to be occurring simultaneously in the English countryside. One is the absolute and tenacious continuity of rural patterns, land use, and physical fabric. The other is the continuous growth and implacable transformation of lands adjacent to regional towns, cities, and all major roadways. One can drive for hours (or days) along roads and highways in any direction throughout England and see little else but urban sprawl, upheaval, dreary commerce, industry, and housing. Conversely, one can leave these corridors of development

65. *Church Street, Longbridge Deverill: above as it appeared looking north in 1900, and below as it is now. Hedgerows, trees, and buildings have been swept away along its length to make way for overhead wires and speeding vehicles. Also, compare this earlier view with the drawing of the crossroads at the beginning of this section (fig. 24).*

66. *Patterns of growth, structure, rhythm, and form — lupine growing from a stone wall. Which art, which life, which world is not made of an endless assemblage, mixture, collage of such events? Porthmeor, Cornwall.*

and drive for hours (or days) through vast stretches of beautiful, unspoiled farmland and countryside. The latter areas are, however, a series of cells between the former, diminishing in area every day. These relatively intact areas also tend to be around the edges of the island and at some distance from the sprawling megalopolis that now spreads from London through the Midlands to Birmingham and Liverpool.

There are large portions in the north, the west and Wales, in East Anglia and the southwest peninsula that have changed little in these last thirty years. Driving through Shropshire near Ludlow this year my wife commented "how lovely the countryside is as far as the eye could see." I responded that it had been true for several hours, that there had been no town with suburbs, and that every one had stopped neatly at a clear edge, with genuine farm and countryside beginning immediately. Towns as large as Hereford seemed to do the same. No sprawl, no mess. There was industry, but it seemed neat and under control. For anyone who might assert that the Welsh border country is unique and out of the way (which is true), I can assert that in both 1995 and 1996 travels through the counties of Gloucestershire, Oxfordshire, Wiltshire, Somerset, Devonshire, and Cornwall produced the same conclusions. Mile after mile and day after day of extraordinarily beautiful countryside, unspoilt villages, robust agriculture, but always, as in the case of the Nadder River valley between Wilton and Shaftesbury, this world is located between the lines of major transportation, off the ordinary map of the urban population, their transportation routes, weekend and vacation habits.

Conversely, one day after remarking on the beauty and extent of this traditional scene we found ourselves battling through the seemingly endless mess that surrounds Bristol, with its tangle of highways, ugly buildings, chaotic uses, and din. Confusing, dirty, wasteful, and choked with vehicles of all sorts, we could have been somewhere just south of London or near Oxford or Wolverhampton. It is possible to move about the country in all directions and hardly leave this ubiquitous scene of petrol stations, abandoned gasometers, confusing overpasses, hideous housing, devastated high streets, out-of-date factories, abandoned buildings of all sorts, dumps, new suburban hypermarkets, and industrial estates with their annular rings of parking. In terms of conservation and continuity, the cup is both half empty and half full at the present time.

FOLLOWING PAGE: *67. Continuity and change: a plastic wheeled trash bin for recycling beneath a seventeenth-century timber dovecote, and a stable converted to a cottage for the retired parents of the owner of an ancient manor — a collage of construction techniques and materials, each representing a different period, economy and resources, needs of the moment. Thatch roof, slate roof, tile roof. Timber, stone, brick. Not quite the three little pigs, but nearly, except that each piece does its job, many have worked successfully for several hundred or dozen years. Words like "organic" will not serve — it is absolutely built, not grown. Northmoor, Oxfordshire.*

The move away from the land continues today, partly as people continue to flock from the rural provinces to the urban centers, and partly as these centers continue to transform the land they continue to engulf. Despite attitudes that guarantee such things as kitchen gardens in both town and country, efforts to streamline agriculture and to produce factory food — coupled with mass marketing and investment techniques, all pushed by the swollen size of the growing population — are further changing society and its landscape. Recent projections indicate that the number of households is expected to increase by 25 percent in the next quarter century. While only about 15 percent of Londoners commute to work by car, at the present time at least 60 percent of the rest of the nation's workforce drive to work. One village after another is becoming a bedroom commuter venue or weekend retreat. The impact of this, plus the increase in goods transportation by highway instead of ship, barge, or rail, has had a devastating effect on countless villages, towns, farms, and estates. The years from 1960 through the 1990s have been fraught with battles over road schemes. The impact of traffic and the accompanying roadwork upon the landscape has been tremendous. The Council for the Protection of Rural England issued a report in 1995 that states unequivocally that the increased traffic of the past thirty years throughout the nation has eroded rural peace and tranquillity in a total amount of area equivalent to all of Wales.

While middle-class businessmen and professionals have been gobbling up former agricultural cottages and village structures for weekend retreats, and the number of dairy farmers has declined drastically, as noted above. Those who remained, many of whom have also taken over the land of those now gone as well, produced so much in 1994 that Britain received substantial fines from the European Union for overproduction. The two most vulnerable physical features in the countryside are hedgerows and parks. The fate of hedgerows is entwined with agricultural developments and the attitudes of the Ministry of the Environment and local planning authorities. There are fashions in government and public policy as well as in other aspects of our lives. What these ultimately will be toward any particular local flora, fauna, and the visual appearance of the landscape is unknown. Dramatic soil erosion resulting from hedgerow destruction, coupled with dwindling

68. A farm, a ruin, fields, and rampant nature: this quiet scene, farmed since Neolithic times and mined voraciously for tin, off and on for two thousand years, witnessed some of the most dramatic nineteenth-century Methodist meetings to rally miners to fight for their rights against the owners. Once teeming with people and maintaining its fires through the night, this abandoned smelter, stamp mill, and farmhouse, engulfed by bracken and gorse, are visited today by vacationers and cows who wander down from the bed and breakfast above. Bosigran Farm, Cornwall.

wildlife and protests regarding the loss of heritage for the past twenty years, however, has led to renewed appreciation and some protection for them.

Likewise, country parks represent an enormous cultural and ecological resource. As one studies the Ordnance Survey maps of southern England, the ubiquitous distribution of these parks throughout the countryside becomes obvious. It is evident that by far the largest amount of wooded spaces adjacent to nearly every urban population is a collection of these historic parks. Nevertheless, despite the optimism of some writers, their eventual widespread destruction seems almost assured. Seen as unused and empty space by many of the general population, one proposal after another to invade or replace them with highways and with bypasses, for sewage works, housing, and industrial works, is put forward. Modern Britain, predominantly an urban society, like other modern industrialized nations, is largely out of touch with its land. These estates, with their remarkable architecture and breathtaking parks, are almost universally in serious decline. Trees are dying, ponds silting up, ungrazed meadows returning to scrub; houses, bridges, and pavilions are crumbling with no maintenance. Even the history of these parks is as ill understood by the English as if they belonged to another culture, which in a sense they did. Furthermore, they are still perceived by many as the symbols and playthings of a privileged class that has been under savage attack since the Great Depression. The dire economic straits of much of Britain today, and the general shortsightedness of every government in the world regarding its physical environment, lead one to the inevitable conclusion that despite the remarkable achievement of the National Trust and the tenacity of some property owners since World War II, at most several hundred landscape parks will remain at the end of our century — designated as national treasures and overrun by tourists — of the thousands that existed in 1900.

The factors that will determine the fate of the land will be as many and complex in the future as they have been in the past. Inevitably, it will be a landscape of ideas interacting with physical heritage and resources. In England, two elements of the many centuries of interaction between man and environment are the patterns of village and farm and parks, great and small. Together they have provided a remarkable continuity in history and landscape that is unequaled in any other modern nation — a hard pragmatic life and a rich, Arcadian dream.

69. The layered landscape of enclosure: mature hedgerows and trees planted to enclose once common land and medieval open-field farms dwarf this grazing herd. The thousands and thousands of miles of these hedges play a vital part in the visual continuity and ecological health of southern England, masking the density of population and development, creating the illusion of infinite vastness and a distant forest that recedes steadily as one approaches. Oxfordshire.

70. *Timeless and tranquil, wildflowers — poppies and daisies — in a wheat field, and a view of the same wheat field with its oak trees, now protected by law: shifting scales and time frames that summon echoes of seventeenth-century naval policy in the curved branches of the elderly trees, memories of terrible wars in the fragile annuals, blood-red drifts across the pale hillside, the ancient struggle of farmers against weeds. Buckland, Oxfordshire.*

Et in Arcadia Ego
Landscape Gardens and Parks

Other sweet and delectable Country Seats and Villas of the Nobless,

rich and Opulent Citizens (about our August [i.e., London]) built and environed

with parks, padocks, Plantations, &c. adapted to country and rural Seats,

dispersed through the whole nation, conspicuous not only for the Structure

of their Houses, built after the best rules of Architecture, but for Situation,

Gardens, Canals, Walks, Avenues, Parks, Forests, Ponds, Prospects and vistas,

groves, woods and large Plantations, and other the most charming and delightful

Recesses, natural and artificial: But to enumerate and describe what were

extra ordinary in these and the rest, would furnish Volumes.

JOHN EVELYN
Sylva, 1662

Happy is England! I could be content

To see no other verdure than its own;

To feel no other breezes than are blown

Through its tall woods with high romances blent:

Yet do I sometimes feel a languishment

For skies Italian, an inward groan

To sit upon an Alp as on a throne.

JOHN KEATS
"Happy Is England," 1816

LOVE AT FIRST SIGHT

I HAD BEEN IN ENGLAND for the first time for all of eight hours when friends took me out onto a terrace overlooking a private park in Oxfordshire. It was a lovely July evening with the sun flooding a meadow below, and across the golden wheat fields of the Thames valley and the hills of the Cotswolds beyond to the north. A herd of fallow deer silently grazed belly deep in the meadow grasses and wildflowers between us and a lake several hundred yards downhill. Dark cedars towered over the honey-colored pavilions to our left and right that were the music room and library of an imposing villa behind us. In the distance on a hill to the left, a small domed temple was silhouetted against a dense plantation of tall elms and oaks. Herons poked in the rushes of an eel pond near the lake. Ducks and moorhens paddled about. Pigeons exploded into flight out of what appeared to be a ruined classical structure that was dwarfed by a group of full-blown trees standing apart in the meadow. Billowing clouds climbing up into an eggshell blue sky held the light and turned from white to cream as shadows began to spread across the park, leaving a reflection of silver on the lake where it disappeared into the distant woods near a rustic boathouse.

It was an extraordinary and sweeping panorama, as Arcadian and Virgilian in mood and detail as any scene I'd ever beheld. My hosts began to tell me a little about the park and house. In answer to my questions they explained a little about eighteenth-century gardens in general, the sort of information that every English elementary school student would know. Later I was to learn that the house in the small village of Buckland a few miles west of Oxford had been designed by John Wood the Younger of Bath and that the park was the work of Richard Woods, a contemporary of Lancelot "Capability" Brown. The entire composition — house, terraces, drives, dams, lakes, plantations, pavilions, grottoes, all of this extensive and beautiful ensemble — had been designed and built in a brief ten-year period from 1757 to 1767. As a young architect from the Pacific Northwest of the United States who had only recently begun to see my work built, I was stunned by the skill and artifice before me. I realized what an achievement in artistic vision and technical mastery I was gazing upon. My entire vacation and professional life took a new direction that evening. Although I eventually went on to spend considerable time looking at the agricultural landscape that forms the setting for such parks, and since have studied a wide range of gardens from oth-

FOLLOWING PAGE: *71. An Arcadian view of the deer park of Buckland House, Oxfordshire, with its eel ponds, Roman folly, and mixture of old and new trees in the meadow; beyond the lake and boundary plantation in the distance lies the Thames River valley and the Cotswolds.*

er periods and countries, I retain a particular fondness for the parks and gardens I first visited and scrutinized as examples of the art of landscape design. It also became obvious to me while engaged in my exploration of the villages and countryside of southern England that the gardens and parks were an integral part of that landscape, despite a pronounced separation between the scholarship and literature of each, a situation that is only somewhat better today.

Both Buckland and Longbridge Deverill turned out to be fortuitous locations from which to set forth to study the design of English landscape gardens. Day after day that first summer I walked about and drew in the grounds and park of Buckland House, learning its dimensions and parts as much with my legs as my eyes. A brisk hike of a mile south through the fields took me to another of John Wood's country villas, Pusey House, which had an overlay of modern developments by Geoffrey Jellicoe from before World War II and which at the time was relatively unknown and could be visited whenever and as often as one wished. Five miles to the west was Buscot House, another eighteenth-century work but with remarkable early twentieth-century additions by Harold Peto, and a mile beyond it was Kelmscott Manor, a medieval establishment that had been the home of William Morris. Twelve miles to the northeast of Buckland as the crow flies, but eighteen by roads and lanes, was Blenheim, one of the greatest parks of Capability Brown, and only six miles further was Rousham, the best surviving work of William Kent, the acknowledged "father" of the English landscape garden. Oxford with its bookstores and train station was only ten miles away. Soon I was journeying to London to see its parks, to Chiswick, Kew, Richmond, Greenwich, and further afield to Stowe and Woburn Abbey. Motor trips were launched with friends to Bath and Montacute. In the period between July and October I pickled myself in several centuries of landscape design with extensive forays on foot with camera and drawing materials, maps and books. The effect was so great that it took me years to digest it all.

As with most autodidacts, my course was circuitous, jumbled, and full of surprises, gaps, omissions, and delayed understanding. But I had the extreme pleasure of personal experience and direct contact with the material I was curious about, and I had time to move about at a slow pace, to sit still and to take things in on foot. I looked with equal attention at large famous works and little-known and less important ones. I began with an interest in the work of the eighteenth century, especially those works known as "landscape gardens or parks," which became so popular that they inspired widespread imitation on the continent in the name of the *jardin anglais*. Unlike the repetitive and uncompromising parks, with their mechanically curving paths and compulsory grottoes and dizzying rockeries one finds in Germany, France, and Italy, however, the parks and gardens that I kept finding and visiting were nearly as variable as the individuals who made them and the locations in which they were created. With the exception of a few of the largest parks by Capability Brown, most of the works that I visited were highly personal and quite different from each other, despite some of their common elements, shared ideals, or purpose. Many of them had been worked over by several generations and had become a mixture of different periods, styles, and personal talents. While many people studying English gardens and "landscape parks" or attempting to copy them have focused on their common features and characteristics, the English who invented and perpetuated them (until the very recent past) appear to have concentrated on their potential to express variety and to exploit the unique possibilities of particular terrain. In what may be the most famous gardening quotation of all time, Alexander Pope exhorted his countrymen to "consult the Genius of the Place" while creating private realms of artifice within nature.

Few products of the recent past in Western art are as beautiful or as ambitious as the English landscape garden. The wealth of literature — both popular and academic — devoted to English gardens and parks is by now so extensive that one hesitates before attempting to add much more to the subject. Nevertheless, the importance and role of country houses and their extensive settings must be acknowledged in any examination of the English countryside. It is impossible to move in any direction in southern Britain without encountering land that was originally enclosed and developed for the pleasure of some well-to-do landowner. Some parks began as portions of enclosed hunting preserves and were gradually transformed into ornamental and quasi-agricultural parks. Many were created out of difficult marginal lands that had proved unrewarding for agriculture because of their awkward topography, harsh exposure, or poor or badly drained soils. Mirroring changes in art, fashion, politics, and economic cycles, a panoply of country parks and gardens, numerous examples of which survive in varying states dating from the Elizabethan era to the present, pepper southern England in a quantity and extent that no other country can equal. The region around Longbridge Deverill, to which I returned two years after my sojourn in Buckland, is no exception. Despite a great void of stream courses and settlements on nearby Salisbury Plain, the number and distribution of such "ornamental" lands within close proximity to this village are remarkable and include some of the most ordinary and some of the most famous and important gardens in the country. Within a five-mile radius of Longbridge are to be found six such houses and parks, including Longleat, Sutton Veney, and Maiden Bradley houses. Within ten miles are eight more, including Stourhead, Fonthill Abbey, and Wardour Castle; within sixteen miles are Great Chalfield Manor, Prior Park, and Wilton House, among others. This amounts to roughly one park for every four square miles, some consisting of thousands of acres, some hundreds, and some quite modest with only a few acres. They range from fortified manor houses and grounds created during the period of the Wars of the Roses to Palladian villas with parks by Lancelot Brown and Richard Woods executed in the eighteenth century, to works by Humphry Repton, various Victorian and Edwardian gardeners, and Russell Page in our own time.

HABITS OF MIND

It is difficult to determine why a people or nation develops some of its habits. Why does one country raise to a higher art something that in a more rudimentary form is common to many others? Consider gardens. More than anywhere else that one can think of in the West, England is a nation of gardeners. France, Germany, and Italy all have great gardens and rich agricultural areas also. All have a tradition ranging from high-art to kitchen gardens, but none has developed such a great or long love of growing things, nor has it become such a part of the national character. This may in part be related to the fact that there are little or no truly wild areas left in England, nor have there been for centuries. It is a small island with a dense population. While an appreciation of nature may be found among some individuals in all the world and all periods (it was in Provence, for example, that Petrarch was the first modern European to write about the pleasure to be derived from climbing a mountain), it is England that has produced a vast body of nature writing and painting, not France or even Italy — where animals are still treated brutally, songbirds hunted with shotgun and net, the rugged landscape held at arm's length — and it is human works that amaze and inspire.

An awareness of natural forces and rhythms runs deep in English literature. It has been so since the beginning of the culture. The anonymous verse of Old and Middle English is peppered with fowls, freshets, and fruits. Langland's Piers Plowman struggles in the cold and the wet, the rough changes in the weather and seasons of the soul. Chaucer's pilgrims begin their journey in April showers. Wordsworth stumps about the Lake District, and Dylan Thomas is overwhelmed by the "force that through the green fuse drives the flower." None was more effective in linking the imagination of the English to their island garden than Shakespeare. Like his contemporaries — one also thinks of Andrew Marvell in the next generation — the well-tended garden and nature in its wilder aspects provided him with complex and rewarding imagery to discuss the temporal and metaphysical problems of man's life: analogies, metaphors, and similes for death, rebirth, responsibility, corruption, strength, and growth.

The land of Shakespeare, Wordsworth, Constable, and Turner also produced Gilbert White, the first modern naturalist, the revolutionary biologists Alfred Russel Wallace, Charles Darwin, and T. H. Huxley, and pathbreaking botanists and plant hunters such as

72. What is more English than a rose, where love is described in terms of one and rivals for the crown fight brutal wars blazoned with them? Probably first brought to Europe by Roman horticulturalists, this Asian plant had already reached England by the fifth century. Today it is still the most popular garden flower, whether in tiny back plots by railway sidings or enormous terraces on country estates. Longbridge Deverill House, Wiltshire.

PRECEDING PAGES: *73 AND 74.* *Pleasure and pragmatism in a kitchen garden: between and around the lettuces, beans, and radishes, as a matter of course, one finds hollyhocks, marigolds, lupine, stock, snapdragons, nasturtium, and morning glory. Some of the flowers attract pollinators like bees and butterflies; some repel leaf-eating predators with their pungent odors or provide a base of operations for insectivores; together they provide beauty and utility in a modest setting. Warneford House, Buckland, Oxfordshire.*

David Douglas and Archibald Menzies. It produced the Royal Society, which had an agricultural committee in the 1660s, the Royal Horticultural Society, greenhouses, organic gardening, scientific farming, and that strange phenomenon, the flower show, as well as Francis Crick and James Watson's discovery of DNA in our own day. One of the most astonishing outgrowths of this gardening tradition and the literary preoccupation with man's place in nature was the landscape garden of the eighteenth century. Along with its language, literature, and technology, the so-called informal or landscape garden or park has been one of England's most popular exports. All over the world today, people relax, stroll, play, and picnic in large public estates composed primarily of undulating lawns, trees, ponds, streams, and winding paths. Around the world, whether built by dictators and business moguls or utopian reformers and liberals, these parks are all derived in one way or another from the landscape movement of the seventeenth and eighteenth centuries in England. Many of these parks — like those designed by Hermann Fürst von Puckler-Muskau in Germany, Frederick Magnus Piper in Scandinavia, Adolphe Alphand in Paris, or Frederick Law Olmsted and Calvert Vaux in the United States — are brilliant, original works of art in their own right, but most are pallid versions of the originals. Grand English landscape parks such as at Blenheim and Stowe, and the smaller, more literary ones such as Rousham and Stourhead of the eighteenth century, share with the carefully wrought farms surrounding them a considerable evolution that has its roots in the countryside of classical antiquity, Saxon and Norman hunting parks, and recent developments in Italy and the previous century in England.

While each generation likes to think of itself as new and unique, living in a time such as no one has ever had to cope with before, and that their own great art is fresh and unprecedented (which in some ways is usually true), ideas originating in Republican Rome regarding man's place in nature have played a significant role in the stimulation, building, disposition, and uses of country retreats, as well as in the art of constructing gardens containing natural and artificial elements and that are rich in literary and philosophical allusion. Revived in the Italian Renaissance, much of this theory and literature found its way to England as early as the end of the sixteenth century. Throughout the seventeenth century there was a great outpouring of pastoral literature and art throughout Europe, including England. Despite a disastrous civil war, subsequent Puritan rule, a war with France, the Restoration, and the "Bloodless Revolution" of 1688, which firmly established the constitu-

tion and the principle and practice of limited monarchy, the construction of country houses and the creation of various kinds of gardens and parks were widespread. Recently generated capital resulting from agricultural and trade expansion of the period allowed a
rising middle and the upper classes to embark on an unprecedented construction binge.
Moreover, ties with Europe, never severed, were reinforced by the temporary exile of

*75. Gardening is also a craft: the standards and success of the English gardener are well
explained by the apocryphal tale — I first heard it at Blenheim and years later at Hampton
Court; a friend heard it at St. John's, Cambridge, and there must be countless other sources
— of the American tourist who asks a gardener how he has achieved such a magnificent
lawn; the gardener replies, "It's easy, guv. You roll it and water it regularly" — pause — "for
three hundred years." In truth, they also cut them, weed them, feed them, aerate and grade
them carefully. One should also note that the climate in England is ideal for certain kinds of
grass: moist, cool at night, warm during the day, and that in years when it has been unusually hot and dry, as in 1973, 1995, and 1996, lawns all over England looked as bad as or worse
than in other parts of the world. This is a lawn roller used at Buckland House, Oxfordshire.*

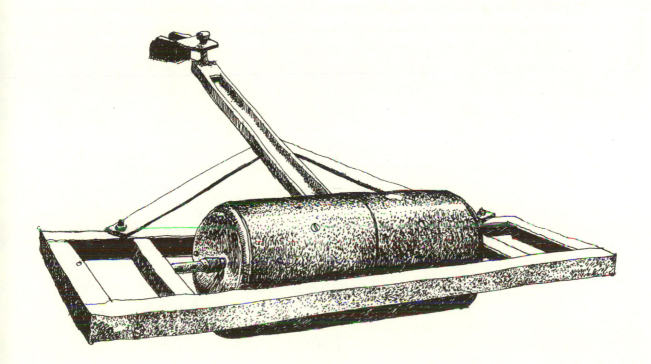

numerous aristocrats during Oliver Cromwell's tenure. The grand tour to Italy and points en route became a requirement for men of taste and ambition. Italian developments were quickly and eagerly absorbed. Gentlemen turned archaeologist-collectors ransacked historic sites, studios, and shops of the Continent, carrying home to England vast collections of antiquities, books, prints, sculpture, and painting. The eye-popping gardens and villas of France and Italy provoked emulation as often as they did appreciation and envy. One interesting result is that the places these cultural pilgrims made upon their return somehow turned out to be genuinely English, so much so that no matter how considerable the precedent and influence, the resulting parks have consistently been dubbed "English," not Italian, landscape parks.

The widespread desire to create or rebuild one's country seat coincided with the Enclosure Acts, which were transforming landholding patterns throughout the countryside. Entire villages and many hundreds of farms were moved, rearranged, or abandoned. As hedgerows appeared in the older open fields and the shift from medieval farming to that of the modern capitalist system discussed above was taking place, a plethora of new estates and parks were being carved out of former woodland or created on what had been sheep walks and barren wastelands.

In the seventeenth century, astute figures such as John Aubrey restated what was even then an old observation: the distinction between the motives, attitudes, and effects upon the countryside of the urban, industrial entrepreneur and that of the educated, agriculturally minded country gentleman. The belief that the country is a more wholesome place than the city is easily as old as Rome and recurs again and again in our literature from Varro through Lewis Mumford. Summarized, the position usually holds that urban people are unwholesome in spirit, ruin the countryside, promote greed and irresponsible government and that it seems in the nature of commerce (or more recently of manufacturing as an industry) to treat people and their environment as material to be exploited for an abstract gain of doubtful value. Behind these country gardens and parks, as well as the more recent garden city movement and modern flight to the suburbs, lie the ghost of Virgil and the image of Horace's farm.

By 1750 throughout southern England literally thousands of parks and gardens were under construction, many comprising hundreds — some thousands — of acres of land. Their number, estimated conservatively at more than one hundred thousand in 1828, and their total acreage are easily larger in proportion to population and cultivated land than anywhere else in the world, at any time. Among the greatest were those constructed by a

76. Artifice and dream: in a ravine within a sheep walk on the chalk downs, this lake, island, vegetation, and park, one of many inspired by classical literature, were all created and planted by its owner, an imaginative banker. Built in a brief space of time, it has provided pleasure to hordes of visitors for more than two hundred years. Stourhead, Wiltshire.

small circle of intellectuals, most of whom were allied to the political fortunes of the Whigs, who swept to power after engineering the accession of King George I, as well as a few Tories like Alexander Pope, one of the most important polemicists of the new "natural-artificial" gardening movement. Coinciding with this development was the rise of neo-Palladian architecture, first introduced to England by the Renaissance genius Inigo Jones and reintroduced a century later by Colen Campbell and his patron, Lord Burlington. The impact of this development upon Western architecture over the next two hundred years has been enormous. Its Arcadian dream can be summed up in the images of classical domes and pediments within pastoral landscapes of full-blown trees reflected in undulating bodies of water, replete with grazing cattle and sheep, billowing clouds, and the distant sun-lit vistas that one sees in the paintings of Claude Lorrain and Nicolas Poussin. There is hardly a city in the world where some derivative of this dream has not been attempted — from Buenos Aires to Vancouver, from Weimar to Hong Kong. In Russia, Italy, and the United States, one eighteenth- and nineteenth-century private landscape park after another was created, and now just as frequently in this century has been opened to the public. An integral part of the local economy in rural England as a source of employment — initially in their construction and then in their maintenance and operation — once again these parks are potentially important as a source of revenue in the rapidly growing tourist and recreation industry.

LONGLEAT

The closest such park to Longbridge Deverill is Longleat, belonging to the Thynne family. Best known as a place of public entertainment and recreation and as the first drive-through wild animal park in Europe, a visit today can become a very mixed experience, combining a handsome arboretum and sweeping pastoral park, serene vistas, and classical architecture with traffic jams, boat rides among barking sea lions, a carnival midway, great art, and vulgar displays of family memorabilia, junk, and shops. In the late 1960s, as part of their effort to raise money without parting with their land, the family struck a deal with Jimmy Chipperfield, a Spitfire pilot and war hero, who was the heir to a long line of circus owners and wild animal trainers. By 1970, when I first visited Longleat to meet the head animal keeper to discuss their techniques for research I was engaged upon for a zoological project in the United States, I was astonished to find a browse line established by grazing giraffes among the two-hundred-year-old oak trees planted by Capability Brown in a valley within the northern portion of the park. The "Lions of Longleat" were the talk of the region, and a local veterinarian at Warminster had become one of the leading authorities on African big game, their health, parasites, and nutrition. The situation was and is bizarre, attracting many thousands of visitors a year. Visitors are instructed to stay in their cars with the windows rolled up as they drive through the park, where there are rhinos, baboons (the most destructive creatures in terms of the landscape), and lions. People invariably get out of their cars among the giraffes and antelopes, who sensibly wander slowly away from them. This wildly successful financial experiment inspired other estate owners, and within a few years the duke of Bedford had created a rival wild animal park closer to London at Woburn. The increasing burden of taxes and staggering maintenance costs of properties such as these in recent times have prompted many families to strike a deal with the National Trust, English Heritage, or some other public charitable organization, thus preserving and opening up a considerable portion of this once private realm. Some landowners unwilling to part with their property, no matter what, have followed the Thynne family's example and set up private theme parks, entertainment, and festivals of all sorts throughout England.

Since the sixteenth century, events at Longleat have often been in advance or at the height of fashion and ambition. Despite the circus atmosphere of today, one can still see the overall structure and large portions of a justly admired landscape park created here in the eighteenth century by the most famous park designer of all time, Capability Brown. Among the best ever, Brown's landscape parks were designed and built in an era of widespread park building, or "improvement" as it was termed during the latter half of the eighteenth century. This movement, initially inspired by classical Italian gardens and *vigne*, began with the creation of highly geometric and elaborate gardens to accompany a new wave of architecture that began in England in the seventeenth century and was well represented in this portion of Wiltshire with the work of Inigo Jones and Isaac de Caus at Wilton downstream on the Wylye, by that of Robert Smythson, John Thynne, and later George London and Henry Wise at Longleat, and by Smythson, Lord Arundell, and London again at Wardour Castle ten miles south in the Nadder valley. It is an irony that if the subsequent landscape movement, with its rejection of these earlier geometric and highly regular and symmetrical gardens and its substitution of undulating meadows, curvilinear paths, water bodies, and decidedly asymmetrical groupings of trees and structures, had not occurred, many of the gardens it eradicated would now be equally thronged with visitors and considered masterpieces of the formal garden to be conserved and protected. As it was, all of the great early Italianate, Anglo-Dutch, and baroque gardens of this region were ripped out and rebuilt in the new pastoral mode. Many critics have remarked on the frequency with which Brown demolished great gardens of the previous era in order to build his own. In fairness, however, one should note that his clients' zeal for the new manner then coming into fashion often matched and encouraged his own. Longleat, the estate of the Thynne family, lords of the manor of Longbridge Deverill, in addition to the Renaissance palace mentioned earlier, once possessed magnificent gardens in the continental manner. Depicted in engravings by Kip and Knyff, they were described by John Britton thus: "and when the Dutch taste of gardening was introduced into the Kingdom, at the ascension of William and Mary, he [the first Lord Weymouth] ornamented the grounds with the chequered gardens, canals, fountains, vistas, and avenues, in all the extravagant,

77. View of Longleat from Heaven's Gate, looking north toward the Mendips.

expensive taste of that region, and left it the equal if not superior, to any seat in the King-dom."

Two generations later, in 1751, Thomas Thynne, the third viscount Weymouth and the first marquess of Bath, succeeded to the estate at the age of seventeen. Six years later he engaged Brown and work commenced on a total revision of the estate. Again in the words of Britton: "finding the gardens and improvements in the grounds made by the First Lord Weymouth, quite in ruins, and the taste of the times entirely altered, he, with the advice of Mr. Brown, planned the park and grounds in the way they are now laid out; and from that time unremittingly pursued it until his death in 1796."

Beginning with a first contract for £1,450, Brown was commissioned to rebuild certain aspects of the park adjacent to the house. He replaced the Renaissance parterres with a lawn that sloped down to a series of ponds arranged to resemble a broad river in place of an earlier composition of canals that he demolished. All but one of the allées was broken up into groups of trees. A curving drive was substituted for the former axial approach. Beyond the pastures of the immediate farmland, on the surrounding uplands, he planned and began to plant the vast circumferential belts of beech, oak, and chestnut, which, despite the destruction of thousands of trees in two hurricanes that struck in the late 1980s, largely remain. A second contract with Brown followed in 1759. It included the relocation and construction of a new kitchen garden, curving gravel walkways and shrubbery near the house, the reconstruction of the road leading to neighboring Horningsham, and the draining and replanting of meadows there. Another contract was begun the following year and produced more sunken pales (or ha-has, as these ditches to contain livestock came to be called), the relocation and reconstruction of the road leading to the neighboring town of Frome, as well as the continuation of the plantations and alterations to the water bodies.

Despite Horace Walpole's doubts about the success of a cascade built within view of the house and rebuilt in the next century by Humphry Repton, visitors were in agreement that the park was as magnificent as it was ambitious. Like John Evelyn earlier and many landowners elsewhere, William Thynne had developed a passion for planting and kept at the work laid out for him by Brown, working on the improvement of Longleat for forty years, "during which time he planted, without intermission at least fifty thousand trees, on an average, annually." One little-known aspect of this activity, in keeping with the strongly Italian flavor of several of the avant-garde gardens closer to London, was his father's intro-duction of conifers. The conifer plantations that have troubled many in the reforestation schemes of our era could be said to have their roots here. (To many they seem foreign and alien in appearance in the English landscape, where large stands of conifers have not exist-ed naturally since the end of the Pleistocene era.) Between 1705 and 1710 the previous Lord

Weymouth began planting American white pines (*Pinus strobus*) at Longleat and then gave seedlings to friends for their estates. The tree soon became popular and is still known as the "Weymouth's pine" in Europe. Forty years later Brown made extensive use of these, the tallest conifers native to New England, in his peripheral screen plantations.

The next major figure in English landscape design, Humphry Repton, also worked at Longleat. Self-educated and a self-appointed heir to the practice of Capability Brown, Repton embarked upon his practice in 1788, a few years after Brown's death. Continuing work on many of the same estates as Brown and those of new clients of his own, he put down in writing and graphic form his theoretical and artistic ideas in a series of publications: *Sketches and Hints on Landscape Gardening* (1795), *Observations on the Theory and Practice of Landscape Gardening* (1803), and *An Inquiry into the Changes in Taste in Landscape Gardening* (1806). Repton's series of Red Books (so called because of the color of their leather bindings) contain narrative text and illustrations of "before" and proposed "after" conditions of his clients' properties. Working on the grounds at Longleat over an eleven-year period, he also sited the new stables subsequently designed by Jeffry Wyatville that now house much of the commercial services and public entertainment. He revised Brown's "river" into more of a lake, adding an island covered with trees, and began thinning the dense park plantations, opening up views and creating a covered seat and pavilion in the park. Eventually he was to work further afield on the estate, designing one of his rustic cottages with attendant planting for Sheerwater Lake adjacent to Crockerton on the northern edge of Longbridge Parish. Although not all the proposals in his Longleat Red Book were acted upon, the path toward subsequent heavy Victorian planting was opened.

The next two generations of owners unleashed upon the estate a panoply of imported plants: rhododendrons, azaleas, and other Asian shrubs in particular, as well as trees from around the world ranging from redwoods and giant sequoias to monkey puzzle trees. Today much of Repton's work, especially the terraces and floral beds he reintroduced near the house, is hard to detect, partly because these areas have been reworked yet again in our own time. Despite Victorian planting, hurricanes, wild animals, and time, the attitude and outline of Brown's work as Repton modified it can clearly be seen today. This is largely due to the work of Russell Page.

A predilection of the lords of the manor of Longbridge and Longleat to engage the most prominent and talented landscape designer of the time didn't end in the nineteenth century. In our own period, Page, yet another in the long line of England's self-educated garden makers and one of the finest artists in the medium of landscape in the twentieth century, worked on the grounds at Longleat from 1932 to 1955. While employed as a landscape draftsman in London, the very young Russell Page met Henry Thynne (then Viscount Weymouth, later marquess of Bath), the heir to Longleat, who was also young, exuberant, full of energy, and in charge of his father's estate. Page, in his autobiographical *Education of a Gardener*, describes the scene as he first found it in 1932: "In the middle of the nineteenth century the deer park had been planted with ugly round clumps of mixed conifers and deciduous trees, and the woods with a profusion of exotic trees and shrubs. Mauve Rhododendron ponticum and the common yellow azalea had rolled through the woods like a heavy sea and eighty years later formed thickets fifteen feet high and more."

That year the two walked the estate over and over, marking vast quantities of trees and shrubs to be removed, groves to be restored and reshaped. This drastic editing restored the park to a clarity it hadn't seen for a hundred years. Page's description of the fun and difficulty of his task should warm the heart of any landscape architect who has attempted anything like the task he undertook that year, especially the difficulty of laying out clumps of trees so that too many of them wouldn't end up falling into lines. Page and his client then turned to the lakes, clearing them of a clutter of unnecessary small islands and shrubs that had come to engulf them, and to the long entry drive from the Warminster Road and its tangled aspect. With the absolute ruthlessness of serious gardeners, they set to work:

With the help of a tractor we uprooted the ponticums and burned them on the spot. Only then could we see that the ground lay level for a few yards and then banked steeply upwards to the Beech Woods on either side. Once the rhododendrons had gone we found a few large isolated trees, one or two thuyas and monkey puzzles and some very large specimens of the blood-red Rhododendron arboreum. This sheltered valley was enclosed by the surrounding beech forest, so here we felt we could try out all kinds of trees and shrubs which would look too exotic in a wider landscape. . . . [Page goes on to describe many of the specific plants they introduced along this drive.] Here was a fine field for two energetic and enthusiastic gardeners and now, twenty-five yeas later, the park and woods begin to take the many colored shapes we then devised for them. Near the house we did not get: Henry's father still lived there and preferred that the view from his windows should remain as he had always known it.

At about this point in their adventure, the future Lord Bath asked Page to help him develop the public facilities for one of the caves in Cheddar Gorge nearby to the west that his family owned. Uncertain about how to achieve the architectural portion of the resultant scheme, he approached another promising soul, Geoffrey Jellicoe, a young architect who had recently completed a now classic study of Italian gardens and was then in the process of setting up an organization for landscape architects in England modeled on the older American Society of Landscape Architects and the Royal Institute of British Architects. They got on well, solved Bath's problem, and formed a partnership that produced several important works and ended only at the outbreak of World War II. After a stint in the Office of Political Intelligence that took him to France, the United States, North Africa, Ceylon, and India, Page was discharged and unemployed. Despite a handful of gardens done for wealthy clients and his participation in the planting for the Festival of Britain in 1951, which earned him an OBE, Russell Page largely worked abroad for the rest of his life, mostly in America and France with forays to Italy, Spain, and South America. One of the few English exceptions was his continued work at Longleat, where he now turned to the reorganization of the area around the great house. Faced with enormous taxes imposed by the Labour government after the war and his father's death, Bath decided to open his property up to the public and asked his old friend Page to help him rearrange and adjust the grounds to accommodate the anticipated crowds of visitors and their vehicles.

Page set to work. Time had given him the perspective to reorganize the relationship of the Renaissance building to Brown's pastoral park. In the nearly twenty years since he had first begun to work here, Page had spent a lot of time in France and had closely studied the gardens of Italy, France, and Spain. He had become a designer of tough and austere geometries that were at the same time remarkably beautiful and serene gardens. Having begun with rock gardens, primulas, campanulas, little ponds, and rivulets as a schoolboy in Lincoln, he was now in the process of becoming one of the great classicists of the twentieth century. He had lost patience with the "informal" school of landscape. He felt that Brown had "encourage[d] his wealthy clients to tear out their splendid formal gardens and replace them with his facile compositions of grass, tree clumps and rather shapeless ponds and lakes. Such vagaries on a huge scale may appear irrelevant to the problems of garden designers in the latter half of the twentieth century, but I can only think that the formlessness of so many modern gardens stems from this earlier decadence." At the same time, he had a clear opinion of how such things should be organized: "Most houses need anchoring to their setting, and for traditional houses some formal extensions of the straight lines and rectangular shapes of the buildings is usually the most effective way of doing so. The shapes and even the volumes of the interior of the house should find some echo on the larger, outside scale. Curved or straight walls and hedges, a line of clipped trees, a more or less formal pattern of flowers, a change in level with a bank or retaining wall are all useful devices to this end."

Clearly disagreeing with Brown's removal of the interlocking geometries of the seventeenth century and the parterres, hedges, terraces, and basins of London and Wise, he reasserted them using devices he had catalogued. Partly to help accommodate the new situation of public visitation, partly to help resolve the riddle of how to maintain a stylish garden with fewer staff and resources, and partly to satisfy his own taste in composition, Russell Page simplified and reorganized the grounds around the main buildings. First he swept away the Victorian garden beds that had been furnished with forty thousand new bedding plants every year, replacing them with four squares of boxwood and a circular fountain all set in lawn. Next he added a grassed allée with fifty-two pleached lindens — the same number as chimneys on the house — backed by clipped yew hedges and cypresses. There wasn't time to start new shrubs and grow them up before the public was let in, so he simply moved an existing, massive yew hedge near Wyattville's Orangerie twelve feet in order to open up the space. His study of seventeenth- and eighteenth-century French gardens had taught him that not only could traditional spaces made with tall hedges and garden architecture accommodate crowds, but also they could hide them from view, something anyone who has ever become lost or disoriented in a baroque garden can affirm. Page even designed a topiary room to show off several white peacocks (which he hated) that Bath had added as crowd pleasers.

In the front of the entry facade he reorganized things as well. The elms lining Brown's curving drive had recently been felled, having succumbed to Dutch elm disease. Here he reestablished London and Wise's earlier axial entry drive to the south lodge, lining it with American tulip poplars that have done well. Next Page installed the two superb basins in the lawn immediately in front of the facade, flanking the entry drive. Tight and flat with a recurving rococo medallion form, these pools seem so perfect in character, scale, and proportion that it is hard to imagine they have not been there as part of the composition since the beginning. Also in the 1950s and early 1960s he created a series of linked garden rooms

79. Hedges reintroduced near Longleat House by Russell Page.

behind the Orangerie. The centerpiece, planted with circular beds of shrubs and roses, is a small statue of Sir Jeffrey Hudson, a dwarf whom, it seems, was once presented to King Charles I in a pie! Next to one side is an elegant evergreen room of lawn, clipped hedges, and strict upright Irish yews. Further along by the water come weeping willows, urns, and railings. Closer to the building he laid out a simple quadripartite scheme using Japanese crabapples and musk roses while incorporating a one-hundred-fifty-year-old American black locust that remained from earlier adventures in collecting exotic foreign plants.

Also nearby in the back of the house is one of the most impressive, extensive, and delightful pet cemeteries I've ever seen. While reading the names of overly loved dogs, cats, and birds interred with amusing and touching remarks from those left behind, I couldn't help thinking of the arch (and unfair) joke about the English upper class which holds that they are a strange people, packing their children off to boarding school as soon as possible so they could fill their houses with dogs. It is true, however, that they do love dogs. From rat catchers to pit bulls, from whippets to brachets, whether poachers or gamekeepers, each with their dogs, from the relationships between shepherds and sheepdogs of the lower class, to the packs of hounds and spaniels of the upper class depicted in paintings and prints from Van Dyck and Hogarth to Wootton and Landseer, the English have bred, worked, beaten, loved, and spoiled their dogs.

Taken singly each of these projects was a minor effort in Page's career, but together they form a masterpiece and do, indeed, restore the balance between the buildings and the larger park of Brown that Repton would admire and had sought unsuccessfully to achieve himself. The particular essays in garden design that came from his many years of visits are characteristic of Page's sensibility and touch. He had a great eye and a sophisticated cunning that characteristically produced a feeling of classical order, calm, and simplicity. Within traditional forms and ordinary layouts, his work is uncommonly lush. Page was a deeply learned plantsman and horticulturalist. He was also an unremitting sensualist, although under strict self-control. At Longleat in the secret garden and the terraces between it, the house, and the lake, he establishes — as he often does — simple bilateral, four-square symmetries in plan, but also, as time after time in his work, he overlays and varies one or more of the elements. In a physical/spatial equivalent to that of offbeats in jazz or the pleasing dissonance of some modern music, he wittily plays against the grain and the potentially stiff pattern of the plan, producing a scheme that is calm and orderly in one dimension while lively and surprising in another. At Longleat Page rescued the pastoral park and produced several rooms of private gardens that dazzle the eyes and delight the nose with simple variations of what in other hands would have been numbingly archaic and dead compositions. How many people coming to see the lions and giraffes, the Dr. Who exhibit, the erotic paintings of the current and aging hippie lord, or to use the rest rooms and have tea in the stables notice the remarkable display of English garden history that Longleat presents is an open question. I doubt that it is very many these days.

80. Hedges north of the house framing garden rooms created by Russell Page when Longleat was opened to the public after World War II.

ITALIAN MOODS, PALLADIANS, AND THE LANDSCAPE

Twenty-five years ago there was only a handful of scholarly books on English gardens. Since then landscape and garden history has emerged as a rich field of scholarship, loosing a torrent of work, some by cultural historians, some by art or architectural historians, and some as well by geographers and literary scholars. An information lacuna similar to that of the so-called Dark Ages has now been filled by a spate of articles and books detailing developments in English gardening of every period, style, and century. One hardly needs to turn to such literature, however, to discover that, just as in other social and economic endeavors discussed above, southern Wiltshire and the area around Longbridge Deverill was in the thick of developments in gardening from medieval times on. One has only to look about to see considerable evidence. Even so, some of the earliest and transitional works have been altered or have disappeared. John Aubrey, writing in the latter half of the sixteenth century in *The Natural History of Wiltshire*, gives us a glimpse of an early transitional garden and its builder, Sir John Danvers:

The garden at Lavington in this country [Wiltshire] and that at Chelsey in Middlesex [near London], as likewise the house there, doe remaine monuments of his ingenuity. The garden at Lavington is full of irregularities, both natural and artificial, so, elevations and depressions. Through the length of it there runneth a fine clear trout stream; walled with brick on each side, to hinder the earth from mouldring down. In this stream are placed several statues. At the west end is an admirable place for a grotto, where the great arch is, over which now is the market roade. Among several others, there is a very pleasant elevation on the south side of the garden, which steales, arising almost insensibly, that is, before one is aware, and gives you a view over the spacious corn-fields there, and so to East Lavington: where, being landed on a fine levell, letteth you descend again with the like easinesse; each side is flanked with laurells. It is almost impossible to describe this garden, it is so full of variety and unevenesse; nay it would be a difficult matter for a good artist to make a draft of it.

Although Italians had been working in England since the time of Henry VIII, Aubrey's description is the first of a full garden and park with all of the elements that were to be developed into the landscape manner. Construction continued or was resumed at Danvers's garden twenty miles to the north of Longbridge about 1686 when the earl of Abingdon, who had acquired the property through marriage, "built a noble portico, full of waterworks, which is on the north side of the garden, and faceth the South. It is a portico and grott, and was designed by [a] Mr. Rose, of Oxfordshire." By then architectural features

FOLLOWING PAGE: *81. An aged American black locust in Page's north garden at Longleat.*

of Italian influence and associated with villas near Rome and Florence, such as terraces, levels and walls, pools, basins, and fountains, were becoming common enough throughout southern Britain at fashionable estates.

It is now known that long before the eighteenth-century work of neo-Palladian amateurs and Whigs, experimentation in the creation of parklike spaces had begun. Views of country houses in the seventeenth century, especially those by Kip and Knyff, frequently indicate a combination of older houses with recent classical additions, of walled terraces and gardens embracing or overlooking adjacent parks and natural features. Gardening and landscape appreciation had become important aspects of cultivated life by the beginning of the seventeenth century and by the end of it were almost ubiquitous, appearing in drama, painting, literature, and the lives of the upper middle class as well as the leaders of society. Among the many verses inspired by the subject, Andrew Marvell, in a poem simply titled "The Garden," writing far from London and urban life just after the English Civil War, set down the following justly famous lines that refer to the ancient Roman tradition of retirement to the country for moral and aesthetic reasons:

> How vainly men themselves amaze
> To win the Palm, the Oke, or Bayes;
> And their uncessant Labours see
> Crown'd from some single Herb or Tree....
>
> Meanwhile the Mind, from pleasures less,
> Withdrawn into its happiness:
> The Mind, that Ocean where each kind
> Does straight its own resemblance find;
> Yet it creates, transcending These,
> Far other Worlds, and other Seas;
> Annihilating all that's made
> To a green Thought in a green Shade.

The outburst of gardening and country and nature verse in seventeenth-century England was not merely an expression of a desire for escape, although it was partly that. Like Virgil and other Latin poets who lived through the disastrous years of the first century B.C., Marvell, Cowley, Evelyn, and their friends were "sick at heart, exhausted, nearly maddened by the worst of all wars — civil war," as Gilbert Highet observes in his superb study *Poets in a Landscape.* Far from being escapists, Horace and Virgil, their models, were two of the great moralists of their age, urging their readers to accept order — natural, divine, and human (legal) — and to respect and practice the archaic values of industry, thrift, family and civic loyalty, and religious faith. Both of these Latin poets rose from rural backgrounds to artistic fame and great favor with Emperor Augustus, yet each maintained his independence. Each also contained within his own work and life a philosophical ambiguity, a contradiction that haunted Roman society and reappeared in the art and lives of Renaissance personalities in Italy, such as the architect Palladio's patron, Daniele Barbaro, and again in certain Englishmen of the seventeenth and eighteenth centuries. This was a vacillation between Stoic and Epicurean philosophies, a polarity of values that underlay the town versus country argument then, just as it does today in both England and America.

The public life and success of Rome was solidly built on Stoic principles of duty and self-abnegation, of endurance and humility. This was the grim, tough, stern, and chaste face seen by Rome's enemies, whether abroad in battle or at home in the courts and temples. This was the Rome of aqueducts and highways, the hearth of Vesta, the honorable suicide, the cold breakfast, and the forced march. It was a country firm, fair, implacable, and ordered. But there was another side — voluptuous, hedonistic, self-indulgent and overwhelmingly sensual — at its best, rich and deeply aesthetic; at its worst, vulgar and obscenely cruel. The mind's pursuits can lead in many ways, and the private lives of many of Rome's greatest men led among other things to the art, philosophy, literature, and lives of the Greeks. On one hand were Pericles, Phocion, Plato, and Socrates; on the other Epicurus, Sappho, and Dionysos.

In Virgil's *Bucolics* — a touchstone for the English pastoral movement — the verse veers from authentic Roman hardships to dreamy Greek landscapes and mythical figures; from hardworking and dispossessed northern farmers to pleasure-taking Arcadian shepherds and nymphs. Pastoral literature of the first century B.C. recommended both traditional agrarian values and an attitude of hedonism: that within a difficult and pragmatic world, one must seize the pleasures of each situation as the opportunity arises. For those educated in what are now referred to as the classics, whether one was rich and powerful or not, the concept of *retirement* was an important one. In England and northern Europe prior to the seventeenth century, most of the population was still rural. Large country houses with their gardens and hunting parks belonged to a very few extremely wealthy and powerful hereditary lords. By the beginning of the seventeenth century, however, a new class of people with money began to emerge. Urban areas began to grow rapidly, and, as noted earlier, the countryside began to become more open and less populated. Many of those with new wealth were not established landowners but derived their fortunes from politics, wool, manufacturing, and trade or a combination of these. At the same time many of the older aristocracy were forced to follow their lead into commerce if they were to survive, a situation not dissimilar to that of recent times. Simply owning land in the countryside no longer guaranteed power or money. The newcomers into the upper classes had no traditional holdings in the counties, or if they did, these were often modest or remote from the urban centers. Many of these newly arrived landowners soon embraced the values of their predecessors and peers, among which was the classical tradition of the country retreat and its trappings. For this reason and rarely for financial gain — in fact they spent fortunes, at times beggaring themselves — the nouveau riche of the seventeenth and eighteenth centuries spread out into the countryside, buying and building country estates in large numbers.

Their desire and ambition for urban success and country retirement were no more cynical or false than that of their predecessors or more established families. Nor is there any doubt concerning the fact of the increasing chaos and squalor of the cities from which they sought release, exactly as did the Romans before and Americans after them. Throughout northern Europe, not just in England, this period witnessed the rise of the country house, the promulgation of pastoral literature that included a whole subset of country house verse, and the rise of landscape painting. Like Horace and Martial fifteen hundred years earlier, literate men retired to the country or bought small places as soon as they could and began to improve them. Many of these latecomers had to settle for difficult or barren sites, as we learn in John Evelyn's *Diary*. Those with access to great funds built palaces with enormous parks like Longleat; those with only modest means, like the poet Abraham Cowely, followed Juvenal's advice in his Third Satire: "If you can tear yourself away from the circus, a fine house at Sora or Frosinone can be bought for no more than a year's rent of your super-slum in Rome. You'll have a tiny garden, and a shallow well which needs no bucket to help irrigate the tender plants. Live with spade in hand, the boss of a neat garden which could provide a lavish vegetarian banquet. After all, it is something, even in a lonely corner, to make yourself the landlord of a single lizard."

The seventeenth century in England opened with the artistically isolated polymath Inigo Jones designing a handful of buildings based upon personal study in Italy and presenting on stage a vision of pastoral beauty derived from ancient and modern Mediterranean sources. It ended with a considerable avant-garde actually building such scenes amid the general construction boom. Evelyn, both leader and barometer of taste, noted in his compendium *Sylva* that the wave of country house and park building had transformed the countryside during his lifetime. In the opening years of the eighteenth century the political and dynastic revolution that maneuvered a German from Hanover onto the throne, thereby ending the possibility of a Catholic succession, also marked the beginning of a new era in taste and design. In Whitehall the transcendent Whigs were to hold power for two generations, while their supporters were to advocate distinct moral and aesthetic values that departed from established standards. Baroque architecture and landscape design as promulgated by Sir Christopher Wren and his followers were eclipsed by what came to be known as Palladian (although it was an amalgam of disparate influences and precedents in addition to those of Palladio). The Whigs were supported by an overwhelming majority of wealthy and educated landowners who were allied to the successors of nonconforming, urban, mercantile empiricists who had on several occasions asserted their independence of established order and were implacable opponents of the Tories, who in turn were allied to retreating feudal interests including the Stuart and Catholic causes and who viewed the acquisition of wealth (especially through commerce) and taste with disdain. For a great number of these Whigs a gentleman's education was founded upon wide reading in the classics, the grafting of the rudiments of Platonism upon Protestantism, and a grand tour of Europe to become familiar with the visual and physical background of classical civilization as well as the latest developments in art, architecture, science, and industry. For them land and property were more than a secure investment: they were a key to political and social influence that also offered the possibility of a retreat to the country in order to cultivate the land, the mind, and the arts.

In 1715 a young Scottish architect, Colen Campbell, published the first volume of *Vitruvius Britannicus*, and Giacomo Leoni, an Italian architect living and working in England, brought out the first volume of his translation of *I Quattro Libri*, the books of the sixteenth-century Venetian architect Andrea Palladio. Both books were in effect pointed attacks on baroque architecture and other contemporary styles, and both recommended instead an architecture that the authors considered to be more truly classical, pure, and historically derived. Both authors used the work of Palladio as an example to be emulated. Campbell also made a point of praising the work of Inigo Jones, the first thoroughly classical Renaissance English architect whose works had been executed in the previous century. This triad of classical example, Palladian revival, and reverence for Jones formed the theoretical base for the Palladian movement in eighteenth-century England.

Campbell, originally trained as a lawyer, was an architect with a meteoric career in a period containing some of the greatest figures in English architectural history, whose rivals included John Vanbrugh, Nicholas Hawksmoor, James Gibbs, Thomas Archer, and William Talman. The entire body of work upon which his fame rests was produced in the fourteen years between the appearance of *Vitruvius Britannicus* in 1715 and his death in 1729. Almost single-handedly he invented the English Palladian country house and worked out the principal variations on the theme. Strict in adherence to the canons and classical authority set forth by Palladio, Campbell was, nevertheless, his own man. An extremely talented designer, he possessed an instinct for mass and plasticity usually associated with the baroque architects he opposed.

Like other successful self-appointed revolutionaries from Alberti to Le Corbusier and Robert Venturi, Campbell understood the importance of publishing. Also like them he had an eye for the main chance. His book, containing some of his own early work as well, established him in the company of more famous architects like Vanbrugh, Talman, and Archer, and, as the self-proclaimed heir to Jones, placed him ahead of Leoni in the favor of men looking for a talent to entrust with the construction of their buildings.

The centerpiece of Campbell's book was a presentation of his scheme for Wanstead, a large country house then under construction in Essex. In its boldness and classical purity, this building was noticeably equal to the work of the most famous architects then alive and also presented in his book, such as Wren and Vanbrugh. Shortly after its publication, William Benson, the sheriff of Wiltshire, who was to execute several modest early Palladian buildings himself, replaced Wren as surveyor-general of the Royal Office of Works and in 1718 named Campbell his assistant, a position he held for a year. Among the first to recog-

FACING TOP: *82. Palazzo Antonini as published by Andrea Palladio in his* Quattro Libri.

FACING BOTTOM: *83. The Villa Rotunda at Capra near Vicenza by Palladio.*

nize that the cool Palladian classicism and antibaroque message in these books could well give form to refined taste and independence from current European fashions and the Tory establishment and to employ him was Richard Boyle, Lord Burlington. He dismissed James Gibbs, who had been working on the reconstruction of Burlington's London residence, and turned the work over to Campbell. Burlington was not disappointed. For him Campbell produced another touchstone of eighteenth-century architecture, Burlington House. During the next few years, Campbell produced designs for numerous buildings, several of which, although heavily derived from Palladio, were themselves to become prototypes for dozens of other country villas. The most notable were: Stourhead, 1721, based on the Villa Emo and commissioned by the banker Henry Hoare, who was Benson's brother-in-law and cousin; Mereworth, 1722–23, based on the Villa Rotunda for Colonel Fane, another powerful Whig; and Houghton Hall, 1722, partially derived from Inigo Jones's own Palladian exercise at Wilton, executed for Sir Robert Walpole, the first Whig prime minister under George I. Of these buildings, writing in his now classic 1953 study *Architecture in England, 1530–1830,* Sir John Summerson states flatly, "it would be no exaggeration to say of Campbell that between the years 1715 and 1724 he set up the models upon which the whole of Palladianism was to depend."

It is not possible to discuss the Palladian movement in England without mentioning Lord Burlington and William Kent. This is because Burlington, wealthy, attractive, powerful in government and society and an amateur architect himself, was an extremely important patron of others, building, publishing, and promoting a large body of work in the new style. A friend of writers and journalists, influential at court, he established a salon that aspired to being an academy of sorts. Bringing important figures from the Continent, such as the composer George Fredric Handel and the architect Fillipo Juvarra, to London, he sponsored and pushed his friends, their work and publications, upon others. In addition to employing Campbell for his own imposing residence in London, he designed and built a casino at his country place in Chiswick a few miles up the Thames that outwardly recalls Palladio's most famous building, the Villa Rotunda near Vicenza. The interiors and furniture were eventually designed by his most interesting discovery, William Kent.

A designer of remarkable imagination and mercurial abilities, Kent is the oft-acknowledged "father" of the English landscape garden. While true enough in some ways, this attribution doesn't adequately acknowledge the long and convoluted history of Eng-

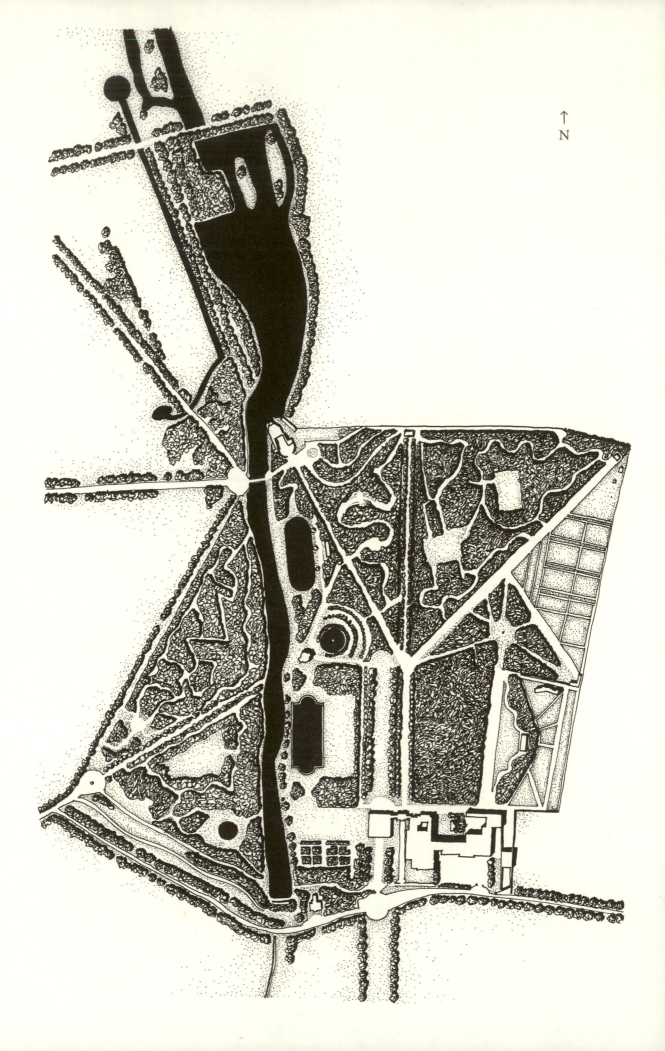

lish gardening, which is beyond the scope of this work. Suffice it to say that many others played a significant part, not the least of whom was Alexander Pope, the poet, neighbor, and close friend of Burlington. Other important figures — William Chambers, Stephen Switzer, and Batty Langley — published works advocating versions of the new manner of gardening in the opening decades of the eighteenth century.

Burlington's contribution to landscape design consists of, first, sponsoring a publication written by Robert Castell, *Villas of the Ancients Illustrated* (1728), which presented a

FACING PAGE: *84. Chiswick villa plan as recorded in 1730. Note the baroque allées, "goose-foot" trident of walks and wilderness, the placement of pavilions, and alignments that underlie the softening of Kent, as well as the extent of the water body and meadows to the north and west at the time.*

85. Chiswick villa plan as it exists today in its reduced state, absent the manor house and full park and ponds.

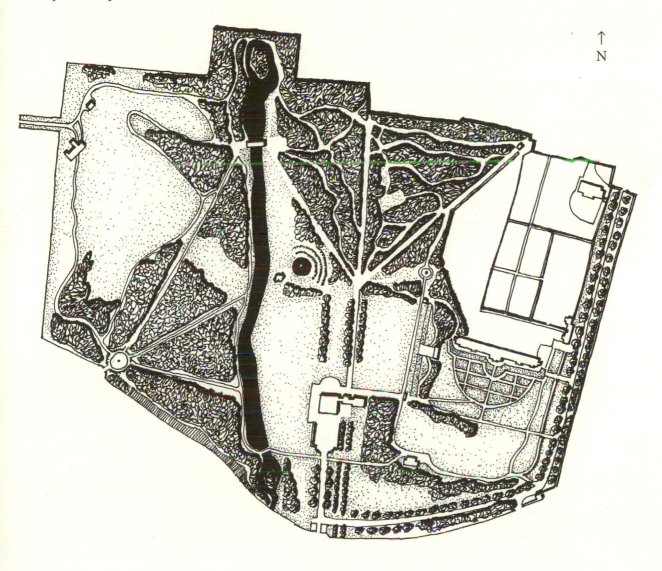

↑
N

discussion of ancient Roman villas and their gardens, some of it based on archaeology, some on ancient literary sources, and some on imaginative speculation; second, his own experiments and constructions at Chiswick; and, third, his employment and subsequent sponsorship of William Kent, who became his house guest and remained so for more than twenty years. Kent, originally from Yorkshire, began his career as a painter and lived and studied in Italy, where he met Burlington and other English nobles for whom he was later to execute work. Returning to England, he painted frescoes and designed furniture and interior decoration, only to end up designing gardens and establishing a manner of working that evolved into what is referred to as the English landscape park (or landscape garden). Kent's first work in this medium seems to have been at Chiswick, where he had been living off and on since 1725. Here he experimented with nearly all of the elements that were to become identified with him, an undulating body of water, lawn leading directly from the house down to the water, clumps and groves of trees standing in meadows, the sinuous grading of earth forms, and the use of conifers, evergreens, classical statuary, and architec-

BELOW : *86. Entry approach from the south and cedar allée, Chiswick villa.*
FACING: *87. The south entry court at Chiswick (above) and the west facade with its lawn facing the canal (below).*

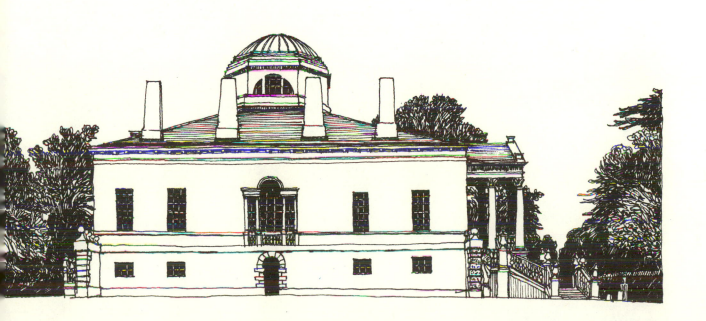

88. *Entry stair and orange court with the small pavilion by William Kent that formerly linked the Casino to the older manor house, now demolished, Chiswick.*

tural elements to recall Italian scenes — all arranged in a landscape setting, albeit softer and more lush than those of their Mediterranean predecessors.

A visit to Chiswick seemed essential as I embarked on my examination of this period and its figures. I wasn't prepared for the combination of marvelous and peculiar remains that I found. Like much of London, Chiswick was heavily bombed by the Luftwaffe in the early years of World War II. Afterward Burlington's rotunda and portions of the park were restored or reconstructed, but an older medieval and Jacobean manor house to which they were appendages was not. Additionally, a dense and sprawling mass of suburban houses begun before the war and continued afterward completely engulfs the remaining fragment of his estate. Playing fields have chewed up the meadows and Kent's first broad essay in pastoral planting. A highway with traffic headed for Heathrow airport occupies the site of what was once a watery island terminus to the canal. On my first few visits, a decrepit neoclassical bridge built by the succeeding generation interrupted what was left of the canal. The remains of Victorian flower beds and a recent greenhouse occupied an area where the manor house garden should have been. It was an eye-opener regarding the fate of landscapes and gardens, my first reckoning with their ephemeral and fragile nature. In the next months and years, I was to visit countless gardens that no longer resembled the designs that had once existed, and I was to learn how to see them for what remained, what they had been, and what they might be next. I also saw that all over England trees planted in the eighteenth century were now crashing down with great frequency. Most of the parks I was interested in were on their last legs and would have to be replanted or rebuilt soon, or they would be changed forever or perish. I am happy to say that in the past twenty years many of the greatest have in fact been taken in hand, and restoration has occurred. Blenheim, Stowe, Prior Park, and Claremont are good examples. Chiswick Park and its architecture, partly threadbare, partly overgrown, and a crumbling shambles in the 1970s, have been largely restored. Nevertheless, even in the sorry condition that I first knew, Chiswick was clearly a masterpiece of invention and integration of architecture with landscape. The relationship between what happened here and what came after was obvious.

By the time Kent began contributing to the garden scheme, Burlington had already executed several pavilions, and one of the last and best landscape designers working in the previous Anglicized-baroque style, Charles Bridgeman, had been working there for several years creating a series of radiating paths, allées, basins, and ponds. Within young groves planted between radiating hedges and walks, a series of meandering paths were under development, which strongly resembled those shown by Rubert Castell in the plates of his *Villas of the Ancients Illustrated*. Kent was responsible for three areas executed from 1730 on: a large area to the west of the stream, the stream itself, and the two spaces adjacent to and leading away from the garden facades of the Rotunda. The first seems to have been west of the stream. Here he created dense plantations with winding walks bounded by avenues that converged upon a Roman obelisk and gate. This area was not merely a reprise of Bridgeman's and Burlington's work in other parts of the garden, but was noteworthy for its reference to a well-known landmark in Rome, the Piazza del Popolo with its gate and obelisk, known to all visitors as the entry (or exit) to the ancient city. Here Kent began what was to become a series of compositions in this garden and elsewhere that evoked specific memories of Rome, its topography, particular buildings, and garden furnishings that he admired through the creation of a "scene" somewhat in the manner of building a theatrical image.

An equally important area was the meadow immediately to the west. Here he experi-

FACING: *89. Allée of cedars and exedra by Kent at Chiswick as it appeared in 1730 and today. Note the small seedling replacement between the urns on the right as these handsome giants finally begin to die.*

ABOVE: *90. An Italian mood is established by the choice and arrangement of plants. Here cedars are seen from inside the villa at Chiswick.*

mented with the first version of what was to become a hallmark of the landscape garden: a large, open meadow with irregular clumps of forest trees artfully scattered about. Similar situations had evolved over time owing to grazing herds and natural succession in the older parks and *vigne* of the villas in and around Rome to the point of being commonplace, and had come to be one of the most familiar elements in late seventeenth-century landscape drawing and painting. As an idea or device for planting from scratch, however, this was so new in French and English circles that a draftsman who recorded the plan of this area in 1736 had no real understanding of it, nor any convention with which to convey such

BELOW: *91. The garden front of Chiswick villa; Kent's linking pavilion in the foreground and Burlington's Rotunda with stairs leading from the salon directly to the garden beyond.*

FACING: *92. Radiating paths by Charles Bridgeman leading off into the park with wilderness plantations in between.*

a scheme, resorting to dotting trees about in the field like so many measles. In all fairness, this first attempt of Kent's may well have looked awkward and spotty, but the effect made an impression on those who visited Chiswick. A new vision and manner of working were launched.

His next project here was more radical and was to become one of Kent's most highly regarded activities: the reshaping of the principal water feature on the site, in this case a stream that had been channeled into a straight-sided canal. Damming it so as to increase the quantity of water, he widened and softened the banks along its entire length through the property. He created several islands for the distant end in the woodland and erected a rusticated, triple-arched stone grotto with a cascade near the casino. It was a master stroke. The creation of a pseudo-natural, undulating body of water suitable for small boats, with grassy banks and heavy plantations of trees and shrubs along its course embracing two small classical buildings of Burlington's, all reflected in the water, was an immediate success. Among the many sketches by Kent from this period, now at Chatsworth, is one that shows the far (north) end of this water with its islands. Although a loosely drawn design study, it depicts mature trees and shrubs and vestiges of the wooden stakes and planks used to stabilize pond edges during construction at the time, as if drawn after the fact. It also demonstrates a highly developed sense of where to place shrubs and where to leave them out, so that one's eye is led on through the scene to more distant elements. The sources of inspiration for the elements of this early work of Kent's are fairly clear, ranging from seventeenth-century masque drawings of Inigo Jones and sketches by Claude Lorrain from the Vigna Madama outside Rome, to several cascades at the Villa Aldobrandini, Frascati, and parks in Rome.

It may be that Kent had made studies for the space immediately adjacent to the villa before the implementation of his forest and water gardening, but an impetus to implement such schemes apparently came with the successful completion of the water course. On the southwest side toward the water, he again did something that in England at the time was bold and original. It, too, was to become a precedent, although, as with his other work, prototypes had been at hand in the theater, painting, and Italian villas for ages. Treating the west facade as fronting a rustic private space, he dispensed with terrace and railing and swept a carpet of lawn in a swath as wide as the villa all the way from the base of the building down to the gentle bank at the water's edge. Flanking this sloping lawn, he planted on one side a dense grove of trees and on the other a maze of tall, clipped evergreens. Mixed into plantings on both sides and on the opposite bank were firs and cedars. Even some of

93. A water gate designed by Inigo Jones for Somerset House that was moved to Burlington's garden. Although Jones was revered for his work and the fact that he was the first English follower of Palladio, it should be pointed out that this gate was copied from that of the terrace of the Villa Lante by Vignola.

94. Undulating earth forms reminiscent of natural features in Roman vigne, as shaped under the direction of William Kent to the west of the villa (above), and a curving path within a woodland plantation (below), Chiswick.

the deciduous trees were pruned up to reveal tall trunks with their foliage high above, a reminder of the pines, elms, and oaks of Italy in his day.

Although the grounds of this estate were relatively small and episodic, the key elements that were to characterize the Landscape movement had been brought together: classical architecture (especially of a Palladian sort) sitting in a lawn leading directly to grounds with Anglicized Italian park features; soft bodies of water; curving walks, contrived woodland, and clumped plantations laid over a baroque plan with diagonal views to distant elements — pavilions, architectural ornaments, and classical sculpture; an avoidance of floral beds of any sort, with instead a palette of greens comprised of evergreen shrubs and a mixture of full-blown deciduous forest trees and conifers forming shelter belts and screens around the periphery, thereby creating a coherent and controlled vision. While the contrivance was considerable, it produced a result so dramatically different from the neat, clipped, geometric parks and gardens of the time with their absolutely flat terraces, polychromed floral beds, and straight rows of trees and canals, that it seemed positively "natural" and almost not designed.

95. A view of the canal after Kent had demolished Bridgeman's rectangular masonry edge; note one of Burlington's pavilions standing in lawn and the clumps and groups of trees that have replaced earlier rows and allées.

96. *Lush vegetation today overhangs Kent's only surviving island in the northern portion of the canal.*

By 1730 Palladian architecture was firmly established as the most fashionable mode for country estates and civic buildings. Politicians, writers, retired generals, and a cross section of hereditary lords were all building gardens and structures in the new manner. Henry Flitcroft and Isaac Ware, trained at Burlington House and Chiswick, went on to execute numerous commissions and to publish books of their own on architecture. Two of Burlington's social peers, Richard Temple, Lord Cobham, the presiding genius at Stowe, and Henry Herbert, the ninth earl of Pembroke and heir to Inigo Jones's early Palladian villa at Wilton, also became accomplished designers working with Colen Campbell and Roger Morris. Others, such as John Vardy, James Paine, and William, John, and Robert Adam (father and sons) in their early work, contributed excellent buildings in the Palladian mode. None was more accomplished than John Wood of Bath and his son. Outsiders, and not part of Burlington's circle in London, the Woods produced a series of buildings in Bath under the patronage of Ralph Allen, that, beyond making it a fashionable spa of the day, established it as a landmark in urban design history. These are the buildings comprising Queen's Square, the King's Circus, and the Royal Crescent. With the exception of Prior Park (1735) executed for Allen on a hill overlooking the city and Avon River valley, their superb country villas are not particularly well known. Of these, Pusey and Buckland houses in Oxfordshire — discussed in detail below — stand out as superb examples of the villa as derived from Palladio, *Vitruvius Britannicus*, and Colen Campbell's work.

STOURHEAD

In 1743 on the old manor of Stourton, which lay within the former Saxon forest of Selwood, only seven miles southwest of Longbridge Deverill, a wealthy London banker, Henry Hoare, began to build a remarkable garden while mourning the recent death of his wife. This manor, with all of its property — houses, mills, rivers, pastures, as well as traditional rights and obligations — had only recently been acquired by the widower's father in 1720. His grandfather, Richard Hoare, had been one of a group of goldsmith-bankers who had helped to underwrite the Crown's debts and to develop the commercial banking system near the end of the seventeenth century. In 1673 after a financial crash precipitated by the monarchy's overextended debts, Richard had founded Hoare's Bank in Fleet Street. The business prospered: Hoare went on to represent London in Parliament from 1709 to 1713, becoming lord mayor of London in 1712, and was later knighted by Queen Anne. Although nearly all of his eleven sons went into commerce, only two, Benjamin and Henry, were to become partners in the bank. A patriarch imbued with the Puritan ethic of prudence and diligence, he pressed moral and economic virtues upon his sons, constantly exhorting them to tend to their business, family, and church.

Sir Richard, who died in 1718, had been a founder and director of the famous — or

257

97. Woburn Abbey as transformed by Henry Flitcroft and James Paine, one of many such impressive products of the Palladian fashion.

infamous — South Sea Company. In 1720, the year of the great "bubble," its stocks rose to £1,000 per share before suddenly plummeting to £132. In the wild speculation accompanying this event, fortunes were to be made and subsequently lost. Apparently the elder Henry Hoare and his brother were shrewd enough to make a sizable profit and to withdraw in time, and, like the disgraced chancellor of the exchequer, John Aislabie, shortly thereafter bought country estates, a move that, then as now, was considered to be one of the only investments that would safeguard their money in a volatile economy.

Henry Hoare senior was married to Jane Benson, the sister of William Benson. Benson, a Whig representative to Parliament from Shaftesbury, had erected one of the first Palladian revival buildings in England, Wilbury House, in Wiltshire in 1715. Appointed surveyor of the royal works in 1718, he had named Colen Campbell, the probable designer of his house, as his assistant. It was quite natural, therefore, that when Hoare desired a new villa on his estate in Wiltshire, he should turn to his brother-in-law's assistant, the brilliant young author of *Vitruvius Britannicus*. Pulling down an old manor house on the property, Campbell produced a design based on Palladio's Villa Emo, the structure of which, with the exception of the entry portico added in the next century, was largely complete by 1722. Henry didn't live to see the interior completed. After his death in 1725, his widow stayed on in the country, eschewing the hectic life of London, and their son, also named Henry (later called "the Magnificent" to distinguish him from his father, "the Good"), began to help out with the completion of the villa.

Born in 1705, the younger Henry was nineteen when his father died, and he joined his Uncle Benjamin at the bank. Although a dedicated banker and used to the life of commercial and social activities in London, he had spent much of his youth at another country estate of the family, Quarley, in Hampshire. As well as enjoying the lively and boisterous life of country houses with its hunting and parties, Hoare seems also to have developed a regard for classical literature and the more bucolic aspects of the countryside. At the age of twenty-one he married an heiress, Ann Masham, who died the following year in childbirth. A year later he married another heiress, Susan Colt, and although they generally lived in London or elsewhere, he continuously contributed toward the improvement of his mother's residence at Stourhead between 1726 and 1734.

During this period, young Henry seems to have been befriended and influenced by his late father's brother-in-law, Benson, who apparently introduced him to the artists John Wootton and Michael Rysbrack and the architect Henry Flitcroft, whom Hoare employed on his estates at Stourhead and Clapham for the next twenty years. Also, following his grandfather's and Benson's lead, he became a member of Parliament from Salisbury in

1734. That same year he began to spend more time in the country. Benson was fond of Virgil and Milton, both of whom eventually were to become the two most influential authors in Hoare's personal pantheon. At some point, probably in 1737 at the age of thirty-two, Henry went abroad for a long period of time, of which almost nothing is now known. Most likely it was an exhaustive trip including many sites in several countries. It definitely included Italy, as he subsequently paid sums to agents in Leghorn (Livorno) and Venice for works of art, classical antiques, and paintings, purchased on the trip.

98. The east or entry front of Colen Campbell's villa for Henry Hoare at Stourhead of 1721. The library wing to the left and gallery wing on the right were added later in 1796. Note the condition of the oak planted in the 1720s and the recent replacement clump to the right.

At the same time, Hoare attended to business and family. Both were precarious ventures in the eighteenth century. Death was never far from his thoughts. By our own standards, medicine and public health were in their infancy. Hoare's father died in 1725. His first wife died in 1728; in 1735 a daughter died. As Kenneth Woodbridge has remarked, "it was the beginning of a series of bereavements which touched him deeply and which followed regularly through the remainder of his long life." In 1740 a son died at the age of seven. In 1741 his mother died, after which he took up residence at Stourhead, directing his business affairs from there, with visits to London. Then, in 1743 his beloved second wife, Susan, also died, leaving him with a son of thirteen and two small girls of eleven and six. Nine years later in 1752, almost as a final blow, this son, Henry III, died in Naples at the age of twenty-one while on a grand tour that was intended as part of his grooming to become

the appropriate heir to the extraordinary estate that even then was only partially complete.

Although a man of talent and independent thought, Hoare didn't conceive of the masterpiece of garden design at Stourhead in seclusion from Burlington and his Palladian circle. The connections between Hoare's Elysium and the work of Kent were both direct and indirect. Kent died in 1740, three years before Hoare embarked on his project. Burlington died in 1753, long before Stourhead was completed. Nevertheless, Burlington had kept an account at Hoare's Bank from 1717 to 1736, the major period of construction at Chiswick, and he had borrowed large sums, somewhere in excess of £20,000. The two men were on excellent social terms. Mutual friends and several artists of the Palladian circle maintained their accounts at Hoare's Bank, and later his daughter married into Burlington's family.

More important, however, was Hoare's long-term patronage of Henry Flitcroft and John Wootton. Flitcroft, whose father had been an assistant gardener to Henry Wise, was a protégé of Burlington and Kent. He was discovered as a likely sort among the workmen and elevated from the building trades during the construction of Burlington House; Burlington provided his architectural training, and Kent taught him how to draw. As Kent's assistant at the Office of Works and on private commissions, Flitcroft worked on illustrations as well as on architecture and landscape projects for nearly twenty years until Kent was too ill to work. Wootton, best known today as a painter of hunting and sporting scenes replete with portraits of landed gentry, was, it seems, one of the first — if not the first — of the English landscape painters of the eighteenth century. An acquaintance of Kent's, he had only recently returned from Italy in 1725, when Hoare commissioned a painting from him. Two years later, he and Kent produced a series of pastoral illustrations for John Gay's *Fables*. In 1728, Wootton was commissioned to paint three more pictures for Hoare, two of which were landscapes. All told, Hoare ended up with twelve paintings of his at Stourhead, most landscapes, one of which was done as a companion piece for a copy of a work of Claude Lorrain. Hoare also utilized sculptors who regularly executed work for Burlington and Kent and subscribed to publications promoted by them. Like Richard Temple of Stowe and Charles Hamilton of Painshill, although considerably younger, he must be seen as one of Burlington's cultural equals. Not only did he create the great emblematic landscape of Stourhead, but also a Palladian mansion at Clapham and the design for a landscape park at Barn Elms for his nephew, Richard Hoare.

99. Ha-ha on the garden side of the house at Stourhead (above), separating the lawn on the right from the pasture on the left, with the view from the front salon across this scene (below) with the obelisk standing among the grazing cattle. The valley with the pleasure garden, lake, and temples, lies hidden beyond the trees across the pasture.

The Itinerary of Stourhead

Off and on for two years I prowled around the grounds of Stourhead in different seasons and was graciously allowed to use the family library by the manager for the National Trust, who had recently taken charge of the operation and rehabilitation of the estate. Retreating into the kitchen with selections of books and folios that Hoare and his family had acquired (so as not to impinge upon the visitors), I pored over them, studying the plates and browsing through writing and treatises that had played a role in the formulation of this great garden. Of particular interest to me were those illustrated by Kent and Wootton, the 1771 edition of two hundred etchings with mezzotint after Claude Lorrain's *Liber Veritatis* by Richard Earlom, and the various classical texts of which Hoare had availed himself. Because Stourhead is absolutely one of the most beautiful and most important of all the English landscape gardens, a considerable amount is known and has already been written about its evolution and iconography to which I can add only a little. Nevertheless, a brief synopsis of its contents and itinerary is appropriate at this point.

Prior to 1743, a few improvements had been made to the grounds of Stourhead adjacent to the house. None was related to the project that Hoare embarked upon after his wife's death. Below and southwest of the house, past an ancient church and a small collection of cottages making up the tiny hamlet of Stourton, was a valley with a stream, several springs, and a livestock watering pond. On the surrounding hills were a few scraps of the former forest. Beyond in all directions lay the chalk downs, recently reallocated and subdivided by the Enclosure Acts.

By 1744 Hoare had begun to work on the major landscape space that unifies the garden — or "Pleasure Ground," as it came to be known — and was eventually to be filled almost entirely by a large lake. The low bottomland where this lake was to be, a rough and poorly drained pasture called Black Meadow, contained several springs from the chalk banks on each side as well as the stream. By the simple means of a carefully placed earthen dam and the selective removal of a mill, some trees, a few walls, and other utilitarian objects, he created a meadow as well as the first version of the lake. Simultaneously he began to lay out a circumferential path around the space and to establish background plantations. Then, steadily for the next twenty-seven years, he continued to plant, build, and adjust the elements within this park to create a picturesque itinerary rich in allusion and meaning.

The first building on this itinerary was to be the Temple of Ceres, designed by Flitcroft and completed in 1745. Next was an obelisk (1746–47), then the lakeside Grotto of 1748 and the Pantheon (1753–54) by Flitcroft and Hoare. That same year he raised and completed the dam, enlarging the lake until it nearly filled the entire foreground formerly occupied by the meadow and smaller body of water. Then came the Temple of Apollo (1757); a five-arched stone Palladian Bridge from 1760 on (a single-arched wooden bridge based on a design of Palladio was added at the upper end of the lake but has since disappeared); a hermitagelike structure called the "Convent" in a distant wood; a roadway underpass in the form of a grotto below the Temple of Apollo (1760–70); the erection of the Bristol Cross near the Stourton church in 1765; and finally the Hermitage in 1771. Alfred's Tower, which could be seen but not reached from the circumambulatory lakeside path, was completed in 1772.

All these items were carefully chosen, placed, and woven into a circuit contrived to allow the strolling observer to see them in sequence, to lose them, to find them again, to see one from another, and finally to see all of them together as a unified composition. There was a "correct" sequence, and visitors were carefully directed to begin at the Temple of Ceres, keeping to the right, and to continue around the lake in a counterclockwise direction, finally ending back at the little valley with the Stourton church and its cemetery. The whole ensemble was in some degree a memorial to the dead — in this case, the numerous family members mourned by Hoare — and a testimonial to the perseverance of the survivors: to the founding of a family dynasty and to English, Puritan, agrarian, mercantile, and cultural values. The unifying theme was that of the voyage of Aeneas and the Trojan survivors, their piety and trials that led to the founding of Rome. Particular passages and key images of the epic were selected, which related to Hoare's desire to establish an elegiac tone.

The first scene to greet the visitor is a breathtaking view presenting a vision of the Pantheon from Rome seen across a lake with swans and verdant islands. Here, in one bold image, ancient Rome, the pastoral paintings of Claude, Poussin, and Domenichino, the verse and landscape of a golden and remote age, are summoned up before one's eyes. The path to the right leads immediately to a small Doric temple dedicated to Ceres, goddess of agriculture, beneath which in a rusticated grotto a river god originally presided over a spring that poured forth water into the lake. Over the doorway to the temple is carved a quotation from part 4 of the *Aeneid*, which sets the tone and theme for the journey about to be undertaken around the lake: *Procul, o procul este profani* (Away, away all who are profane, or unworthy). These are the words Virgil gives to the Cumaean Sibyl before she leads Aeneas down into the Underworld, where he sees the souls of the damned, consults with his beloved father, Anchises, in the Elysian Fields, and sees a vision of those who will eventually live in the city he is to found (Rome).

From here one walks up the valley away from the temples toward a small vale with groves and ponds known as the Baths of Diana. Diana, Apollo's twin sister, was also a goddess of agriculture as well as hunting, and because, according to legend, as the first born she had assisted her mother, Leto, with the difficult birth of her brother, she was also the

FOLLOWING PAGE: *100. The Pantheon, lake, and islands at Stourhead as seen from the circumambulatory path between the Temple of Ceres and the Bath of Diana.*

goddess of childbirth. Not only did she help to bring life into the world, but also this aloof, chaste goddess could bring death to humans, whether swiftly and painlessly with her arrows, or terribly as in the death of Actaeon or the agony of childbirth. Here, however, gazing across the water all is serene, hauntingly sylvan. From this glade of Diana's, one can also look back down the entire length of the lake. The only visible work of man, high on a hill in the distance, is the seemingly small Temple of Apollo, the prophet, the healer, the god of light, of crops and flocks. Apollo was the god to whom Aeneas made offerings at several key moments on his voyage and who was responsible for Aeneas's guidance and hope during his long quest for peace and a home.

From the upper end of the lake, the path leads along the shore that had been opposite to that upon which the visitor first began. Gradually and gently it descends, leading into a dark rocky grotto, suddenly opening into a vaulted, sky-lit underground room. Here beneath a sculpture of a sleeping nymph, a spring splashes into a basin, the edge of which is graced with a quotation from Alexander Pope, and an arched opening with a window seat looks out at water level across the lake to a charming scene containing the small temple where the journey began. Like the first temple, this complex structure was developed by Flitcroft and was directly derived from an earlier design of Kent's at Richmond called Merlin's Cave. A conflation of the descent into Hades and a cave of the Muses, it emphasizes the classical character of the park with its general references to Aeneas's journey, and specifically in this case to the cave by the sea in which Dido and Aeneas pledged their love. It is also a memorial to Hoare's lost loves, especially to his second wife, who is invoked by the graceful figure of the sleeping nymph, a copy by John Cheere of a well-known antique that had been in the papal collection at the Belvedere of the Vatican since the sixteenth century.

Leaving, the visitor steps suddenly out into the light beside a steeply winding and seemingly dangerous set of stone steps, to face yet another cave with a handsome and gnarled figure of a river god, here called Father Stour, astride a tipped urn, from which more spring water pours out into the lake. Again the reference is to Aeneas, who was befriended by water gods: first Neptune, who calmed a storm that Juno had set upon his ships, thus driving him away from the Italian shore to North Africa where he met Dido; and later by the river god, Father Tiber, who counseled him that he had found his long-sought home, advising him to form an alliance that was to save his colony and provide him with a second fruitful marriage. The hoped-for parallel between the Roman myth and Hoare's efforts to create a prosperous and virtuous family dynasty with Stourhead as its spiritual home was there to be seen by family and visitors alike.

The steep stairs refer to Aeneas's descent into the Underworld. It was easy to descend into Hades but difficult and nearly impossible to return — to climb out of death once again into the light and life — and in Hoare's case, to emerge from despair; so, too, with this subterranean pavilion into which it is easy to descend and from which difficult to ascend. Reaching the path at the top of the stairs, the visitor proceeds along the lakeshore on a path through lush planting with occasional glimpses across to the first temple and up above the lake to the Temple of Apollo, now looming larger on the hilltop ahead. Suddenly, on rounding a bend, one comes out of the trees, and there is the Pantheon immediately ahead, far larger and more imposing than expected. This structure had been out of sight ever since the approach to the Baths of Diana, and the sudden appearance of this half-forgotten object is a powerful experience indeed. Also designed by Flitcroft (presumably with Hoare), this building is the quintessential symbol of Rome — of both the city and its artistic legacy — which were the fruit of Aeneas's labors. The original Pantheon by Hadrian, which this pavilion handsomely evokes, is not only one of the most unforgettable architectural compositions and experiences in the world, but to the informed was a symbol of ancient piety, dedicated as it was to all of the major gods, the Penates.

It is important in the consideration of Hoare's intentions here to recall that the piety of Aeneas is emphasized throughout Virgil's epic and in this garden. The poem begins with the striking image of Aeneas emerging from the flames of Troy, carrying upon his shoulders his aged and lame father, Anchises, who devoutly clutches the images of the Penates. He is accompanied by his young son Ascanius, but his wife has been tragically lost in the chaos of the burning city. Aeneas has been spared by the gods and the victorious Greeks because of his valor, piety, and family loyalty. The parallels to Hoare's own life and attitudes were undoubtedly not lost on his contemporaries.

So, too, in his selection of which statuary to place within his Pantheon, Hoare reinforces the themes of husbandry, love, death, and triumph over death developed earlier in the garden. Outside, on either side of the portico are placed the classical deities of Venus and Bacchus, Venus representing the mysterious, ancient force of love and its effects — in this case good ones — upon men. Bacchus, another name for Dionysus, represented far more than wine and revelry to the ancients: as a god who, like his grapevines, rose repeatedly from the dead, he represented the cycles of nature and the mystery of rebirth. Just inside the door were Diana and Meleager, one of Jason's Argonauts, who slew a great boar sent by Diana to ravage the crops of a people who offended her, and who was then himself killed by the goddess. Finally, facing the viewer, are five more figures, two on either side of the central figure of Hercules. The other four are Isis, Flora, Ceres, and a woman referred to as "Saint Susanna." All are associated with positive aspects of life: Isis, a mother goddess, was associated with the triumph of life over death, childbirth, and the assurance that joy grows out of sorrow; Flora, associated with spring, was the protector of everything that blooms — not only flowers but also fruit trees, vines, grain, and vegetables; Ceres was specifically associated with harvests and autumn and was the protector of grain, the principal crop of the region; St. Susanna refers to more recent women of virtue in Western history as well as to the Old Testament figure who rejected the advances of licentious elders. Susanna was also the name of the thirteenth Book of Daniel in the Apocrypha; moreover, she combined the names of Hoare's two wives, Ann and Susan, and that of his daughter Susanna.

Then there is Hercules himself, whose most difficult trial and greatest deed was his descent into the Underworld, where he triumphed over death and Hades, capturing and taming the dog Cerberus. This central figure, in a heroic sculpture by Michael Rysbrack, is not depicted in repose or as static, but rather as turning toward two of the four women, choosing from among them, thus staging a "Choice of Hercules." This mythical figure was a mortal embodiment of heroic virtue, and as such his image was frequently to be found in gardens from classical antiquity through the Renaissance in schemes that elaborated upon a theme of the triumph of virtue over adversity and temptation. Moreover, Hercules was the "destroyer of lions and boars that ravage harvests and fruitful countrysides," and when upon Father Tiber's advice Aeneas had visited the Arcadians to seek their aid as allies, he found their king "paying anniversary honors to Hercules, who had killed Caus, the destroyer of herds on that spot."

The theme of a choice between pleasure and virtue was a common one in Puritan and post-Puritan England and was elaborated in the works of numerous writers, including Marvell and Milton, and other texts used in grammar schools at the time, such as *The Choice of Hercules* and the *Tabula Cebetis*, which traces the rocky path to virtue in the manner of Bunyan's *Pilgrim's Progress*. Hoare owned such a painting by Nicolas Poussin, *The Choice of Hercules*, which has hung in the house at Stourhead since 1747. However, he had Rysbrack's statue placed in the Pantheon in an arrangement that shows Hercules choosing not between virtue and pleasure, the more usual didactic situation, but instead between different virtues. His head is inclined toward Ceres and Susanna. By means of this gesture, Hoare deliberately paid homage to his wife in the form of Susanna, and to the fruit of one's labors in life and maturity in the form of Ceres.

On leaving the Pantheon, the visitor steps back out into the sunlight and is suddenly presented with a new and dramatically different scene. Across the lake, beyond a charming foreground island, is a vision of rural England, both historic and contemporary. There in a small vale, catching the afternoon light, are the medieval church and cottages of Stourton. Between the hamlet and the lake, Hoare placed an ancient market cross that was originally erected in 1373 in the city of Bristol but was removed as a traffic hazard. In front of this tableau is a handsome stone bridge, both classical and medieval in character. To the left, embraced by trees, is the small Temple of Ceres. From this view it is startlingly reminiscent of the ancient shrine of Clitumnus, which stood within a sacred grove over the source of the Tiber in the heart of a rich agricultural valley in Umbria, north of Rome. To the right and above on the hill stands a round Temple of Apollo, its dome gleaming in the late afternoon sun. Seen in the afternoon light, this striking composition has never failed to dazzle me, regardless of season. Here these passages of classical landscape are used to form a proscenium, to frame a vision of England, its religious faith, history, villages, and landscape as if seen upon a stage. What Hoare and Flitcroft have literally done is to present one age and culture so that it is seen and framed in terms of another. The journey is building toward a climax.

Leaving this scene and the Pantheon, the path leads across the large earth dam. The top has been planted with yews and trees, blurring its edges and shape, making it seem a relatively natural extension of the surrounding park. From here one can catch glimpses through the trees down the valley of the Stour, away from the pleasure ground toward another small hamlet called Gasper after Poussin's son-in-law, the landscape painter, and beyond to the farms of southwest Wiltshire. Close by and above on the hill with the round Temple is a waterfall reminiscent of the most beloved and famous sacred landscape of the Roman Campagna, that of the so-called Sibyl's Temple and cascade at Tivoli. Again the path leads away from the lake into a wood and begins to climb. It leads to a curious and steep, winding rockwork and stair. Turning about this way and that, the visitor is made to look in all directions while ascending this "Grott-esque" structure. Surely this must be the steep and rocky path of virtue, which in both classical and Christian literature leads inevitably to a "Temple of Wisdom" high on a mountaintop. Again a physical device brings forth our consideration of the appeal of the tales of Hercules and Aeneas to Hoare and his generation of Christians in general, and the manner in which they could be read as parallels to or similes of the journey of the soul through life toward holiness, Christ, or heaven, and especially each of these heroes' trials and sojourns in Hades before their eventual triumph and return (or resurrection).

At the top of this rocky climb, the path enters a cool wood and begins to level out. Again and suddenly ahead in a clearing stands the Temple of Apollo. As also happened upon approaching the other temples, it now appears large, crisp, bold, and far more powerful than one imagined from the distant and fleeting glimpses of it along the way. Designed and supervised by Flitcroft, this temple is several monuments in one. Its architectural form and details are not Palladian in the least, but instead are derived from the Temple of Venus at Baalbek, which had been illustrated in a recently published volume on the ruins of Baalbek by John Wood of nearby Bath (1757) that Hoare and Flitcroft had purchased. Probably one of the most animated or "baroque" structures of classical antiquity, this small building has had an impact far in excess of what one might expect from a structure of its size and relative remoteness in Asia Minor. From below, as mentioned, the juxtaposition of Flitcroft's temple and the waterfall is reminiscent of the Temple of Vesta at Tivoli. Here, however, other associations occur. First, there is that of the Roman site of Baalbek and of Venus, goddess of love. Second, and more important, because of its dedication at Stourhead to Apollo, it is most certainly a "Temple of Wisdom." From here, standing on its steps like the god whose temple it is supposed to be, high above the world, one can look back and down upon the entire journey made through the grounds, and by inference and reflection the passage through one's own life. It is a place for contemplation, for recollection, memory, and vision.

As in the Pantheon, Hoare's desire to portray his aspirations and values through association and the presentation of classical tales and iconography is evident. The images and multiple associations provided by Apollo to a visitor well read in classical literature are many. Inside the temple is a copy of the Apollo Belvedere at the Vatican, one of the most famous sculptures of all classical antiquity. Apollo, the only one of the Greek gods not to receive a Latinized name, this god of golden locks, brother of Diana, son of Zeus and Leto, was the god of light, of prophecy, music, and healing and, as a guardian of fields, crops, and herds, was worshiped in numerous forms. Apollo Parnopios wards off locusts; Apollo Eruscidios prevents rust on cereal crops; Apollo Lykeios protects herds from wolves, and so on. Apollo had many herds of his own, and while watching over them he would sing and play on his lyre (the patron saint of singing cowboys!). Even the wild beasts came to hear him sing. As the god of music, he brought order, grace, and beauty into the life of men.

In ancient Rome there were numerous shrines to Apollo. One was built by Augustus on the Palatine to house the recordings of the Sibylline oracles brought from Cumae, the most ancient shrine to Apollo in Italy. This shrine north of Naples was located near a cave and lake that were believed to be the entrance to the Underworld. At Stourhead, as at the temple to Diana in the Alban Hills at Lake Nemi, the juxtaposition of an agricultural landscape, a sacred lake, an entry to the Underworld, and references to Diana and Apollo were associations that those with a classical education, and especially those who had traveled through southern Italy, would be able to read, understand, and reflect upon. Here in late afternoon, visitors can sit in the sun as shadows lengthen below and the blue of the lake deepens and gaze out across to the fields, flocks, and distant woods of southern Wiltshire as in Henry Hoare's day. It is a scene as rich visually as it is economically. The sounds of men at work, although faint and far away, can also be heard, reminding us of Peter Brueghel's great painting of Icarus plunging into the distant ocean as some nameless peasant plows a field in the foreground: that despite the adventures of the high and mighty, despite whatever our own personal tragedies and situation might bring, for others as well as ourselves life and toil go on as they must.

Finally, when ready, the visitor leaves, descending rapidly to the lake, and arrives back in the present and the world of mortals at the Bristol cross. The Stourton church stands just beyond where so many of Hoare's family are buried. From here it is a short walk back to the house or to the small inn that Hoare was forced to build to house the numerous visitors who came to see his private Elysium.

101. Plan of Stourhead House, Pleasure Ground, and the hamlet of Stourton.

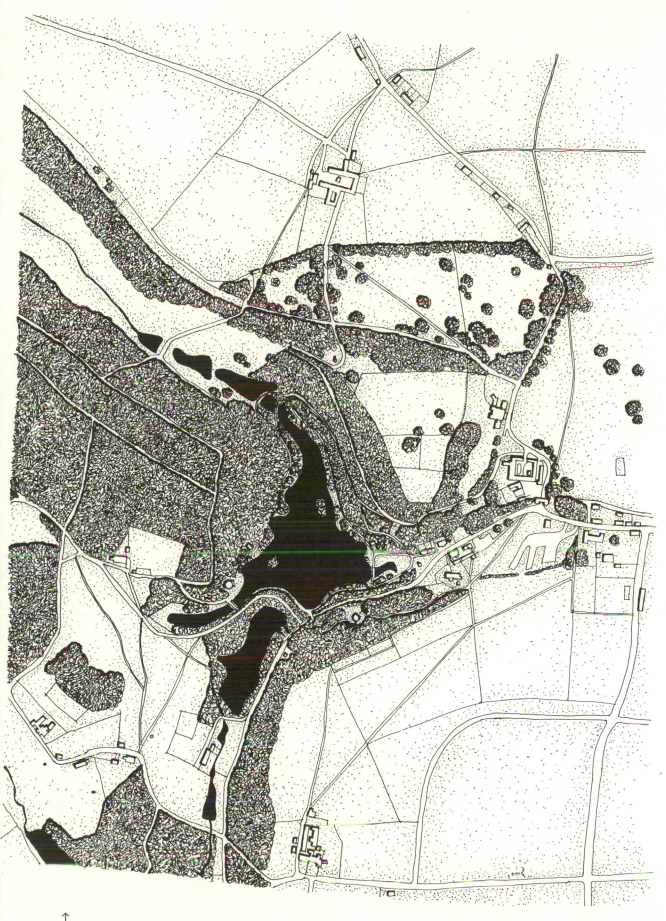

↑
N

The Significance of Stourhead

In his garden and lake at Stourhead, Henry Hoare, with the assistance of Flitcroft, raised the vision, method, and manner of William Kent to a new level. Never in England had a garden been so carefully organized around an emblematic "circuit" of such complex sensibility. At Stourhead thematic content and physical form are so well integrated as to be indistinguishable. More than a few scholars and visitors have suggested that Hoare may have based the initial composition on two specific paintings of Claude Lorrain. It is highly likely that this is so. Although Hoare pursued Claude's paintings for most of his life, he was only able to acquire a copy of one. He did acquire two Poussins and several other fine Italian paintings, including a Gaspard Poussin. Undoubtedly he had seen several Claudes at friends' homes in England and in the great collections on the Continent. More important was the fact that he had been to Italy and very likely had seen many of the scenes that inspired Claude, and it is this — the general imagery, mood, classical structures, landscape, and allegorical settings present throughout the work of Claude — that inspired the design of Stourhead. Hoare followed the literature and painting of his time, and worked for more than twenty years with Flitcroft, a key member of Burlington and Kent's circle. Finally, one must acknowledge that he was a man of great sensibility who labored long and hard over a personal vision until here on the edge of the Wiltshire Downs he produced one of the consummate works of art achieved by Western culture.

In particular, the striking image of the Pantheon reflected in the lake has no precedent in classical antiquity. It seems to have been an invention of Claude, who used it several times: twice in paintings that contained references to Aeneas or Delos and once in reference to the nymph Egeria and her transformation into a spring near the sanctuary of Diana at Lake Nemi after the death of her husband, the Roman philosopher-king Numa, a descendant of Aeneas. Filippo Juvarra, who was probably familiar with two of these paintings that were displayed in a prominent and well-visited collection in Rome, seized upon this image for the backcloth of his set for the opera *Iphiginia in Tauris*, performed in Cardinal Ottoboni's theater while Kent was in Rome. Kent and many others, possibly Henry Hoare, had seen some if not all of these paintings of Claude, and Kent seems to have known some of Juvarra's designs for the theater. Whether Flitcroft and Hoare had any of these specific images in mind hardly matters. The combination of a small classical temple in conjunction with water not only runs throughout the work of Claude and Poussin, but was an inevitable combination once Hoare embarked upon his scheme of damming up the stream.

Many writers have known and remarked on the possible influence and relationships between the seventeenth-century paintings of Claude Lorrain and Nicolas Poussin and the landscape gardens of the next century in England. While it is true that there was some influence, the extent was never so specific or total as is commonly supposed. Their paintings drew upon the art, literature, and intellectual currents of their time, and in Claude's case were themselves heavily influenced by gardens, parks, and rural landscapes in and around Rome, many of which were well known to foreign travelers. The principal appeal of many of these paintings for English collectors was that of treasured souvenirs, works of art to be carted home that were filled with visual images of places visited and a climate of thought. For many of the landowners and designers in an age before photography, they functioned as memory theaters and visual guides, as mementos of their experience in Italy. Even more central to such memories were the actual gardens and ruins, the theater, and the landscape of Italy that was and still is so hauntingly beautiful.

The skill with which the Pantheon at Stourhead is designed, placed, and set off by foreground, middle ground, and background in the view from the entrance is unparalleled (see fig. 100). The foreground, with the Doric Temple to the right, the Palladian Bridge to the left, the grassy slope and soft curving bank, leads the eye gently onto the broad sheet of water that comprises the middle ground; its two small islands, with clumps of trees placed asymmetrically in front and to the side of the temple, make a brilliant restatement of the clumps of trees on lawn found in a conventional park. Then in the background is the vision of this particular white building catching the shifting light throughout the day, placed firmly on a gently rounded grassy bank, embraced by a dense plantation of hardwoods and reflected with its green backdrop in the deep blue of the tranquil lake. This unforgettable image, ruffled occasionally by the passage of Apollo's sacred swans, is as haunting as that found anywhere in any medium.

It was what today we would call a smash hit. People flocked to see it. Horace Walpole praised it. Artists came and sketched or painted its varied scenes: C. M. Bamfylde, J. M. W. Turner, Piper, and Constable. Moreover, it was the high-water mark of a particular sensibility. Nowhere since has anyone constructed so ambitious a landscape composition with such an extensive literary structure. At the time Henry Hoare began working on his garden, the health of William Kent, the initiator of this style of garden design, was failing, and Capability Brown was beginning his career at Stowe. By the time the garden was complete, Kent, Burlington, Temple, and Flitcroft were all dead, Britain was at war with France, and the grand tour nearly impossible. Trouble was brewing in the American colonies, and an agricultural crisis had developed. The economy was faltering. Brown was still alive, but his major work was behind him. The people who owned country estates now had different concerns from those of the previous generation: the upper classes were more isolated from the general populace, less secure, and in many cases more beleaguered or arrogant than the circle of men who had supported King George I and produced the Palladian movement. Understandably, the fashion in landscape design, as in everything else, was to change.

Life went on at Stourhead. Henry Hoare's grandson and heir, Colt Hoare, continued to build and to plant. The carefully wrought scheme was overlain with Gothic Revival touches, such as the thatched cottage between the Grotto and the Pantheon and a castellated entry gate to the house. New wings were added to the sides of Colen Campbell's simple Palladian villa. Exotic plants were introduced into the park — American conifers and hardwoods, flowering shrubs from Asia. Romanticism, with all that the term implies in art and sentiment, was to flourish at Stourhead as in the nation as a whole. A tempest between advocates of the "picturesque" and those of the "gardenesque" was soon to dominate the writing and practice of estate design. Some, who in earlier times would have devoted themselves to the arts and the "improvement" of their parks, turned instead to the sciences, to new agricultural enterprises, or to interests in emerging industrial technology. By 1785 when Henry Hoare died, the humanist tradition that had influenced the design of landscape gardens from the beginning of the Renaissance was in decline and largely over.

LANCELOT "CAPABILITY" BROWN

William Kent may be the father of modern landscape gardening and the link between the eighteenth century and the garden art of an earlier period, but it is Lancelot Brown who is the most famous practitioner of the art as it evolved. Although some gardeners, scholars, and landscape architects know of Kent's existence and a smaller number are aware of what he actually did, entire generations of English children know about Lancelot Brown. Known as Capability Brown because of his habit of announcing that an estate or piece of land possessed certain potential or "capabilities" that could and should be developed, he is lionized like Francis Drake, King Alfred, and Dick Whittington as a self-made man and one of the architects of the nation. Brown's fame and Kent's relative obscurity are partly due to the fashionable surge of activity in park construction that swept England in the eighteenth century, providing Brown with the opportunity for numerous commissions, and partly due to the personality differences between the two men. Although as gregarious as Brown, Kent is reputed to have been somewhat lazy and is known to have detested traveling, preferring to spend his time at the houses and estates of his friends in and about London. Brown, on the other hand, was a tireless and ambitious worker, endlessly traveling from one project to another, even when ill and elderly. We know this from numerous letters from clients beseeching him to come to their estates, while his own letters constantly refer to juggling dates and visits, trying to fit them all in.

There is, too, the difference in their gifts. Kent's work was finely wrought, at times almost precious or small in scale. It appealed to intellectuals. Brown's work and reputation didn't possess much in the way of literary underpinnings. From the start he worked at a larger scale, composing parks with a thorough knowledge of construction and horticulture gained in his youth in the north. Virtually none of his work relies on a circuit or itinerary, and none has the layers of meaning associated with the work of Kent or Hoare. The parks of Brown, as exemplified by Petworth and Blenheim, are a watershed in social order, sensibility, and art. Visually, formally, and to a degree ecologically, they are the last wave of the humanist love affair with pastoral artifacts and manners. At the same time, the age of a formal abstract art, stripped of literary and historical allusion — of an art that deals primarily with formal problems within its own particular medium — had begun. In his own lifetime Brown was accused of producing vapid and inhuman landscapes, enormously monotonous and dependent on a single formula — the same charges used to attack other, more recent artists, especially in our own time, those considered to be the most abstract or minimalist.

Contrary to popular myth, Brown did not begin as an apprentice in the kitchen gardens at Stowe and work his way up to become head gardener, only then to be launched on a great career after being befriended by Kent and Temple. Instead, as is often the case, the real facts are at least as interesting and better help to explain his remarkable achievements. Born in 1716 in Kirkharle, Northumberland, near the Scottish border, Brown was fairly well educated in village schools, leaving at age sixteen to go to work for the largest landowner in the valley, Baronet William Loraine. This nobleman had been active in local and national politics until middle age. After 1720 he began to withdraw to spend more time on his estate. Like many of his friends and contemporaries in London and neighboring Yorkshire, Loraine was interested in improving his property in the fashion of the times. Acting as his own architect, he rebuilt his house and set to work redeveloping the extensive grounds of the estate. Removing an old village near his house, he rebuilt it farther away on high ground. He demolished parterres developed in the previous generation, replacing them with a sweeping lawn, while maintaining mature trees in groups within the scene between house and village. Loraine planted more than twenty-four thousand slow-growing trees, five hundred thousand of quick-growing varieties, and five hundred eighty fruit trees during the remaining years of his tenure.

For six years of this endeavor, the young Lancelot Brown was employed by Loraine. Although little is known about Brown's duties on these projects, it is known specifically that he was responsible for the draining, regrading, and replanting of a large boggy vale and that his efforts were so successful that it was later termed a "woody theater of stateliest view." Thus from the start of his working days, Brown was engaged in the craft of landscape construction, working with beech, oak, and chestnut, which were to become his staples for plantations. He was moving earth and redirecting water. Furthermore, from the beginning he worked on large-scale projects, requiring the careful organization of numerous men, trades, and quantities of materials.

This is an important point, for *scale* in design is as intangible and important as it is difficult to describe to those who don't customarily work in three dimensions. Even among architects, sculptors, and painters, who generally know and consider it, one can observe that different individuals will gravitate toward working at particular scales. This is not merely a matter of luck in obtaining commissions, nor a function of some "spirit" of an age or style, although these can be factors to a degree. The individual temperament of an artist plays an important role. It is a truth that of all architects, only a small number can work effectively at a heroic or monumental scale. So, too, some are far better working at a domestic or more intimate scale than others. Why this should be so is probably related to many influencing factors: the landscape of one's youth, the nature and emphasis of one's training, the scale and nature of the early work upon which a young apprentice learns his craft, and so on. As a colleague of mine once remarked, "it seems that we spend our career trying to re-create a version of the landscape of our youth and early enthusiasms." In any case, it is a fact that Brown, who grew up in a broad, open, rolling region of Northumberland, began his career working for a man who late in life committed himself with confidence to large-scale works of vision. Throughout his life, Brown also radiated a self-confidence and generosity, artistically and socially, that I would associate with his early experiences in the north.

In 1738 both Henry Wise and Charles Bridgeman, the two most successful and traditional (baroque) gardeners and nurserymen working for the Crown and on large private estates, died, leaving a gap in the leadership of the gardening industry. Shortly thereafter, in 1739, Brown left for the south. He traveled to London, visiting numerous estates and parks, as any young aspiring artist or architect would. Hoping for work, he carried references and introductions to relatives and friends of his former employer. By 1740 he had his first project under construction in Buckinghamshire at Kiddington. Modest in comparison to his later work, it contained an important element that was to become his hallmark, a lake. Damming up the River Glyme, he produced a serpentine pond with a small, tree-covered island. This device, coupled with a bridge at the upper, narrow end and a broad lawn sloping gently away from the house and nearby medieval church — judiciously planted with groups of trees — were the elements with which he was to work for the next forty years.

Shortly afterward he came to the attention of Richard Temple, whose head gardener, William Love, had left Stowe after fifteen years. Brown, already established as a landscape gardener, took up the post of head gardener at Stowe in 1741 and almost immediately found himself directing forty men. Proving himself reliable and honest, he rapidly became clerk of the works on other construction, directing carpenters, carters, masons, and plasterers. In his early years at Stowe, Brown studied diligently to increase his knowledge of architecture, observing ongoing work and availing himself of Temple's superb library. Because of the varied works in progress, Stowe was a perfect training ground for a bright young designer. By 1747 he had become competent in drawing, a key skill needed for his subsequent career. In this he was influenced by Kent's manner of delineation as well as by his formal ideas.

Love, his predecessor, had supervised the making of an eleven-acre lake under Bridgeman and the creation of the Elysian Fields of Kent. Brown was to preside over the next period of construction, which included the revisions and pavilions of Hawkwell Field and the Grecian Valley. During this period, he executed design ideas by Kent, Temple, Gibbs, Borra, and Leoni, a formidable group. In 1743 he supervised the demolition of Bridgeman's terrace and the creation of the great South Lawn. Simultaneously he was breaking up the avenues of trees, continuing to alter and soften the lakes, and planting thousands of trees. He also organized the work of three separate quarries and four masonry crews for the construction of the Palladian Bridge, the Gothic and Lady's Temples, a grotto, the stables, coach house, chapel, and library of the house. For the Grecian Valley, one of Temple's last endeavors, he directed the removal of more than twenty-three thousand cubic yards of earth.

If Brown had arrived in the south with self-confidence and a good, solid background in horticulture and landscape construction, at Stowe he continued his architectural education and honed his landscape design and construction skills. Equally important, he was well placed to come to the notice of other wealthy landowners. During his last years at Stowe he began to work for other clients, being "loaned out" by Temple. In 1749 his patron died, and in 1751 Brown left Stowe for London, where he set up practice in Hammersmith, which in those days was the abode of many nurserymen and landscape contractors.

Brown was industrious, and work came flooding in. Most of the Palladians were dead — Kent died in 1748, Burlington in 1753 — and William Chambers and Robert Adam had yet to arrive on the scene. Not only did Brown have landscape commissions, increasingly he was called upon for architectural advice as well. He was competent as an architect and, in a lesser age, might also have been known for his endeavors in that field. As it was, in the mid-eighteenth century, his architectural abilities were far overshadowed by his predecessors and the next wave of architects. Nevertheless, he was skillful, and at times — as in the Gallery at Corsham Court — good in a restrained, Kentish sort of way, but not so good as to be remarkable. Then as now, he was sought out for his parks, for his sense of which attributes of a piece of property to seize upon: his exploitation of its "capabilities." As his contemporary William Mason wrote to Humphry Repton in a letter of 1792, part of the reason for his efforts in architecture was that the work was often forced upon him by the lack of others to do the work properly, a circumstance that many in practice today may appreciate as a familiar one: "I am uniformly of the opinion that where a place is to be formed, he who disposes the ground and arranges the plantations ought to fix the situation at least, if not to determine the shape and size of the ornamental buildings. Brown, I know, was ridiculed for turning architect, but I have always thought he did it from a necessity having found the great difficulty which must frequently have occurred to him in forming a picturesque Whole, where the previous building had been ill-placed, or of improper dimensions."

Over the next ten years, many of his greatest commissions were begun: Petworth, 1752; Moor Park, 1753; Burghley, 1755; Longleat, 1757; Bowood, 1757; Harewood, 1758; Blenheim, 1758; Syon, 1760; Chatsworth, 1760; Corsham, 1760. The work went on until his death in 1783 without letup. Some of the projects kept him actively involved for more than twenty years. How many projects he actually worked on is unknown. Hugh Prince lists 189 parks, Dorothy Stroud lists 211, some of which only amounted to brief advice or consultation, or just architectural work.

In 1764 Brown was honored by the Crown and made head gardener of the Royal Parks. This was partly as a result of his work for the duke of Northumberland at Syon House — where he cleared a view to the river and Royal Park of Richmond opposite while

102. Possibly the most famous of all Brown's parks is that of Blenheim near Oxford, with its magnificent lake, seen here with Nicholas Hawksmoor's monumental bridge.

simultaneously creating a lake opposite the house (a showplace by Robert Adam) amid new plantations — and partly as a result of his growing fame and entreaties by friends, clients, and confidants of the king. In his new post, Brown was to contribute designs for the garden at Buckingham House (now Palace), for St. James Palace (some of which was not to be implemented until the time of John Nash), for Richmond park, for Windsor Park, and for Hampton Court, near to which he moved, residing and working there until his death. Like his predecessor Henry Wise, Brown continued to execute private commissions during his tenure as royal gardener: Luton Hoo, Claremont, Milton Abbey, Burton Constable, Temple Newsham, Rycote, Grimsthorpe, Ashburnham, Compton Verney. The list of works goes on and on, each name evoking a particular place and mood.

Brown's parks offer far more than a period flavor of knee breeches and hose, great coats and perukes, of carriages crunching toward country houses on gravel drives so familiar to Jane Austen fans and addicts of BBC television specials produced for export to America, those images projected by our nostalgia onto the past. They are works of art, in many cases as alive today as when they were built. Some are decrepit, some are immaculate, and nearly all are vastly different from when they were first planted. Examining prints and paintings of the period, one sees that these parks were once rather bald and new looking. The trees were small and often far apart, despite their arrangement and "clumping." Today the horizontal distances between the masses of planting seem smaller, more in scale with the height and mass of the trees. This was part of Brown's true genius — to understand the dynamic changes of time and growth that would produce the parks we revere today. The other part had to do with his extraordinary skill in the handling of water.

These parks, large in conception and in their elements —lakes, valleys, massed tree plantings — are also as impressive for their subtlety of feeling as for their size and expense. Brown understood light, modeling, atmospheric conditions, and the latest technology, whether of hydraulics or horticulture. His handling of water and tree masses in the middle distance has never been surpassed for its variety and pictorial "conviction." This may seem an odd phrase, but there is about his compositions such a thorough balance and adjustment to all the parts that one rarely can imagine moving any element without the whole scene coming unraveled.

Brown: Achievement and Critics

In his own lifetime Brown was attacked by William Chambers, who despised him and his work on political, social, and aesthetic grounds, and later by Richard Payne Knight and William Robinson, who found his work too uniform, tidy, and simplistic, preferring instead landscapes that were both wilder, more contorted, and profusely planted. For reasons deriving from Brown's own education as well as the changing social climate and artistic fashions, the era of poetic gardens constructed around an itinerary of complex literary

FOLLOWING PAGE: *103. Vista at Blenheim to the Wellington monument with Brown's characteristic clumps and single specimen oaks carefully placed to frame the view, delineate depth, and explain the land form — here with the help of late afternoon sun, but equally effective on a foggy or rainy day.*

themes and allusions was over. Nevertheless, Brown was highly regarded by the surviving members of Burlington's circle. Employed by Henry Hoare's son-in-law, Lord Bruce, he consulted on Bruce's property at Tottenham Park with the older Hoare, who later produced a sketch to explain an idea of Brown's to Bruce. Brown's parks were to set the standard of excellence and the formal norm for the next century in England, which in the hands of his followers was transmitted to Andrew Jackson Downing and Frederick Law Olmsted in the United States, setting the direction for public and private parks there for the next hundred and fifty years.

If there is any aspect of Brown's work rarely matched by other landscape designers before or since, it is his genius for working with water. Whatever sameness his planting may exhibit, his manipulation of the placement and scale of ponds, streams, serpentines, cascades, and lakes was done with endless variety. Each and every water feature of his is particularly apt for the property, house, and landscape where it was built. From the small ponds glinting in the shadowy vale at Prior Park to the broad, curving rivers at Burghley and Audley End, and the spectacular lakes at Petworth, Sheffield, and Blenheim, Brown is the master of land form, large masses of trees, and above all water and light.

During Brown's long career, architectural fashions changed. The Palladian generation was mostly dead by 1750. Although architects like Talman and Flitcroft, whose careers began during Burlington's later years, were to continue building with the ideas and compositional methods developed by Campbell, Burlington, and Kent, fashionable architecture from 1760 to 1790 was soon dominated by the work of two new figures: William Chambers and Robert Adam. Both were to broaden the architectural vocabulary of their period in England. To a degree, they were similar despite their apparent differences and animosity toward each other. Both drew upon the traditions and work of the preceding generation as exemplified by Burlington and Kent. Both men were extremely well traveled and educated in architectural history, and both were highly imaginative and innovative in their application of this knowledge of the past. Chambers had grown up on the Continent, traveled to the Far East, and carefully studied the works of classical antiquity. Despite numerous large or urban projects, he was always best when working within the country house or palace idiom. Adam, the son of Scotland's first native classical architect, whose three brothers all were to practice some version of architecture, had spent more than four years in Italy in the company of some of the best French and Italian artists and archaeologists at work there at the time, particularly Charles-Louis Clérisseau, Giambattista Piranesi, and Julien-David LeRoy. Both men were conversant with recent archaeological findings in Greece, Asia Minor, and southern Italy. Unlike the Palladians, they embraced a much wider spectrum of art — classical, Renaissance, and modern — and were to develop a greater personal freedom with classical material, allowing them to work in the "manner" and "spirit" of the ancients, not merely replicating portions of a handful of famous monuments. Both were also familiar with new developments on the Continent, particularly in

France, where a more eclectic and scholarly movement was under way, a neoclassicism that focused more on Greece than Rome.

Adam was clearly indebted to Kent, Vanbrugh, and Hawksmoor in his enthusiasm for "movement" in the composition of buildings — a conscious emphasis upon developing a rhythmical composition of diverse, often dramatically opposed elements within a facade or plan — and to Kent, Vardy, and Flitcroft for his drawing techniques. His principal effect upon his contemporaries and successors was in the field of decoration and the design of interiors, although the delicacy of his slender Greek columns and frequent use of plain surfaces on exteriors were to show up in numerous subsequent country houses and garden pavilions. William Chambers, on the other hand, was to adhere to a cool and conservative, although personal, form of classicism that virtually set the standard for public buildings and country houses. An interesting by-product of his architectural services for the royal family and of his publishing activity was that he became embroiled in a bitter feud with Brown and devotees of the landscape movement.

Although not a motivating force, a certain knowledge of garden and landscape sentiment in China had been filtering into the thought of English intellectuals since the seventeenth century. This came first in the prints, paintings, and descriptions brought back by traders and missionaries and then in essays and studies. The Chinese passion for curvilinear shapes and sudden changes of scene, for contrasts between simple, strong geometries and wildly irregular natural formations; for circuitous itineraries about gardens conceived as microcosms; and for a variety of garden structures that included temples, bridges, tea houses, and fishing pavilions was made known to English connoisseurs and amateur architects through a manuscript, *Upon the Gardens of Epicurus*, written by Sir William Temple in 1685 and published in 1697. All of this confirmed rather than deflected the direction that the Whig philosopher-gardeners were to take. Later essays by Temple and Batty Langley drew upon China as an example of the natural wisdom and logic of the poetic landscape garden. By 1749 the first recorded Chinoiserie pavilions, the so-called House of Confucius, had been erected in Kew Gardens and William Horne had erected his innovative boat house in Gopsall Park, Leicestershire. The way to such a change in sensibility that welcomed these exotic structures had been opened in the previous decades by the fanciful Gothic works by Vanbrugh, Kent, and Walpole while at the height of their most supposedly "classical" powers.

Chambers returned to England from a tour of Europe in 1755 and shortly thereafter became the architectural tutor to the prince of Wales and architect to the princess dowager. In the latter capacity he began building garden ornaments at Kew Gardens, one of which was his celebrated Pagoda of 1761. Even before this, he had published his first work, *Designs of Chinese Buildings, Furniture, Dresses, Etc.*, in 1757. Regardless of Chambers's own motive or feelings, an absolute rage for novelty of all sorts was developing. A desire for things Chinese was added to the growing list of styles: Moorish, Gothic, Greek, Roman, Egyptian.

At the same time, however, Brown's career and circle of acquaintances and clients were developing parallel with that of Chambers and Adam. Apparently on decent terms with Adam, Brown worked on many projects for the same clients, usually during the same years. Chambers took a dislike to both Brown and his work, and soon they were powerful adversaries. Chambers accused Brown of having a poverty-stricken imagination and implied a lack of class and education on his part. In 1772 he published a querulous book, the *Dissertation on Oriental Gardening*, purposely aimed at Brown and his "common meadows." Chambers miscalculated: Brown's work was too highly regarded, his friends too numerous and powerful for the attack to damage his career. Walpole laughed out loud at it, and the rebuttal of William Mason, a poet in the Whig tradition, cleverly embodied an anti-Crown, anti-Tory political tract, *An Heroic Epistle to Sir William Chambers*, which became so popular that it went into fourteen printings. Mason managed to attack the character of Chambers, recently appointed comptroller general of the Royal Works, as a servant of tyrants who understood neither the overwrought and artificial gardens of China nor the landscape gardens of England, which supposedly had grown out of a long desire for liberty. Brown may not have been laying out gardens with a panoply of symbolic emblems like the preceding generation; nevertheless, his parks were taken in toto as a symbol of the liberal, constitutional movement and as a physical and natural expression of the English Enlightenment's continuing struggle against oppression.

THE LANDSCAPE MOVEMENT SPREADS

Capability Brown was the central designer and arbiter of taste in the making of country parks for nearly thirty years. During this period the passion for "improvement" of estates continued unabated and was to continue well into the next century. At the beginning of the eighteenth century, approximately 25 percent of the entire agricultural resources of the nation were controlled by only four hundred families. In a land of less than eight million people, nearly half of the arable land was owned by only some five thousand families. Even so — whether one believes it was because of or despite the social system — the other 50 percent of arable land was still owned in countless small holdings, and a complex agrarian capitalism far more flexible and open to innovation than any on the Continent was vigorously evolving. In addition to the better-known, vast parks of the very rich, thousands of smaller parks ranging from twenty to a hundred acres sprang up. The endeavors of the nouveau-riche group that built them were often ridiculed by those with old money and the haut monde, especially in contemporary satires and comedies, as seen in the following lines from *Headlong Hall* by Thomas Love Peacock: "a white, polished angular building reflected to a nicety in this waveless lake; and there you have Lord Littlebrain looking out the window."

As in other things, the southwest corner of Wiltshire was not left out of developments in the Romantic movement in architecture as Georgian tastes shifted to those of the Regency. The outburst of fanciful and exotic architecture that began in garden pavilions and interiors in the mid-eighteenth century was taken up in eclectic revival styles and picturesque, rococo, and wildly eccentric compositions for the villas and mansions as well. One of the most extreme practitioners of this sort was Jeffrey Wyatt, an architect who had participated in the restoration of castles and cathedrals. Between 1800 and 1813 Wyatt engaged in the application of ecclesiastical Gothic features to at least ten large country houses, the largest and most (in)famous of which was Fonthill Abbey, built for his equally excessive and fanciful client, William Beckwith. Located seven miles south of Longbridge Deverill, this spectacular and eye-popping concoction of towers, spires, crenellations, crockets, dizzying stairs, and halls came crashing down in an equally spectacular collapse. The feelings such shifts in style and taste bring forth is well evident in a remark by Christopher Hussey, a twentieth-century writer and critic devoted to the classical, baroque, and Palladian architecture and the landscape parks of the eighteenth century, who coolly wrote that "its collapse in 1825 was perhaps a greater loss to literature than to architecture." Like the original abbeys after the dissolution, the ruins of Fonthill Abbey, consisting largely of local Chilmark stone from the Nadder valley, became a quarry for several undistinguished houses built later on the estate and nearby. Of Beckwith and Wyatt's fantasy, however, virtually nothing remains.

The creation of these parks was not as negative in social or agrarian terms as has sometimes been asserted. Despite increasing practices of ruinous rack-renting, enclosure, and the occasional wholesale relocation of entire villages, the amount of arable land increased continuously throughout this period, just as the yields per acre continued to improve with constant experimentation in farming methods. Many of the new country houses and parks were built on lands that had been of marginal or poor agricultural quality. This accounts for the ease with which they were purchased and the lack of any real negative impact on agriculture and the economy. It is this frequent peculiarity in the origin of their siting that leads to an intrinsic variety in topography and prospect, and that created so many problems for the gardeners and designers called upon to create them. Poor soils were probably their most common feature.

In his expansion of Daniel Defoe's *A Tour Thro' the Whole Island of Great Britain* (1742), Samuel Richardson documents how one such site was transformed from a wasteland into a remarkable park:

At *Painshill* near *Cobham* in *Surrey*, is the Seat of the Hon. *Charles Hamilton*, where is a great Improvement making by inclosing a large Tract of Land designed for a Park, which was most of it so poor as not to produce any thing but *Heath* and *Broom*; but by burning of the heath, and spreading the Ashes on the ground, a Crop of *Turneps* was obtained; and by feeding Sheep on the *Turneps*, their Dung became a good Manure to the Land, so that a good Sward of Grass is now upon the land, where it was judged by most People impossible to get any Herbage. . . . The lands which Mr. *Hamil-*

104. Brown's influence is recorded in many ways. The sketch above is taken from a painting of Steepleton House, Dorset, depicting the progress of a fox hunt across one of the vast meadows planted with clumps of trees (elms in this case) and villa in the new manner beyond. The sketch below is taken from one of George Stubbs's many depictions of horses and groom that often utilize Brownian landscape compositions as a stage set, much as they functioned in reality for the lives of their owners.

ton has inclosed, have fine Inequalities; for every 100 yards there are great Hollows, then rising Grounds again, so that the Prospect is continually changing, as you walk over it.

Hamilton's success was nearly as spectacular as that of Henry Hoare at Stourhead, creating an itinerary of enchantment and illusion in a linear development along a seemingly endless body of water that was created not only with grading, planting and dams, but also by means of a mechanical device that raised water fifteen feet from the diminutive River Mole. Among the countless examples of this tendency to wrest verdant and pleasurable parks from bleak sites, one of the best is that of Petworth, one of Brown's great works, where Arthur Young wrote that the northern part had originally been in the roughest state, consisting only of "bushes, furze, some timber and rubbish of no kind of use."

Even while Brown was alive and vigorously practicing, others less famous were successfully engaged in the design and supervision of projects begun in this wave of park construction. Partly because they were not prominent at the time, and partly because the history of art and especially of landscape architecture is a recent development, we are just beginning to know more about some of the other practitioners of this period. Because only a handful of these other designers' names and projects were known until recently, many parks have been erroneously attributed to Brown. For many the only link to Brown is the desire of latter-day owners and visitors to believe that one exists. In fact, other designers of genuine ability were working at a slightly smaller scale on countless parks during Brown's era. A good example of this can be seen in a group of houses southwest of Oxford that I stumbled upon the first summer I visited England.

Located on one of the chalk ridges radiating to the north and east of Salisbury Plain, the region around Oxford has also been a highly successful agricultural landscape for thousands of years, like that of Longbridge Deverill and southwest Wiltshire. Just south of Oxford is an older market town, Abingdon, from which a road leads west to Faringdon and the Cotswolds. This road lies along an ancient trackway on what has been called the Golden Ridge — a reference to both its prosperity and color in late summer, when vast fields of ripe grain cover the chalk. Dotted along this ridge are several small villages that are overshadowed by a group of houses and parks. In one stretch only fourteen miles long there are eleven country houses and parks, each within a quarter mile of the road and none more

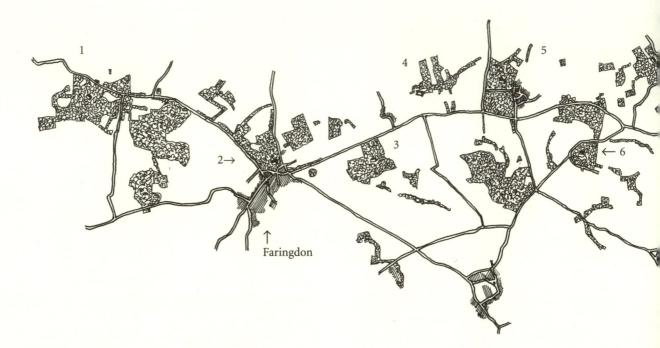

1. Buscot House
2. Faringdon House
3. Wadley House
4. Barcote House
5. Buckland House

6. Pusey House
7. Hinton Manor
8. Kingston Bagpuize House
9. Appleton Manor House
10. Tubbney Warren House
11. Sheepstead House

105. The numerous parks and gardens located along the road between Abingdon and Faringdon can be seen in this plan. Buscot House lies to the west with Buckland and Pusey Houses near the middle of this limestone ridge with its ancient and wealthy farms.

than a square mile in area, although several subtend farming estates and holdings that stretch for several miles from the road, either toward the Thames on the north or south toward the Vale of the White Horse. Not all of these houses are products of the eighteenth century, of course. One, Appleton Manor near Wytham Woods, is an amazing survival

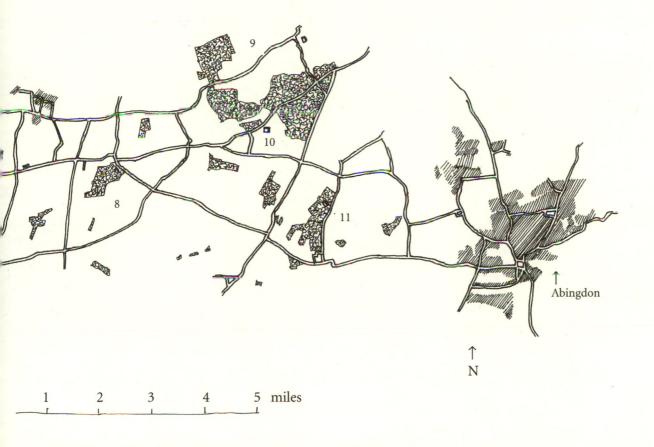

1   2   3   4   5 miles

↑
N

Abingdon

from the twelfth century. Another, Hinton House, dates from the sixteenth century. Most of the others, which date from the eighteenth century, are built on or near sites of earlier houses. Of the eleven, there are four well-developed eighteenth-century houses and parks of note, none of which Brown had anything to do with: Faringdon, Buscot, Pusey, and Buckland.

PUSEY HOUSE

The second English garden I explored that first summer was Pusey. It lay only a mile south of Buckland. Taking less than an hour to reach by footpath through the fields from Buckland, it was even quicker to visit by bicycle. In recent times most visitors have come to see the remarkable garden of flowering shrubs, perennials, herbs, and exotic trees created in this century within the grounds of an older park by a pair of superb gardeners, Michael and Nicole Hornby. Beginning in 1935, with the assistance of landscape architect Geoffrey Jellicoe, they rescued the estate from decline. The principal elements of an eighteenth-century park remain, providing an excellent miniature example of a Brownian park reduced to its essential parts. The entry faces a large tree-studded meadow backed by a screen of trees to the north; a driveway curves up to the door and away again into the grounds. The south front of the house, possibly designed by John Wood the Younger of Bath, looks out across a serpentine of water and a meadow flanked on either side by woods to a distant cornfield that has several carefully placed clumps of elms and oaks, and beyond to a valley and the distant chalk escarpment of Uffington. Despite what seem like natural shapes, there is a firm underlying geometry. Diagonally to the right, at the end of a long, curving wall replete with aedicules and classical busts that hides the kitchen garden and a stable block, is a small domed temple providing a seat at the head of the long, curvilinear pond. From here one can look back to the house on the left, to the nearby wood across the water on the right, or straight ahead down the length of the entire pond past a tree-clad island to a lovely Chinese bridge.

This handsome piece of Chinoiserie is the product of the flurry of exotica let loose into the gardening world after William Chambers, Batty Langley, and others began writing about Oriental gardens and pavilions. The taste for things distant, strange, and somehow picturesque, which began with an appreciation of wild or unique sites and artifacts in the seventeenth century and was reinforced by the work of Kent and Chambers, led to the widespread production of garden structures such as this Chippendale Chinese bridge. Other gardens of the period sprouted Turkish tents, pagodas, and Gothic temples with little of the literary meaning found in the best work of the previous generation. The bridge at Pusey is among the best surviving examples of the genre. Long, low, and delicate, its intricate white wood railing arches across the pond just before the water turns and disappears into the wood to the east of the house. Placed symmetrically opposite the temple seat and diagonally related to the south facade of the house, it provides a focal point for several views and a link to the circuitous walk that lies across the lake from the house. This distant

106. Plan of Pusey House and garden.

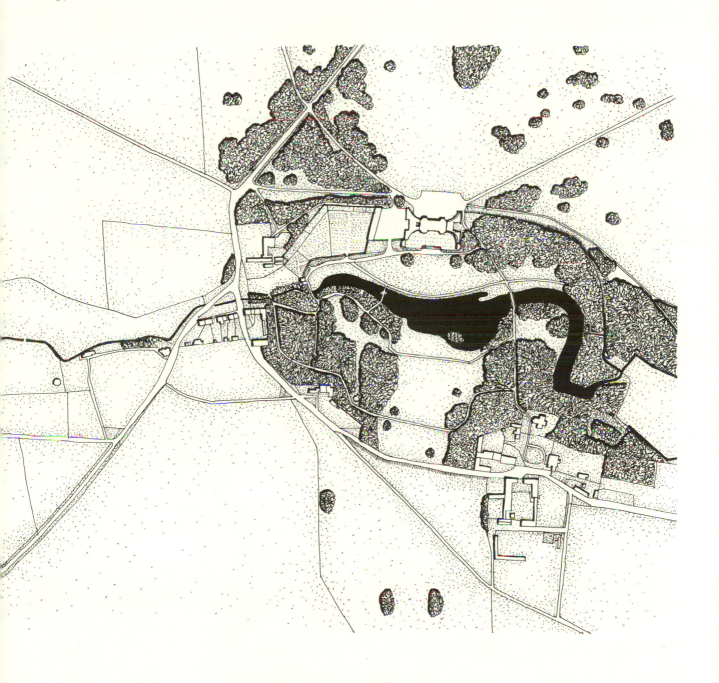

107. The Chippendale Chinese bridge at Pusey House, one of many exotic garden features introduced in the early decades of the eighteenth century.

108. This border at Pusey, like many of those developed in England between 1900 and 1950, while lovely and original when created, looks quite modest today, as we have become overwhelmed by the vast quantity delivered month after month in popular garden books and magazines. Bigger and more florid, at one estate and garden or another in France, England, Italy, and the United States, derivative and repetitive herbaceous borders have become cliché today. By comparison, this thoughtful display against the curved wall, with its niches and classical busts leading to the garden seat, remains a delight.

path connects a small church, All Saints, built by John Allen Pusey in 1743, to a small cluster of farms that lie hidden behind the plantations to the southeast and southwest. A road linking these farms together into a dispersed village passes across an open vista to the distant valley. It has been lowered from sight and thus acts as a ha-ha between the meadow within the park and the fields beyond. Each element of the ensemble is of a size and position to work with the others. There is a controlled and gradual shift in textures from the fine lawn at the house to the rougher meadow across the lake, and finally to the fields beyond the road. Whoever besides the owner may have helped to create this scheme is unknown today. Certainly it dates between 1745 and 1760 and shows a firm grasp of the formal devices employed by leading practitioners of the art such as Kent, Brown, Hoare, and Woods.

Shortly after the property was purchased by the Hornbys, they turned to Geoffrey Jellicoe, a landscape architect who had only recently begun practice. His principal achievement was to create a broad terrace that sweeps across the entire facade and reaches out to the garden in both directions to left and right. The center opens to the lawn and lake down a flight of stairs of stone and is planted with an array of sun-loving plants in surprising and superbly unmatched drifts and tufts where portions of the stone have been deleted. As Repton had surmised in a previous era, the introduction of an appropriately scaled and carefully articulated intermediary space between the front rooms of Georgian architecture and the broad, sweeping lawns of a landscape park could add immeasurably to both. Jellicoe's invention at Pusey makes the case as well or better than anything that Repton himself accomplished or those who criticized Brown for his removal of formal gardens adjacent to so many of the country houses upon which he worked. Thus started, the Hornbys moved on to restore the park and walled gardens and to begin the great border leading to the temple garden seat.

Even knowing next to nothing about gardens at the time, I knew at first sight that this garden was particularly lovely and well made. I now know that it is truly a gem among the boulders of English gardens. Virtually complete and perfect, Pusey is unusually successful in balancing a small landscape park with a large cottage garden of the highest style.

109. Jellicoe's terrace at Pusey House as planted by the Hornbys, as much a tribute to Mondrian and modern sensibility as to Gertrude Jekyll and the cottage tradition.

BUSCOT HOUSE

Six miles west of Buckland along the same ridge lies Buscot House and Park, first built between 1770 and 1780. Heavily derived from the style of Adam inside and out, the house had been altered several times and was restored to its earlier appearance just before World War II. Although the main lines of the park are distinctly representative of Brown's manner, its most distinctive feature is a series of handsome Italianate allées, basins, and gardens added by Harold Peto in 1899. The author of the original park remains unknown, which often means that the design was the result of the owner's own efforts with the aid of a skillful steward and local craftsmen.

110. View to Buscot House from the statue of Ceres after leaving the lake and climbing the hill through the woods along the entry drive.

111. *View back to the park and approach drive from the front entrance of Buscot House. This view to the left is mirrored by a similar view to another drive on the right.*

The house sits on a slight ridge facing north toward the Thames and the Cotswolds. The two approach drives from the Faringdon road wind into the park, both crossing bridges that offer views of an extensive lake that curves out of sight. In fact, there really are two different lakes, as one learns only by examining a plan or exploring the park on foot. So carefully placed and made are they that from the lawn overlooking the ha-ha in front of the house, both lakes are visible and appear as one. From the house the visitor looks out to the right and sees a lake in the distance. Straight ahead a grassy vista leads down to a rolling land form to a mass of trees screening the public road running between Faringdon and Lechlade. The viewer does not realize that a second body of water seen beyond yet another meadow diagonally down another vista to the left is not connected to the first behind the central screen of trees.

A short drive to the northwest is now used as the principal entry for visitors. In former times a longer more circuitous route from the northeast was followed from which one first viewed the house from just inside the gate, and subsequently from a situation where it was seen on a rise, across from and reflected in the lake. Both the twenty-acre lake, with its three small islands and curving shape, and the theatrical visual composition are superb examples of the genre. A classical bridge comes next. It is actually a dam in disguise holding back the lake — nearby stands a small temple on the bank by the lake. The drive passes between a wood and farmland and begins to wind up a gentle rise, passing through alternating areas of woodland and meadow until, at the top of a small crest in the wood, the road turns at a statue of Ceres and the visitor sees the entry court of the house in the near distance beyond a small vale at the end of a tree-lined avenue. One descends and climbs again to enter the gravel forecourt of the house. Having arrived, the visitor inevitably turns to look back before entering, to see off to the left the point where the drive came out of the wood and straight ahead to the south a skillfully planted valley opening out to a distant wood. Finally, walking through or around the house, one reaches the front lawn that sweeps right up to the base of the building. From here a broader view opens up to the bridge and temple near the entry where one began. Elsewhere on the property are handsome kitchen gardens, orchards, farms, and a third lake hidden from sight by encircling plantations.

112. The south entrance front of Buscot House (above) and the north garden front of the house with lawn sweeping right up to the base of the building, sans terrace (below).

FACING PAGE: 113. *Two views to the northwest from Buscot House: from the lawn out over the ha-ha down a vista framed by plantations to a meadow and one of the lakes (above), and from the second floor garden front looking down onto the lawn, ha-ha, and pasture that forms the upper portion of this vista (below).*

114. *Plan of Buscot House: note the baroque organization of the vistas from the house that have been overlaid with curving meadows and terminated with irregular lakes. Harold Peto's cascade garden can be seen running almost due east from the house toward the lake aligning with the three islands.*

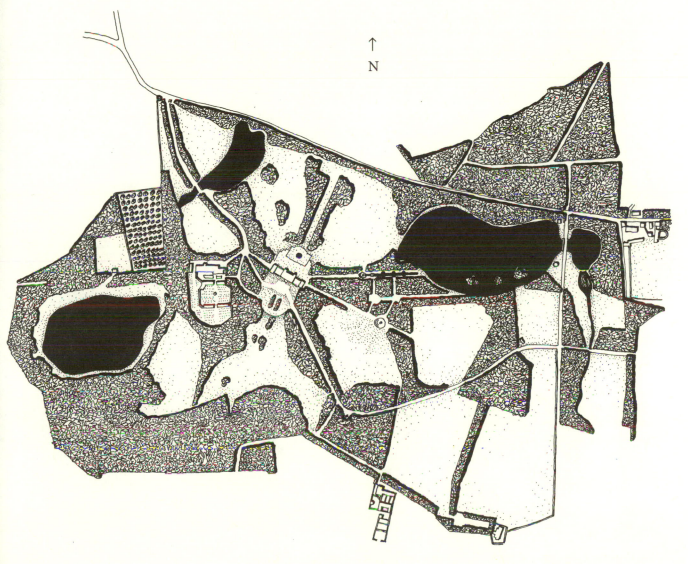

The house at Buscot was refurbished and three-quarters of a mile away a small picturesque village was created at the end of the nineteenth century by George and Peto, a fashionable architectural firm in whose office the young Edwin Luytens, the greatest designer of country houses of the next generation, apprenticed. Harold Peto was deeply interested in Italian Renaissance gardens, so much so that he eventually withdrew from his partnership and the design of buildings and turned instead to gardens and landscape. In the woodland to the northeast of the house, Peto created a long, continuously descending cascade and walk of terraces, basins, bridges, lawns, hedges, and statuary in spaces carved out of the trees leading from the house down to the easternmost of the lakes. Representative of the popular fashion for neoclassical and Renaissance revival design in English and American country estates between 1890 and 1920, this ensemble is one of the very best products of its time. Peto's work sits remarkably well within the older grounds. The reason these allées and terraces seem so sympathetic is that, like the early transitional work of the landscape movement by Bridgeman and Kent at Rousham and Chiswick executed between 1720 and 1740, these crisp basins, herms, and yew hedges are so thoroughly classical, well proportioned, and adjusted to each other and the fall of the hill that they meld into the larger pastoral setting and trees in much the same way that their predecessors, the formal terraces of Italian villas, sat within their estates, leading from villa to *vigne* to wood. It is thoroughly evocative of Italy and a return to the scenes of the original inspiration for the earlier eighteenth-century park while linking it and the lake to the house.

115. The Italianate cascade and terraces introduced by Harold Peto at Buscot House in 1904.

116. *Water lilies in one of Peto's basins at Buscot. The combination of fine detail and broad composition, of classically inspired elements and architecture, combined with horticulture and the agricultural scene, epitomize English gardens in their most evolved condition.*

117. *Romantic gestures at Buscot: a "broken" column at a boat landing on the lake shore at the end of Peto's neoclassical sequence looking across to the classical bridge (a dam) on the entry drive (above), and one of several black swans on the lake, birds from New Zealand that recall Britain's far-flung but fading might and empire while adding an odd exoticism to the scene.*

WARDOUR CASTLE, BUCKLAND HOUSE, AND RICHARD WOODS

By far the most impressive house along the Golden Ridge west of Oxford is Buckland House. Begun in 1757 by Sir Robert Throckmorton, the house was designed by John Wood the Younger, the designer of the Royal Crescent in Bath and son of Ralph Allen's architect at Prior Park. The house, neo-Palladian in design and illustrated in *Vitruvius Britannicus,* volume 2, handsomely furnished with superb details and plasterwork, was completed in 1767. It appears that Throckmorton was prepared to build himself the best estate possible on the manor he had inherited, and, therefore, within two years of the commencement of construction on the house, he had begun work on the surrounding park. The park and its ornamental structures were designed by Richard Woods, not by Capability Brown, as many local residents would like to believe. A contemporary of Brown, Woods built up a substantial practice based in southeastern England, although he consulted on parks as far distant as Wiltshire and Yorkshire. Of the eighteen parks he is known to have been engaged upon, several are noteworthy examples of the genre and compare favorably to the work of Brown. The most famous of these is Wivenhoe Park, the subject of an early painting by John Constable, now in the National Gallery of Art in Washington, D.C. Constable also executed paintings of two other parks by Woods: Alresford Hall, "The Quarters," Essex; and Englefield House, Berkshire, near Reading. The painting of the former depicts a delightful Chinese style fishing lodge by the edge of a pond with a lush parkland of elms and oaks behind. The latter is similar to Buckland in the massing of trees and the placement of the house on a rise above a deer park, but lacks the superb lakes of Buckland.

Woods was a Catholic, and many of his clients were old families who as conservative Royalists were Catholics. Following the Restoration after the Civil War and Commonwealth, many such upper-class families returned to their ancestral homes to rebuild and improve them, some after years of neglect or even military destruction, as at Wardour Castle, another of Woods's projects. This castle, partially destroyed by the owner and Ludlow's troops in a siege of 1642, and converted into a picturesque ruin in the park as a result of Woods's plan of 1766, was the home of the eighth Lord Arundell of Wardour. Located ten miles southwest of Longbridge Deverill in the Nadder River valley of Wiltshire, Wardour Castle possesses as picturesque a composition of ruins and Gothic follies to be seen across water as can be found anywhere. This is a project that got away from Brown, who did come, consult, and draw up plans, only to have them not be executed, while he and the owner wrangled about payment for the next three years — a situation, unfortunately, known to all design professionals and one that I can verify still occurs with frequency in the field of landscape architecture. Nevertheless, the relationship with Woods was more successful, and work at Wardour progressed under his personal direction from 1766 to 1768, continuing for at least another ten years. As in many of Brown's projects, Woods suggested where to locate and build the new house (done thereafter by Paine), and he designed the handsome new garden pavilions. A major unifying feature was the creation of a large lake that lies between the new house and ruined castle. While Brown may have been more famous, there is nothing inferior in this project or the landscape art of Richard Woods.

The earliest recorded park by Woods is that of Buckland. It is interesting to note that of more than two hundred parks attributed to Brown, only twelve were complete or in progress when Woods began work at Buckland in 1758 or 1759. Of these, several were not too distant in Oxfordshire. Another was Belhus, in Essex, a park upon which both men were to work for Lord Dacre. Brown began consulting with Dacre in 1753 for changes in the layout of roads and planting, and by 1759 he had begun plans and preparations for a lake a quarter of a mile in length that would cover about ten acres. For financial reasons, the work was several times postponed. Finally, in 1770, the lake and bridge were carried out under the direction of Woods, who was then living nearby at Ockendon Hall. Whatever their relationship might have been — probably that of normal and professional competition, or of junior and senior colleagues — it is safe to say that from his earliest work Woods shared a vision and self-confidence comparable to Brown's in his handling of water and masses of trees.

The house at Buckland (similar to Wivenhoe and several other of his schemes) is set in a handsome park and follows a general pattern established earlier by Lord Temple at Stowe and pursued by Brown throughout his career. A peripheral mass planting of elm, oak, beech, and chestnut draws in to embrace the house, which is placed near the middle of the park on a rise. To the south lies an open meadow, populated by cows or sheep contained by ha-has and dotted with occasional clumps of large, freestanding trees. An entry drive approaches the house through this meadow, and one first sees it from a considerable

FOLLOWING PAGES:

118. Wardour Castle, Wiltshire, as seen from across the lake created by Richard Woods. Here ruins of the ancestral family home have been transformed into a romantic folly in the distance to be seen from James Paine's fashionable new Palladian mansion (1768–76). Below, an arched entryway within the castle courtyard designed by the early Renaissance architect Robert Smythson.

119. Rock grotto created at Wardour Castle in 1792, inside of which one could sit and look out to the ruins of the castle and Smythson's main entry portal.

120. *A quintessential presentation of an eighteenth-century English country villa within its landscape park: Buckland House seen from the end of the south pasture, a view once available from the Faringdon road immediately behind a recent buffer of trees.*

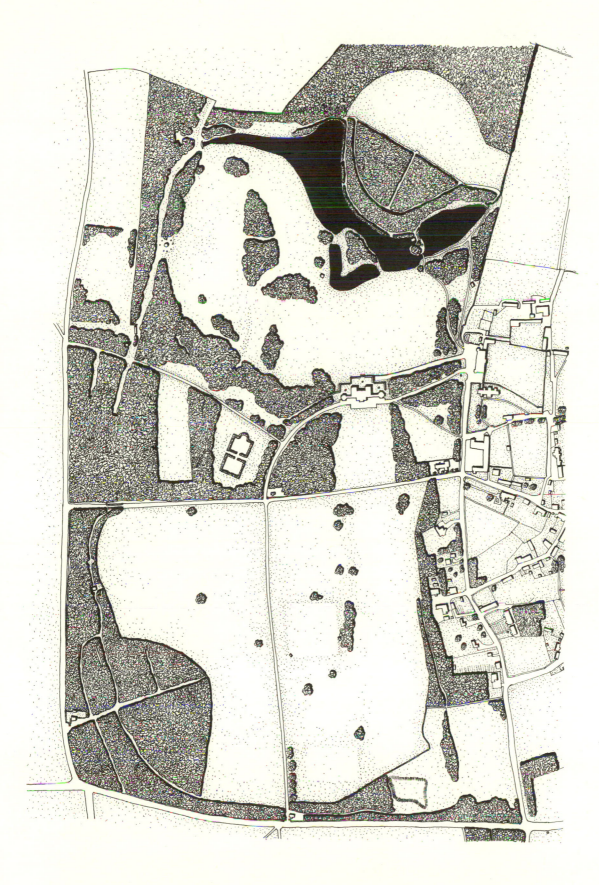

N

121. *Plan of Buckland House Park, Berkshire. The road from Oxford to Faringdon runs along the bottom; Buckland village lies just to the east on the right, with the Anglican church directly aligned with the house and with the old manor, immediately to its north. The various bodies of water created by Richard Woods appear at the top of the plan north of the meadow.*

distance. The house disappears again as the lane enters a last portion of the surrounding wood, only to reappear at the end of a curving drive lined with chestnuts and elms, where one emerges into the open at the house itself.

An aspect of this hide-and-seek approach to the house is the manner in which we perceive the building. First, we are presented with the distant mass and silhouette, the south facade seen against trees and sky. As one moves closer, one sees its golden honey color and can make out the major divisions of columns, windows, and side pavilions before losing it again in the trees. The next sight of it is as one is suddenly brought right up against its base, where one becomes aware of its great height, mass, and volume. Even more important, here where one can no longer stand back to take in the whole composition, there is a presentation of rich and crisp detail: handsome floral swags, Corinthian columns, pediments, moldings, brackets, and the delightful octagonal pavilions set out to each side of the main block, all carved from the rich Bath stone of Ralph Allen's quarries. Off to the left and right, hidden by trees, were the stables and kitchen gardens.

The original building scheme of the younger Wood, now obscured by an inflated nineteenth-century addition, was a stunning visual composition consisting of a solid central sixty-foot-square, three-story-high cube, flanked by one-story wings made of sixty-foot-long corridors and twin forty-foot octagonal pavilions, the entire south front therefore reaching the length of two hundred and sixty feet! The dynamic profile against the sky, the plain and sheer mass of the honey-colored stone, the small windows and heavy floral swags along the cornice of the upper floor combine to give the building heroic and scenographic quality meant to be read from a distance. At the same time it masks the remarkable scene that lies beyond to the north, which can be discovered only by moving through the building or walking around it. This striking and original composition has been severely compromised in this century by the addition of two lumpy wings attached to the central block designed by Romaine Walker in 1910–12.

North of the house lies the deer park. Here, as earlier in Rome and later at Jefferson's Monticello (which seems cognizant of the original building in particular and the other volumes of *Vitruvius Britannicus* in which it appears), a lawn and front terrace were constructed over a series of storerooms, kitchens, and service buildings that have access from a passageway to the side. A spectacular broad view — unseen and not hinted at from the

122. *View from the front entry of Buckland House, Oxfordshire: above, the long view to the south across the gravel court, lawn, ha-ha, and pasture, which also contains a cricket field to the left behind the trees; below, dairy cattle populate the scene, a typical mixture of work, play, aesthetics, and necessity that make up such scenes.*

south approach — opens out across the deer park, sweeps down to a large curving lake and islands, and beyond over the shelter belt of trees to the Thames Valley, Oxfordshire, and the distant Cotswold hills. Visible in the park are several structures. To the right an ice house with arcaded portico and thatched roof nestles into the hillside among the trees where a circumferential path leads down through the park to a bridge disguising a weir and connecting to the large earthen dam holding the lake. Closer examination reveals that the ice

BELOW: *123. The entry facade of John Wood's Buckland House seen from an angle that conveys the original composition before the twentieth-century additions.*

FACING PAGE: *124. Superimposed growth and change occur commonly in landscape, but are rarely so obvious as this collision of Romaine Walker's additions of 1910 to Wood's original central block of Buckland House, Oxfordshire.*

house is a witty piece, for it also can be seen to be a rusticated grotto that parodies the Pantheon, with a conical (comical) thatched roof instead of a dome. The dam has been shaped to resemble an island, and behind it, just visible from the house, is a rustic boathouse of logs and thatch resembling the small cottages and huts that populate pastoral verse, painting, and theater. The walk continues around the far side of the winding shore. From this shady path on the far side of the lake and from the main terrace of the house, one is offered views to a pedimented exedra, a nymphaeum or grotto set on the banks of an upper pond within the deer park. Built as a partial ruin and located in a key position just off-center in the view from the house, it shows Woods's facility with the placement of "eye-catchers" in the picturesque style (see fig. 71).

BELOW: 125. *One of the pavilions and a Lebanon cedar as the deer see them from the park, Buckland House. Used to frame views and as punctuation markers, these towering cedars were commonly used in park planting compositions in the eighteenth century.*

FACING: 126. *Unseen from the entry court and south approach, Richard Woods's deer park at Buckland opens up dramatically as one passes through or around the house.*

Here also Woods displays his mastery of the art of illusion in landscape design. He had only a small stream and a spring with which to work. The configuration of its small valley limited him in the size of lakes he could create. Put simply, the site of the deer park is mostly comprised of hillsides, and the vale they make is not very broad. When seen from the house above or when walking in the grounds, one doesn't fully understand that what he did was to create several ponds, stepping down and along the hillside and vale, linking them together visually so as to appear as one larger body of water with islands. The difference in elevation between the two principal lakes cannot be perceived clearly from the house. The upper, perched, dogleg or L-shaped pond immediately in front of the folly and the lower, longer, and larger body appear to connect somewhere just out of sight behind some trees. There are frequent views from the lakeside walk back to the distant house, backlit upon the hill. Farther along to the west, the source of the lake emerges from a rusticated arch. From here one could see to the upper end of a long, grassy vale and a small, white colonnaded rotunda silhouetted against a tall mass of elms.

Unlike the ponds, recently restored after years of neglect, this scene no longer survives. A once impressive ring of elms planted by Richard Woods two hundred years ago which encircled the small, domed pavilion are gone, victims of disease and storms. The effect intended in Woods's scheme was that from the terrace of the house this small white temple was to be seen gleaming within a grove on a hill slightly above and diagonally to the left of the house, in effect a sacred landscape very much like those depicted in the wall paintings of first-century villas in Rome. A pleasant stroll to this temple, with its Ionic columns and dome, offered a perfect seat to survey the entire sweep of this portion of the Thames valley, the park, house, and estate of the owner. The placement of a large classical urn with the ashes of one of Throckmorton's descendants under the dome adds to the commemorative effect of this ensemble. Finally, one could descend the hill, following the edge of the massed boundary plantations back to the house. With its formal structure, technical skill, and intelligent, even witty architectural elements, Buckland Park — and Woods's work in general — takes a place between the work of eclectic and literary designers such as Kent and Hoare on the one hand and the later, more formalist work of Brown on the other hand.

127. Fallow deer fawns and does keeping to themselves most of the year in the park (above), and diagonal view to the left from the front terrace with the round temple and few remaining elms on the hill (below).

128. *Bucks grazing in the park north of the house in the meadow (above), and parapet rail of the terrace above this meadow, built over service and storage rooms forming the base of the villa (below).*

In Conclusion
Beauty Past Change

BUCKLAND HOUSE may stand, then, for the eighteenth century's great achievement — the image and idea of a park: undulating land forms; trees set out singly and in groves, occasionally with underplanting; a sprinkling of neoclassical features in visually significant locations; gently curving paths and drives; and natural-appearing bodies of water —lakes, streams, and ponds. Brown died in 1783 and Woods in 1793. Their less well known contemporaries faded away. Humphry Repton, John Nash, and others were to continue to build such works, not only on isolated country estates but also in the very heart of London and other cities. The form of what began as a thoughtful, yet self-serving private gesture of wealthy intellectuals had become a public amenity. During Brown's later years, a push for more "natural" gardens and parks began, while simultaneously a rage for trees and shrubs from Asia and America swept gardening circles with the same intensity as the tulip mania of the previous century. Flowers and flowering shrubs were planted in astonishing quantities. Repton reintroduced terraces and updated versions of parterres into one park after another where they had been swept away by Brown. On the heels of the Regency, Sir Joseph Paxton and others developed the glasshouse and horticulture to a new level, further exploring technological aspects of the landscape.

Simultaneously the surface mannerisms — and in some instances, the structural and visual principles — of the landscape gardens of the mid-eighteenth century were taken up by intellectuals and the wealthy elsewhere. While this is especially so in France and the United States, examples of the *jardin anglais* may be found all around the world. For some personalities like Jefferson, Rousseau, and Goethe, who constructed major gardens after the English model, the political and literary content associated with the earlier neo-Palladian gardens of the Whigs continued to resonate. Such men were unusual, of course, and more frequently the gardens that resulted were distorted caricatures of the original models, sprinkled with bizarre pavilions, contorted land forms, rocks, and pools and wreathed in a tangle of writhing paths and a jumble of trees and shrubs. The overwrought and overplanted parks of the picturesque and gardenesque schools, which followed Brown, turned out to be as labor-intensive as the formal parterres that their authors abjured. With their less clear structure and without constant attention, they could rapidly devolve into chaos, and many of them have.

On the other hand, old and decrepit as many of them are, the parks of Kent, Brown, and Woods survive today, usually with the bones of their strong formal organization intact. Although hundreds of country houses have been destroyed or converted into penurious institutions, and an estimated fifteen million trees were blown down in southern England in the hurricanes of 1987 and 1990, landscape parks have often been declared public amenities or even local or national treasures. In the last twenty years, dozens of the greatest of these parks have undergone major restorations, replanting, and rebuilding or have been taken over by government, charitable, or heritage organizations for their preser-

129. *The curving gravel drive to the stables from Buckland House passes between a pair of classical urns on a close-cropped lawn backed by a curtain of oak and chestnut trees.*

vation and upkeep. Superb work has been completed at gardens as important as Stowe, Blenheim, and Claremont and continues throughout the country. One motive is the admirable preservation of a legacy, the other is the compelling forces of tourism and the economics of leisure: the creation of jobs and revenue. There is no question that these gardens are among the greatest tourist attractions in the nation, and that such houses and gardens are extremely important in the postindustrial society and landscape of Europe. This is ironic, or at least can be seen as an echo of the situation at the time of their creation. The English landscape park movement and the creation of these thousands of bucolic scenes

130. *Layers in time and space: a classical carved marble urn in the foreground with the deer fence, deer, and park beyond — flowers gone to seed and antlers full for combat, autumn approaches at Buckland House, Oxfordshire.*

occurred during the same period that England was undergoing the most severe effects of the industrial revolution and was in fact becoming an urban, factory-based society. Like the national park movement in the United States in the next century, wherein a remarkable effort to save, preserve, and protect many of the grandest and most spectacular portions of the wilderness occurred at the very same moment as the most rapacious development and industrialization were ending the frontier, one can only wonder if this movement was not in some way also a compensation for, and a putting off of coming to terms with, the new urban and industrial situation. The English cannot take full credit for having invented the landscape garden (or park) in the eighteenth century — it is inextricably related to the intellectual, economic, and social landscape of both Italy and earlier developments in England. Nevertheless, the evolution of its form and expression in the eighteenth century was one of the great artistic achievements of the West.

131. *Buckland House as seen from a path on the far side of the major lake. This park and lake, overgrown, silted up, and in decline in the 1970s, have been reinvigorated, cleaned up, and partially restored within the past few years as ownership has changed once again.*

Suggestions for Further Reading

In most endeavors, part of the pleasure of pursuing an interest issues from the activity itself. In the case of landscape history this entails the pursuit of information in several forms. First there is that displayed by the land itself, a sample of which is portrayed herein; then there is the vast wealth of information located in archives in the form of letters, deeds, maps, contracts, and all manner of records, public and private. Finally, there are, of course, books, of a wide variety and all periods. In the years since I embarked upon this topic as an amateur without a guide through several libraries and bookstores in England, Italy, and the United States, scholarly research and publication have been transformed by computers, in both the home and library. So, too, there has developed an enormous and ever growing number of books that embrace the many aspects of landscape and gardens in general and the evolution of the many aspects of the English landscape in particular.

While enormous amounts of material have now made their way into paperback editions, and I try to indicate such editions so as to assist students, a certain amount of pertinent material regarding landscape history inevitably still resides in books, often rare books and archives, public and private. In my work I had the benefit of the many rare or merely old books at the American Academy in Rome, the Hoare family library at Stourhead, and the British National Library, then located in the British Museum. Most of the records for Longbridge Deverill, such as the enclosure maps and notebooks, have been transferred from the Longleat estate office to the county records office, necessitating trips to Devizes.

Despite certain efficiencies that may be obtained today through modern technology, there was great personal pleasure to be had in poking about in library stacks and shelves, looking at and feeling the books, in the serendipity of finding unknown works next to that which I had set out after, hefting them, perusing the bindings, and lugging folios to a desk and opening them in genuine curiosity and expectation. On numerous occasions I was able to retire to a cozy room or studio and settle in with coffee or tea to browse or read leisurely. Today, with the recent move to Colin St. John Wilson's new British Library, adjacent to St. Pancras Station (a long-delayed and useful evolution in service, I am convinced), as many thousands of people reflect nostalgically upon the old facility, I can say that it *was* special, just to be in the great rotunda of the old library. While the map room and prints and drawings had their own special aura and tyrannical keepers, the great domed room with its circular catwalk above and central call desk seemed as much like an instrument of some utopian prison system as of a library. On more than one occasion I waited for my requests only to have a slip thrust at me that explained yet another reason a particular book was not forthcoming. The most memorable — I have the slip before me now as I write — stated that it was not available as it was "destroyed by bombing in the war."

Listed below is a selection of some of the many books and articles that I perused and that had an effect upon my knowledge or understanding during my engagement with the topic. Some of these by now are ancient; some are considered old hat or more limited than when they were new or I first encountered them. Likewise, there have been other new and meritorious works that I wish I had found or had been able to read at the time, as well as many that, upon looking into them, I have not found my conclusions in need of revision. Some of the former I note and list, the latter — no small number — I don't. For anyone who wishes to pursue one or more of the topics raised, there are bound to be a few items listed below that will lead to greater depth and other opinions than mine.

Prehistoric and Classical Britain and Wiltshire

In Rome, a few years after I had begun working on this project, Babs Johnson, who wrote under the pen name of Georgina Masson, pointed me to an obscure book that she thought was one of the best she had ever read or found. I borrowed it, agreed, and have recommended it to others and students ever since. It was Charles Glackens's *Traces on the Rhodian Shore: Nature and Culture in Western Thought from Ancient Times to the End of the Eighteenth Century*, University of California Press, Berkeley and Los Angeles, 1967, now in paperback. A survey of Western society's attitudes toward nature from classical antiquity to the end of the eighteenth century by a leading geographer of his era, it is a wonderful history of ideas that retains the complexity and countervailing forces of social movements. Glackens's work can be heavy going, but it is well worth it, if for no other reason than to learn where one's own deeply cherished views come from, and to see them presented equally as intellectual constructs in a context with beliefs that one disdains. Few people actually read this book who do not learn something and have their views changed by it.

The twentieth century has witnessed a revolution in scientific methods as applied to history and especially archaeology, from aerial photography and electromagnetic imaging to radiocarbon dating and genetic analysis of individual plants and human remains. Nevertheless, some of the most accessible and informative works available are quite venerable. I found the early Roman agronomists, whose writing might be considered the foundation works of landscape planning theory, to be clear, articulate, and full of what today we would call common sense. Still in print and available today in the small-format, parallel text and facing translation Loeb Classical Library series, the following ancient Latin texts can be found in bookstores on many U.S. college campuses: Cato, Marcus Porcius, *De Agri Cultura*, trans. Wm. Davis Hooper and rev. Harrison Boyd Ash, *On Agriculture*, Heinemann, London, 1934; the oldest surviving Latin text of the first century B.C., this is a technical treatise on site planning, horticulture, gardening, and farming and still reads well and gives sound advice. See the section on hedgerows, for example. Other later agronomists worth reading also are Columella, Lucius Junius Moderatus, *De Agri Cultura*, trans. Harrison Boyd Ash, *On Agriculture*, Heinemann, London, 1941; and Varro, Marcus Terentius, *Reum Rusticarum*, trans. Wm. Davis Hooper and rev. Harrison Boyd Ash, *On Agriculture*, Heinemann, London, 1934.

A useful and informative modern book on Roman farming practices and how the Romans dealt with some of the various forms of agriculture that they met in their imperial expansion, particularly in northern Europe and Britain, is *Roman Farming* by K. D. White, Thames and Hudson, London, 1970, while Jane M. Renfrew's *Paleoethnobotany*, Methuen, London, 1973, gives an account of earlier prehistoric food plants cultivated in the Near East and Europe.

The archaeology of pre-Roman Britain has fascinated people for centuries, and although the facts have become less conjectural since the seventeenth century when Inigo Jones wrote a treatise asserting that Stonehenge was a great temple built by the Druids, every decade revises and adds to the knowledge of the sequence of events in the settlement of Britain and the evolution of its landscape. Books and articles of great help in my early excursions into the field included: Sonia Chadwick, "Iron Age Enclosures on Longbridge Deverill Cow Down, Wiltshire," in S. S. Frere, ed.,

Problems of the Iron Age in Southern Britain, University of London Institute of Archaeology, London, 1961, pp. 17–28; Sonia Cole, *The Neolithic Revolution*, British Museum, London, 1970; G. W. Dimbleby, *Plants and Archaeology*, John Baker, London, 1967; H. W. Timperley and Edith Brill, *Ancient Trackways of Wessex*, J. M. Dent, London, 1965.

Studies of Roman Britain, likewise, now fill shelves. While I was living there, a new generation of scholars led by Barry Cunliffe published a great amount as well as helping with numerous television specials on the topic (*The Making of the English*, BBC London, 1973, is a paperback synopsis issued to accompany a popular series of the same title). Some of the most cogent of the previous era that got me going included: R. G. Collingwood and Ian Richmond, *The Archaeology of Roman Britain*, Methuen, London, 1969; J. U. Powell, "South Wilts in Romano-British Times," *Wiltshire Archaeological and Natural History Magazine*, 34, June 1904, pp. 270 ff., his "A Sketch History of Hill Deverill," *Wiltshire Archaeological and Natural History Magazine*, 28, Dec. 1895, pp. 235–52, and "The Early History of the Upper Wylye Valley," *Wiltshire Archaeological and Natural History Magazine*, 23, Dec. 1903, p. 109; A. L. F. Rivet, *Town and Country in Roman Britain*, Hutchinson University Library, London, 1958; also edited by Rivet, *The Roman Villa in Britain*, Routledge & Kegan Paul, London, 1969; Charles Thomas, ed., *Rural Settlement in Roman Britain*, Council for British Archaeology, London, 1966.

While there are numerous standard sources useful for checking facts or dates and definitions, one basic reference that makes a good place to start any English rural history endeavor is *The Victoria History of the Counties of England, Wiltshire*, edited by R. B. Pugh and Elizabeth Crittall, Oxford University Press, London, 1955. The Victoria County History is a large and various work containing (at the time I commenced work) 150 volumes. Those on Wiltshire are among those produced after World War II by a different generation of historians than those on the Home Counties and reflect changed methods and attitudes. Written by scholars far more interested in problems of economic and social change than the horsey pleasures of country living expressed in the earlier volumes produced under the direction of Pugh, they are an invaluable starting point and source of raw material and references.

Natural and Rural History of Southern Britain

As noted earlier, of modern societies, England has been particularly interested in all manner of history — natural, social, architectural, agricultural, and so on — at times seeming to be overly obsessed with its own past, so much so as to have Prime Minister Tony Blair remark that, while he was proud of his nation's past, he didn't want to have to live in it.

Among the most obvious and useful earlier works on natural history and its contemporary descendant, ecology, for me were: John Aubrey's *The Natural History of Wiltshire*, written 1656–91, first published in 1847, and edited by John Britton, which can be found in a facsimile reprint by David & Charles, Newton Abbot, Devon, 1969; John Britton's own *Beauties of Wiltshire*, 3 vols., 1801; and the first of its kind, Gilbert White's remarkable and still informative and pleasant to read *The Natural History and Antiquities of Selborne in the County of Southampton*, with engravings and appendix, 1789. Also interesting was George Clark's *The Game Laws from King Henry III to the Present Period*, 1786.

In 1970 when I first began reading about the English countryside, several of the pioneers in the development of modern plant, animal, and human ecology were still alive and actively writing. These included Victor Shelford and Roderick Mackenzie in North America, Charles Elton and A. G.

Tansley in England, and Fernand Braudel in France. I began with Elton, whose slender and eminently readable *Animal Ecology*, Sidgwick & Jackson, London, 1927, laid the groundwork and point of view for the entire field. His *The Pattern of Animal Communities*, Methuen, London, 1966, summarizes several decades of research by himself and his students on a quite ordinary and therefore important (because it is so typical) portion of woods, meadow, and floodplain, basically a leftover portion of downland near Oxford, and his uncanny and prescient *The Ecology of Invasions by Animals and Plants*, Chapman and Hall, London, 1972, which looks at the disturbances and chaos wreaked upon natural systems by the dislocations of all sorts of creatures as a result of emerging patterns of travel, living, and economics in the twentieth century, as well as historically. It is an amusing, entertaining, and deeply thought-provoking work, as well as a good read.

Sir A. G. Tansley's *The British Islands and Their Vegetation*, Cambridge University Press, London, corrected edition, 1949, 2 vols., is exemplary in its field. Before he settles down to move systematically about discussing the enormously variable plant communities of Britain, region by region and in great detail, Tansley provides introductory chapters that give as good a survey of the history of the geology, soils, and climate of the British Isles as can be found.

Other useful guides or in-depth studies of particular topics were: Hermann Heinzell, Richard Fitter, and John Parslow, *The Birds of Britain and Europe*, Collins, London, 1972; A. E. Trueman's *Geology and Scenery in England and Wales*, as revised by J. B. Whittow and J. R. Hardy, Penguin, London, 1971; W. Keble Martin, *The Concise British Flora in Color*, Ebury Press/Michael Joseph, 1965, reissued in paperback by Sphere Books, 1972. The multiple watercolor and gouache botanical illustrations, often with several dozen flowering plants to a page, are such a virtuoso performance that I would have purchased this book even if I hadn't been interested in the English countryside. Other particularly good studies were Helge Vedel and Johan Lange's *Trees and Bushes in Wood and Hedgerow*, Methuen, London, 1960; and Eric Taverner's *The Making of a Trout Stream*, Seely, Service & Co., London, 1952.

There are several topographical publications interesting in themselves that provided information about the disposition and evolution of forests, settlements, and roads from medieval times to the present. One of the earliest is Christopher Saxton's *Atlas of England & Wales*, 1579, a folio of maps — in our case "Wiltoniae Comitatus" of 1576 proved useful. William Camden's folio *Britannica* went through several printings beginning in 1607; the 1623 edition, which I used, gives specific detail about enclosed parks at Longleat and other sites nearby, as well as the river through the Deverills. J. Andrews and A. Dury in the next century prepared *A Topographical Map of Wiltshire*, London, 1773, 2 inches = 1 mile; consisting of 18 sheets plus index for the county, it predates the first ordnance map survey for Wiltshire made between 1805 and 1844. Also helpful was J. B. Harley and C. W. Phillips, *The Historian's Guide to Ordnance Survey Maps*, National Council of Social Service, London, 1964, paperback.

Studies of the rural landscape as a cultural construct are now so well established, with a diversity of topics and distinguished scholars, that it is easy to forget that there were particular individuals who established much of the scope and methodology as well as popularizing the subject matter with academia and the lay public alike. W. G. Hoskins was such a figure, many of whose works have gone into paperback editions with large sales. *The Making of the English Landscape*, Hodder and Stoughton, London, 1955, and Penguin, 1970, was an eye-opening and inspiring book for many besides myself and, as with Cunliffe's work, led to a lengthy documentary series on BBC television and more publications. *Provincial England, Essays in Social and Economic History*, Macmillan, London, 1965, and *Fieldwork in Local History*, Faber and Faber, London, 1967, both in paperback editions, collect several sharply focused studies of his that are small masterpieces of painstaking research, canny intuition, and shrewd fieldwork. What makes Hoskins's work stand out from that of his peers and protégés is his remarkable visual acuity and ability to see and connect what he finds in the landscape to the equally faint and subtle traces contained in documents and records.

Other works that I found helpful regarding rural developments between the departure of the Romans and the modern era were: Eilert Ekwall, *The Concise Oxford Dictionary of English Place Names*, Oxford University Press, London, 1960; H. S. Bennett, *Life on the English Manor: A Study of Peasant Conditions: 1150-1400*, Cambridge University Press, London, 1948, H. C. Darby and R. Welldon Finn, *The Domesday Geography of Southwest England*, Cambridge University Press, London, 1967; and R. E. Sandell, ed., *Abstracts of Wiltshire Inclosure Awards and Agreements*, Wiltshire Records Society, vol. 25, 1969, Devizes, 1971; vol. 2, "Water Technology" and vol. 3, "Agriculture," in *A History of Technology*, Oxford University Press, London, K. G. Ponting, *The Industrial Archaeology of Wiltshire*, Wiltshire Archaeological and Natural History Society, Sherbourn, Wilts., 1972.

In addition to Hoskins there is also a collection of papers from a watershed conference held in 1956 entitled *Man's Role in Changing the Face of the Earth*, edited by Carl O. Sauer, Marston Bates, and Lewis Mumford, University of Chicago Press, Chicago, that helped reshape my views of the environment and the history of design and the land. The book is still in print and worth reading. Some of the papers that related to this project were H. C. Darby, "The Clearing of the Woodland in Europe," pp. 183–216; E. Estyn Evans, "The Ecology of Peasant Life in Western Europe," pp. 217–39; Frits A. Heichelheim, "Effects of Classical Antiquity on the Land," pp. 165–82; and Gottfried Pfieffer, "The Quality of Peasant Living in Central Europe," pp. 240–77.

Just as I am usually at a loss when people ask me to recommend a book that will serve as a general introduction and survey to the subject of landscape architecture, so too I am certain any historian worth his salt would have a difficult time recommending any one single work to represent the field of history or even the history of a nation. This is largely because so much has been written by now that today's scholars, by and large specialists who preside over particular aspects, eras, or individual works, events, or personalities, are deeply suspicious of generalizations or surveys. I confess, however, that there are times when many people need some sort of overview and that there is a legitimate place for such works. For me G. M. Trevelyan's two-volume *History of England*, first published by Longmans, Green in London in 1926 and more recently in paperback by Doubleday Anchor editions in New York in 1952, served such a purpose. Coming before the revisionist histories that resulted from the pervasive Marxist critique that swept the humanities from the 1930s on, it must seem unabashedly "old fashioned" to professionals today. However, this work, along with his later *English Social History* (4 volumes), Longmans, Green, London, 1942, were enormously helpful to me in much the way I believe they were intended, namely, to narrate the broad sweep and significant events of English history — the revolutions, changes, and movements in thought, industry, and social relations, something of art, economics, ideas, and fashion — in short, an introduction to England sufficient to allow a person subsequently to go to more specialized works of particular interest with some sense of how detailed studies of more depth or narrow focus might relate to broader issues and other events or times.

Itinerant peregrinations, whether hiking about for health and pleasure, visiting relatives and friends in the country, or assessing the economy or some particular interest such as ancient architecture or scenery, or exploring distant and exotic lands, is a particularly British custom. So, too, the account of personal travel and observations is a venerable genre of English writing. While some, like Celia Fiennes's descriptions of her visits to country houses at the beginning of the eighteenth century, Boswell's account of his daily travels through London and his trip to the Hebrides, or Wystan Auden's descriptions of his journey to Iceland at the outbreak of World War II, are a pleasure to read and tell a great deal about society at the time, and not just their authors' character and imagination; several accounts and collections of essays or journals were of great interest to me in my perusal of southern England, especially the region embracing Salisbury plain. Among the most entertaining and informative of these were Arthur Young's *A Six Weeks Tour Through the Southern Counties of England and Wales* of 1769, and two from the early years of this century by W. H. Hudson, the author of the once popular fantasy *Green Mansions*. These were *Afoot in England*, J. M. Dent & Sons, London, 1908, and *A Shepherd's Life; Impressions of the South Wiltshire Downs*, Methuen, London, 1910, both of which were illustrated with superb pencil sketches by Bernard C. Gotch. An equally personal work in the same vein is that of Edward Hutton a few years later, *Highways and Byways in Wiltshire*, Macmillan, London, 1917, also illustrated sympathetically with pen and ink sketches by Nelly Erichsen.

There is another source of material, the popular press, once considered beyond the pale by scholars. One winter I stumbled, rather by accident, upon a vast trove of moldering back issues of the magazine *Country Life* in a rarely used room of my in-laws' house in Wiltshire. To my surprise, I learned that for many years, sandwiched between the fascinating advertisements of properties for sale, debutante portraits, grousing editorials about changes in life and taxation, and articles about shotguns, horses, hounds, and auction sales, there had been a steady stream of original articles and research about historic houses, gardens, and natural history. This was partly due to the fact that Christopher Hussey, an architectural historian particular to the Georgian era, whose work is included below, was for many years one of its editors. Not in every issue, certainly, was there anything of interest, but often enough some article would appear with a kernel or nugget to glean. In the case of the architectural and garden items by such writers as Peter Willis, Mark Girouard, and Hussey, many of these would eventually find their way into larger works or become incorporated into their books (see below). The numerous small but pithy and informative pieces about country wildlife, agriculture, and natural history, however, do not seem to have had the same safety net. A selection of articles that caught my eye and led me to look more closely at the land about me and to seek more technical or local references included: John L. Jones, "A Farming Revolution," *Country Life*, Nov. 7, 1957, pp. 972–73, and "Where Barley Is the Only Crop," *Country Life*, Aug. 30, 1962, pp. 462–63; Garth Christian, "Hedgerows as Reservoirs of Wildlife," *Country Life*, April 21, 1960, pp. 868–69, and "The Many Threats to the Barn Owl," *Country Life*, April 6, 1961, pp. 754–55, where he gives statistics on barn owls' capacity to kill rodents in Wiltshire; Roy Beddington, "A Chalk Stream Trout Problem," *Country Life*, April 6, 1961, pp. 751–53; D. S. Martin, "The Plight of Britain's Chalk Streams," *Country Life*, May 16, 1968, pp. 1307–9; and Frank Sykes, "New Weeds for Old," *Country Life*, May 25, 1972, pp. 1349–51, and his "The Future of the Downs," *Country Life*, June 1, 1972, pp. 1394–95.

History of English Architecture and Gardens

As with the history of natural systems and agricultural settlements, the roots of Western architecture and garden design lie in classical antiquity, in its continuity and revivals. The two most important early texts on architecture have been reissued in paperback editions and are readily available today. The *Ten Books on Architecture* by Marcus Vitruvius Pollio, trans. Morris Hicky Morgan, Harvard University Press, Cambridge, Mass., 1914, and Dover, paperback reprint, New York, 1960, a first-century-B.C. text of profound influence in the Italian Renaissance, assiduously studied by Bramante, Michelangelo, Palladio, and Vignola, not only has long sections about the elements of buildings, ornament, and proportion but also directions on urban design and microclimate (bk. 1), the relationship between climate and the style of houses, the appropriate siting of farmhouses (bk. 6) and methods of finding and testing water, plus various machinery (bks. 8 and 10). Dover's 1965 reprint of Andrea Palladio's *The Four Books of Architecture* is a reprint of the 1738 London translation by Isaac Ware, whose plates are the source of so much subsequent design in both England and the United States.

Several studies survey the field of English architecture. Among the very best and indispensable I would include: R. W. Brunskill's *Illustrated Handbook of Vernacular Architecture*, Faber & Faber, London, 1971; Alec Clifton-Taylor's *The Pattern of English Building*, Faber & Faber, London, 1972; and Sir John Summerson's *Architecture in Britain, 1530-1830*, Penguin, London, 1953, paperback, Penguin, 1970.

There are surveys that are geographic and surveys by period or style. The amount of material available is overwhelming. When exploring the countryside, one of the best places to start is with the little handbooks produced for Penguin by Nikolaus Pevsner and his assistants from World War II onward for several decades, in the series *The Buildings of England: Berkshire*, or *Oxfordshire*, or *Wiltshire*, and so on. A monumental task to produce in the first place, they now require an equally serious amount of work to update and correct, for marvelous as they are, they have gaps and are out of date in many instances.

While there is less material on the late medieval period than after, Walter Horn produced several key articles on English construction before moving on to his magnum opus on the monastery of St. Gall. These include: "On the Origins of the Medieval Bay System," *Journal of the Society of Architectural Historians*, 18, no. 2, Summer 1958, pp. 2–23; "The Great Tithe Barn of Cholsey, Berkshire," *Journal of the Society of Architectural Historians*, 22, no. 1, March 1963, pp. 13–23; and with F. W. B. Charles, "The Cruck Built Barn of Middle Littleton in Worcestershire, England," *Journal of the Society of Architectural Historians*, 25, no. 4, Dec. 1966, pp. 221–39.

In Wiltshire, considerable local architectural history can be pieced together from studies regarding major figures in society or design, from period or stylistic evidence, and from local records. In England, however, nearly always someone has gotten there before, and one of the first tasks in local history is to ferret out this work to see if it still holds up. In the case of C. E. Ponting's "Notes on Churches in the Neighborhood of Warminster," *Wiltshire Archaeological and Natural History Magazine*, 27, June 1894, pp. 269–71, nothing had turned up to contradict his research, only to add a few details.

For the Tudor era, I found several works most helpful. One was James Lees-Milne's *Tudor Renaissance*, Batsford, London, 1951, where in chapter 4, "The Protectorate Interlude," he discusses several of the key figures in the development and architecture of southern Wiltshire, namely, Sharington, Seymor (Somerset), Thynne, and Smythson. Later I came upon Roy Strong's *The Renaissance Garden in England*, Thames and Hudson, London, 1979, and John Dixon Hunt's *Garden and Grove: The Italian Renaissance Garden in the English Imagination, 1600-1750*, J. M. Dent & Sons, London, 1986, both of which survey a welter of source material and supply ample verbal and visual descriptions of gardens that introduce ideas from Renaissance Italy and the Continent, while demonstrating the transition and presenting the seeds of what was to come in the landscape movement of the next century.

The first two books on English landscape and gardening that I bought and read cover to cover my first summer in Buckland were Edward Hyams's *The English Garden*, Thames and Hudson, London, 1964, paperback 1966; and Christopher Hussey's *English Gardens and Landscapes, 1700-1750*, Funk and Wagnalls, New York, 1967. They were very fortunate introductions. The first was an unusually balanced and well-considered survey of the major periods, movements, and innovators, with a set of evocative photos and specific sites and gardens that do constitute the range and magic of British gardening. The second was a series of essays devoted to many of the greatest of the English landscape gardens of the Georgian era, with particular emphasis on the influence of Pope, Kent, and Brown. While more detailed research and explication of every one of these gardens have come about since, it was absolutely a classic study. I admired it then, as I do now, for its balance between description and analysis, detail and overall composition, social and aesthetic concerns, plans, photos, and language. Like several of his contemporaries, such as Whistler, Lees-Milne, and Summerson, Hussey had a good eye and wrote well.

Another book that didn't appear in stores until 1975 would have been helpful to me the first summer: *The Genius of the Place: The English Landscape Garden, 1620-1820*, a reader selected, introduced, and edited by John Dixon Hunt and Peter Willis, published by Harper and Row, New York and London, 1975 (rev. ed., paperback, MIT Press, 1988), makes available more than fifty important and historic texts on landscape and garden theory confined to out-of-print tomes, literary studies, and rare book rooms, with commentary by the editors, including practitioners and critics such as William Temple, Lord Shaftesbury, Joseph Addison, Alexander Pope, William Gilpin, William Chambers, Horace Walpole, Humphry Repton, and Thomas Jefferson.

Nevertheless, such anthologies are no substitute for contact with the original works. Inevitably one can learn more and find things unlooked for (and has more fun) if able to work with the historic material. One that I found particularly stimulating and inspiring when I got my hands on it was: John Evelyn's *Sylva, or a Discourse of Forest-Trees, and the Propagation of Timber in His Majesty's Dominions*, London, 1664. There are numerous editions, and I still kick myself for not purchasing a copy I found several years ago because I thought it was too expensive. By now, it costs twice as much. It is a wonderful grab bag, compounded of his reading, experience, and thinking, all of which were wide ranging and creative. Another, John Evelyn's *Diary*, published in an Everyman edition by G. Newnes, London, 1890, and in several editions since (*The Diary of John Evelyn*, 6 vols., Clarendon Press, Oxford, 1955, and more recently selected and edited by John Bowle, Oxford University Press, 1985, paperback), is a fount of information about life, politics, and design activity in London in the seventeenth century. I found it more readable than Pepys's *Diary*, probably because there is less gossip and personal carryings on, and more about his work and art.

At the end of the seventeenth and through the eighteenth century, a flurry of architectural and garden publications appeared, as the subject matter was clearly of great interest to those who could afford books, travel, and the construction of country estates. A large number of the most influential publications of this period, many plates and quotations from which are presented in nearly any survey or study (as those mentioned here), may be found in large or specialized libraries and rare book rooms or private residences in England and the United States. Among the most notable of which I had the pleasure to peruse and highly recommend to anyone interested in these subjects was: Johannes Kip, *Brittania Illustra — Views of the Queen's Palaces & Principle Seats of the Nobility & Gentry of Great Britain*, vol. 1, London, 1707, consisting primarily of extremely careful and useful (from the standpoint of landscape history) aerial perspective engravings; unfortunately many editions have been cut apart to supply the print market.

Equally ubiquitous in influence upon subsequent design in Britain and the colonies as Palladio were the publications of his devotee, Colen Campbell, *Vitruvius Britannicus*, vol. 1, 1715, vol. 2, 1717, vol. 3, 1725, and, after his death, vol. 4 by J. Woolfe and J. Gandon. These are handsome volumes, and the plates of work by himself, Christopher Wren, James Gibbs, William Talman, and others served as patterns for innumerable later works. Plans and elevations of Buckland House by John

Wood the Younger are reproduced in vol. 4 and thus were available to Jefferson, who used its sectional organization and service level for his own house at Monticello.

In the next decades, several authors picked up from Evelyn, contemporary French publications, and the Roman agronomists, carrying on with practical nursery and horticultural advice. Two I enjoyed were George London and Henry Wise's *The Retir'd Gard'ner*, London, 1706, and Richard Bradley's *New Improvements of Planting and Gardening both Philosophical and Practical*, London, 1724. This latter text, although spotty and slow, has a few good plates and is particularly interesting in part about the economic advantages of forest planting and schedules of what to plant, what and when to harvest, and the profits to be expected.

Two recent publications have greatly increased our knowledge of the horticultural details of the landscape gardens of the eighteenth century. Douglas Chambers, in *The Planters of the English Landscape: Botany, Trees, and the Georgics*, Yale University Press, New Haven, Conn., 1993, provides an extensive recent compendium of detailed information regarding the nurserymen, plants, gardeners, seed sources, and construction of the eighteenth-century parks and gardens. Like many (including myself), he has felt compelled to retell the tale of their evolution, sources, and ideas — by now common enough — which, in his hands, is less well done than by others. This book is worth having, however, for the many superb plates and illustrations alone, which offer a wealth of information.

Mark Laird, *The Flowering of the Landscape Garden: English Pleasure Grounds 1720-1800*, University of Pennsylvania Press, Philadelphia, 1999, has produced a startlingly thorough and revolutionary study of the flowers and shrubs that existed in these gardens, most particularly as a wealth of new and striking plants began to pour into England from the colonies, especially from North America. The colors, forms, and textures he documents, the nursery trade, communication between clients, friends, and professionals with a wealth of superb illustrations is a treasure trove.

Four important architectural treatises without which no country house of the first half of the eighteenth century seems equipped are: Robert Castell, *The Villas of the Ancients*, London, 1728, which has his imaginative reconstruction of Pliny's villa in Tuscany, so obviously influential upon the work of Bridgeman and Kent; Sir William Temple, *The Works of Sir William Temple*, 2 vols., London, 1740; William and John Halfpenny's *New Designs for Chinese Temples, Triumphal Arches, Garden seats, Palings, etc.*, London, 1750; and William Chambers's *A Treatise on Civil Architecture*, London, 1759.

While the book is common enough in fine libraries, I had the pleasure of leafing through Henry Hoare's copy of Richard Earlom's *Liber Veritatis, or a Collection of Two Hundred Prints after the Original Design of Claude Lorrain*, 2 vols., 1777, another popular work. Based on an album of sketches in the collection of the duke of Devonshire, which Claude had made as a record of completed paintings to protect himself against forgers, and in an age before photography, these folios were an important vehicle for the distribution of his pastoral imagery.

Both of Humphry Repton's treatises — *Sketches and Hints on Landscape Gardening*, 1794, and *Observations on the Theory and Practice of Landscape Gardening*, 1803 — have gone through several editions, including a couple in our own time, and were readily available in all the libraries I used. John Nolen, one of the founders of the American Society of Landscape Architects, whose town plans have been quoted and emulated by devotees of the New Urbanism movement, edited a reduced-format reprint edition published by the ASLA and Houghton Mifflin, Boston and New York, 1907. This is a marvelous work, and I still do not know of anyone else who has written so carefully and usefully on water and the optics of its light and reflective effects as Repton.

In the twentieth century, studies of English gardening, and especially of the eighteenth-century landscape movement, have undergone quite an evolution as one discipline and generation after another has come to focus upon them. Since so many of these works are still available, a certain amount of warning and selection seems in order for anyone new to the topic. Elizabeth Manwaring's *Italian Landscape in Eighteenth-Century England*, Oxford University Press, London, 1925, and Christopher Hussey's *The Picturesque*, Frank Cass, London, 1927, introduced discussions of the influence of Claude and the masques of Inigo Jones and Ben Jonson (among others), but are now hopelessly out of date. So, too, H. F. Clark's nice little book, *The English Landscape Garden*, Pleides Books, London, 1948, is quite dated in its remarks about Brown and has been supplanted by the work of his students.

Among the more thoughtful books I enjoyed were: James Lees-Milne's *Earls of Creation: Five Great Patrons of the Eighteenth Century*, Hamish Hamilton, London, 1962, which discusses the careers of Allan Bathurst, Henry Herbert, Richard Boyle, Edward Harley, and Thomas Coke; and Lawrence Whistler's *The Imagination of Vanbrugh and His Fellow Artists*, Batsford, London, 1954.

As in America, which received a deluge of scholars and artists driven out of Europe by the Nazis and World War II, England, its universities and institutions, and every field of scholarship including and especially art history benefited from this influx of minds. Among their many other works, Rudolf Wittkower contributed a series of influential essays published between 1945 and 1970, since collected under the title *Palladio and Palladianism*, Thames and Hudson, London, 1974, as did Nikolaus Pevsner, a number of which are collected in *Studies in Art and Architecture and Design*, vol. I, *From Mannerism to Romanticism*, Thames and Hudson, London, 1968; and *The Englishness of English Art*, Architectural Press, 1956, and Penguin paperback, 1964.

The 1960s and 1970s saw a spate of works on the topic by Nikolaus Pevsner, Rudolf Wittkower, Miles Hadfield, Margaret Jourdain, Peter Willis, Kenneth Woodbridge, Denys Sutton, John Harris, John Fleming, and John Dixon Hunt. Each of these authors has significantly added to our knowledge of English landscape and gardening history. Some works are small but fundamental, such as Miles Hadfield's "History of the Ha-Ha," *Country Life*, May 30, 1963, pp. 1261–62; or Hugh Prince's catalogue of the works of Bridgeman, Kent, Brown, and Woods in *Parks in England*, Pinhorns, Isle of Wight, 1967. Others are major monographs: Dorothy Stroud's *Capability Brown*, Faber & Faber, London, 1950, and revised 1975; Kenneth Woodbridge's *Landscape and Antiquity, Aspects of English Culture at Stourhead, 1718-1838*, Clarendon Press, Oxford, 1970; and Peter Willis's *Charles Bridgeman and the English Landscape Garden*, Zwemmer, London, 1977.

The work of several architectural and art historians was helpful as well, especially John Harris's *Georgian Country Houses*, Country Life Books, London, 1968, his *Country House Index*, Pinhorns, Isle of Wight, 1971, his introduction and heavily annotated catalogue of Palladian drawings in the Royal Institute of British Architects collection, Rizzoli, New York, 1982, and his collaboration with Roy Strong and Stephen Orgel on *The King's Arcadia: Inigo Jones and the Stuart Court*, Arts Council of Britain, London, an annotated catalogue for the exhibition on Jones's quarter-centenary in 1973, and their subsequent two-volume work, Stephen Orgel and Ray Strong, eds., *Inigo Jones: Theatre of the Stuart Court*, University of California Press, Berkeley and London, 1973. John Fleming, in addition to numerous articles, published *Robert Adam and His Circle in Edinburgh and Rome*, John Murray, London, 1962; and Denys Sutton, through a series of articles, established the importance and involvement of English painters to the landscape movement, "George Stubbs — Many Sided Genius," *Country Life*, Dec. 5, 1957, pp. 1204–10, and "John Wooton Recognized at Last," *Country Life*, Dec. 4, 1958, pp. 1290–96.

William Kent, a figure who became of great interest to me during my consideration of events in the English landscape, has interested others. Snippets and chunks of scholarship devoted to Kent have appeared at intervals, but with the exception of a recent work by Hunt (see below), I have found them all to be disappointing, thin, and uncomprehending. These range from Margaret Jourdain's *The Work of William Kent, Artist, Painter, Designer and Landscape Gardener*, Country Life Books, London, 1948; to Edward Croft-Murray's "William Kent in Rome," *English Miscellany*, 1, 1950, pp. 221–30; to Michael I. Wilson's *William Kent, Architect, Designer, Painter, Gardener, 1685–1748*, Routledge & Kegan Paul, London, 1984. More recently, however, John Dixon Hunt's *William Kent, Landscape Garden Designer: An Assessment and Catalogue of His Designs*, Zwemmer, London, 1987, has provided a more perceptive and full understanding of his landscape work and a catalogue raisonné of Kent's landscape drawings.

There have been numerous scholars from the field of literature who have assayed English landscape topics. Notable examples in recent decades include Edward Malins, *English Landscaping and Literature, 1660–1840*, Oxford University Press, London, 1966; Peter Martin, *Pursuing Innocent Pleasures: The Gardening World of Alexander Pope*, Archon Books, Hamden, Conn., 1984; Andrew V. Ettin, *Literature and the Pastoral*, Yale University Press, New Haven, Conn., 1984; and Ronald Paulson, *Emblem and Expression: Meaning in English Art of the Eighteenth Century*, Harvard University Press, Cambridge, Mass., 1975, and *Literary Landscape: Turner and Constable*, Yale University Press, New Haven, Conn., 1982. However, none has made such a remarkable contribution nor such a life and career pilgrimage as John Dixon Hunt, who, beginning in the discipline of English literature with — among other works — a biography of John Ruskin, has shifted first to studies of eighteenth-century pastoral literature with *The Figure in the Landscape: Poetry, Painting and Gardening during the Eighteenth Century*, Johns Hopkins University Press, Baltimore, Md., 1976, and *Andrew Marvell: His Life and Work*, Cornell University Press, Ithaca, N.Y., 1978, then the work on Kent (see above), *Garden and Grove*, and *The Genius of the Place* (also above), and more recently *Gardens and the Picturesque: Studies in the History of Landscape Architecture*, MIT Press, Cambridge, Mass., 1992.

New research and publications on the topic of English landscape and gardens continue to stream forth. Two notable recent works are Gervase Jackson-Stops' annotated catalogue, *An English Arcadia, 1660-1990: Designs for Gardens and Garden Buildings in the Care of the National Trust*, American Institute of Architects Press, Washington, D.C., 1991, and the collection of essays edited by James Bond and Kate Tiller, *Blenheim: Landscape for a Palace*, Alan Sutton, Oxford, 1987. For anyone interested in the dilemmas and current state of the art and science of historic restoration, this series of papers and essays by Bond, David Green, Hal Moggeridge, Ralph Cobham, Paul Hutton, and John Campbell should be required reading. It is not only impressive, as is the topic, but also, with the exception of Wilhelmina Jashemski and her colleagues' pioneering work at Pompeii, simply the finest example of its kind.

Books by and about twentieth-century designers and their designs in England that I made use of, or that helped finally to push me into the field myself, included several by Sylvia Crowe, including *Garden Design*, Country Life, London, 1958; *Tomorrow's Landscape*, Architectural Press, London, 1956; and *The Landscape of Power*, Architectural Press, London, 1958; Nan Fairbrother's *New Lives, New Landscapes*, Architectural Press, London, 1970, and Penguin paperback, 1972; the justly famous and respected study by Geoffrey Jellicoe and Jock Shepherd, *Italian Gardens of the Renaissance*, by now through at least three editions, the original published by Ernest Benn, London, 1925 and 1953, then Alec Tiranti's 1966 version, and more recently the Princeton Architectural Press reprint, which was followed by Jock Shepherd and Geoffrey Jellicoe, *Gardens and Design*, Ernest Benn, London, 1927. Geoffrey Jellicoe's *Studies in Landscape Design*, 3 vols., Oxford University Press, London, 1960, 1966, and 1970, I found particularly inspiring at the time I discovered them, for they convincingly made the case that modern landscape designs could be created as works of art, have meaning (just as those of the Renaissance and eighteenth century had), and also make environmentally responsible contributions to a modern working landscape.

When I first found Peter Shepheard's slender and modest work *Gardens*, Macdonald, London, 1969, I realized that it was very much in the tradition of seventeenth- and eighteenth-century practical writing that speaks to both horticulture and aesthetics. It was and still is one of the most sensible of the "how to" tracts of recent times that I have found. In the years since, of course, there have been numerous attractive and helpful books by Penelope Hobhouse and Rosemary Verey about gardening, especially concerning herbaceous plants and borders.

In the 1980s, work by a new figure in English garden studies, Jane Brown, began to appear. Three good and helpful books of hers I recommend to anyone interested in pursuing many of the things I barely touch upon or haven't covered are: *Gardens of a Golden Afternoon, the Story of a Partnership: Edwin Luytens and Gertrude Jekyll*, Van Nostrand Reinhold, New York, 1982; *The English Garden in Our Time, from Gertrude Jekyll to Geoffrey Jellicoe*, Antique Collectors' Club, Woodbridge, Suffolk, 1986; and *The Art and Architecture of English Gardens*, Weidenfeld and Nicolson, London, 1989, which is a nice compendium of drawings, sketches, and renderings from the Royal Institute of British Architects collection ranging from 1609 to the present, with a series of essays devoted to different periods and stylistic movements, along with annotations, many of which amount to small sharply focused essays themselves.

Possibly the best book ever written by a landscape or garden designer is the entertaining and deeply informative series of essays passing as a memoir by one of the few truly great garden designers of our period: Russell Page, *The Education of a Gardener*, William Collins Sons, London, 1962, reprinted with a new preface 1983, and in Penguin paperback, 1985.

Finally, for those who would be interested in reading interviews that amount to memoirs of a number of leading figures in the field of landscape architecture in Britain during the postwar years, there is *Reflections on Landscape: The Lives and Work of Six British Landscape Architects*, edited by Sheila Harvey from interviews conducted by Ian Laurie and Michael Lancaster, Gower Technical Press, Aldershot, Hampshire, 1987; included are Sir Geoffrey Jellicoe, Dame Sylvia Crowe, Sir Peter Shepheard, Brian Hackett, Peter Youngman, and Brenda Colvin.

Acknowledgments

I WOULD LIKE TO THANK the John Simon Guggenheim Memorial Foundation and the American Academy in Rome, for without their generous aid I could never have attempted this project. I owe a particular debt to the late Frank Brown and to Henry N. Millon, the two people most responsible for the vigor of the American Academy during my years there. While in Rome I was aided by a remarkable community of scholars, who offered me the inspiration of their work, the stimulus of their companionship and conversation, and in several instances the opportunity to read and discuss unpublished manuscripts. These included Elisabeth Blair MacDougall, Georgina Masson, William Hood, Charles Hope, John Wright, Harry Evans, and Leo Raditsa.

I am also in debt to the Academy Library and staff, headed at the time by Nina Longabardi and Milton Lord, to Gina Severini of the Phototeca Unione, and to the staff of the Herziana Library of the Max Planck Institute.

Support and interest in this project were given to me at the University of Pennsylvania by Sir Peter Shepheard, dean of the Graduate School of Fine Arts, and Ian L. McHarg, chairman of the Department of Landscape Architecture and Regional Planning during my days there, and by my colleagues and students at the Harvard University Graduate School of Design and the Graduate School of Fine Arts of the University of Pennsylvania, where this work has finally taken form.

Help and the typing of early drafts were provided by Brooks R. Kolb, first as a student, later as a colleague. The final revisions were made by Cristen Gilbert.

At different times throughout the long course of the project I have been sustained by the friendship and patience of several souls, notably Frank B. Holmes, Diana Rose Livesey, and Robert M. Hanna. To each of them I owe the deepest gratitude.

My lengthy sojourns in England would have been impossible without the help of the Guggenheim Foundation and the kindness of many people: first in Buckland, that of Corrine DeLaite Brown; and later in Longbridge Deverill, that of Baroness Nugent, John Latham, Ted Richards, Ray Burgess, Margaret and Arthur Titt, the Reverend Spinney, vicar of Monkton Deverill, and the heirs of Mrs. B. M. White, who allowed me access to her papers. I also wish to thank both F. R. M. Robertson and the National Trust for permission to use the Hoare family library at Stourhead. I am also indebted to Edward Croft-Murray of the British Museum, who allowed me access to the Print, Drawing, and Map Collection, as well as the Library, and to the staff of the Wiltshire Public Records Office in Devizes, and to Derek Lovejoy who opened for me the contemporary world of landscape architectural practice in England.

I am extremely indebted to John Dixon Hunt, chairman of the Department of Landscape Architecture and Regional Planning at the University of Pennsylvania, without whose friendship, example, criticism, and editorial guidance at different times I would probably never have completed this work.

Finally, I must express my deepest gratitude to my wife, Victoria Steiger, who has sustained and encouraged me through the last two decades, who convinced me to return to this once abandoned project.

Needless to say, as in the works of my office where so little of my ideas would be realized without substantial help from others, the faults of the final project are mine.

Index